Dedication

To my wife Meghan, your patience and support fill my life with meaning. Thank you for your love and all that you do.

To my son Michael, your curiosity and love inspire me. As you grow, you teach me what it means to be alive.

To my family, thanks for your support and teaching me so much.

Richard Harrington, PMP, President RHED Pixel

Richard has surrounded himself with media for his entire professional career. He's held such diverse jobs as directing television newscasts and publishing music magazines to managing video production departments and consulting to nonprofit agencies. Currently, Richard is the owner of RHED Pixel (www.RHEDPixel.com), a visual communications company in the Washington, D.C. area.

RHED Pixel is a successful consultancy that provides technical and managerial services to clients such as the American Red Cross, the American Diabetes Association, the National Association of Homebuilders, and the Business Software Alliance. RHED Pixel creates everything from broadcast commercials to live events to interactive projects for a diverse clientele.

The Project Management Institute certifies Richard Harrington as a Project Management Professional. He holds a master's degree in project management as well. Additionally, Richard is an Adobe Certified Instructor, Apple Certified Trainer, and Avid Certified Instructor, and holds two Adobe Certified Expert certificates. Richard is a member of the National Association of Photoshop Professionals Instructor Dream Team.

His personal philosophy is communicate, motivate, create. He's a firm believer that media can have powerful results.

Acknowledgments

Several people have played an important role in this book coming to life:

- Ron Hansen and Michael Davidson who gave me my first job teaching Adobe Photoshop at the Art Institute of Washington.

- Ben Kozuch who believed in me enough to let me teach Photoshop to a room full of media professionals.

- Scott Kelby and the other instructors and staff of the National Association of Photoshop Professionals for their inspiration and support.

- Megan Cunningham for the intro-duction and Marjorie Baer for her interest and support in the book.

- Becky Morgan for challenging me to write the best book possible and Anne Marie Walker for guiding me through the process and fixing my flaws.

- Susan Rimerman and her team for crafting a book that is clean, professional, and useful.

- To James Ball, Jim Tierney, and Abba Shapiro, thank you for your generous gift of photos.

- To my many students through the years, thanks for the challenges and the motivation.

Contents

Introduction

The Role of Photoshop in Education

Learning Adobe Photoshop is essential to success in digital media industries. Photoshop is a gateway into several related technologies. From digital image acquisition and processing to typography and compositing, Photoshop is often your first introduction. If you can master this program, you can go on to success with several other technologies. With this in mind, it is important to learn Photoshop with one eye on the present and the other on the future.

The Role of Photoshop in Professional Industries

It's been said that if you know Photoshop, there's always work to be had. Photoshop is used by everyone from photographers to Web developers, video professionals to graphic designers. In fact, Photoshop is used in more places than you'd expect–including the medical, architectural, and legal fields. Adobe Photoshop is a portal to Adobe's other software applications, but it is also much more. Mastering Photoshop's tools will teach you more about creative technology tools than any other program. With a solid knowledge of Photoshop, you'll be well on your way to being comfortable with the entire digital toolbox.

Purpose of This Book

When I decided to write this book, it was to fill a need. I have worked with Photoshop students of all levels, from the college classroom to working professionals across all industries. What I've heard time and time again is that people wanted an objective book that gave them everything they needed to truly understand Adobe Photoshop. Readers have grown tired of books that talk down to them or waste time promoting only the latest features.

It's not that there's a shortage of good books for the professional; I've read many of them and know several of their authors. But what has happened over the years, as Photoshop has become such an established program, is that we are left with two types of books: those for complete beginners and those for pros looking to dig deep on specific areas of the program. What was missing? A book that addresses the need of the learner who wants to understand the important features of Adobe Photoshop, as well as the core technology behind it, to build a solid foundation for future learning.

This book is for learners who learn best by not just reading but by doing. Every chapter contains extensive hands-on exercises and all of the files you need to practice. You'll also find hours of training videos that bring the most important concepts to life. Finally, interactive quizzes help you check your progress to ensure the knowledge is "sticking." The accompanying DVD-ROM has everything you need, and the vast majority of this book works with all versions of Adobe Photoshop sold within the past 5 years.

If you are learning Photoshop in a classroom, this book should combine with your instructor's knowledge to give you a rich, interactive learning experience. For those working professionals looking to fill in their understanding of Photoshop, this book answers and reinforces the essential information that you'll need. For both audiences, this book teaches you what you need to succeed in the professional workplace. As a teacher and a working professional it is my goal to prepare you for professional success.

WINDOWS USERS

If Windows Media Player prevents you from accessing the DVD, perform these steps:

1. Exit Windows Media Player.

2. Open My Computer.

3. Right-click on drive <d>:\ UAP_DVD, where <d> is the letter of your DVD-ROM drive.

4. Choose Explore. You will now be able to navigate through the exercises and lesson files.

Suggestions on Learning

Photoshop is a very comprehensive program; don't try to learn it overnight. In fact, rushing to learn is often what causes problems. In an effort to learn quickly, skills don't have time be absorbed. To combat this problem, I have eliminated nonessential topics from this book. I've also included a hands-on example or activity for every skill.

The truth is you'll learn best by doing. Don't skip the hands-on activities in a rush to make it through the book. I strongly encourage you to try each one. After completing the book's activities, you should repeat the techniques with your own photos. Nothing makes a topic as clear as you experiencing it interactively and achieving success. With practice—regular and thorough—you can understand and master Photoshop.

Digital Imaging Fundamentals

Many people mistake fundamentals for basics. They are not the same. Understanding how computers represent your digital image data is essential to your career. Being a tech head will not make you a better designer/photographer/videographer but it will make you faster and more confident. While there are a lot of (boring) books on the science of computer graphics, I promise to keep it light and only cover the absolute "must knows" that working pros are expected to understand.

Pixels: Digital Building Blocks

When it comes to digital cameras, most consumers (and salespeople) seem obsessed with megapixels. Because "everybody knows" that having more pixels means better images (it doesn't, by the way). In a similar fashion, I've seen almost as much obsession in the scanner section of the computer store… where consumers are snapping up 9600 DPI scanners with slide adapters.

What's lacking in all of this hoopla is a clear understanding of what pixels are and just how many you need. See, the more pixels you have (whether those are captured with your digital camera or acquired with a scanner), the more RAM you need to buy and extra hard-drive space to store them all. So it behooves you to actually understand a little of the technology behind the images you want to capture, manipulate, output, and store.

ISTOCKPHOTO/PENFOLD

Computers use pixels to build with, like a child might use these wooden blocks.

In the Beginning...

Essentially, computers and video devices use pixels to express image information. Each pixel is a small square of light. The pixel is the smallest portion of an image that a computer is capable of displaying or printing. Too few pixels and images appear "blocky," as there is not enough detail to work with. Too many pixels and the computer or output device just gets bogged down.

ISTOCKPHOTO/ALAN GOULE

A close-up of TV "picture elements," or pixels.

But where did the term *pixel* come from? A pixel is an abbreviation for *picture element*. The word was coined to describe the photographic elements of a television image. In 1969, writers for *Variety* magazine took pix (a 1932 abbreviation of *pictures*) and combined it with *element* to describe how TV signals came together. There are even earlier reports of Fred C. Billingsley coining the word at NASA's Jet Propulsion Laboratory in 1965. While the exact origins of the word may be disputed, the meaning is not. The word *pixel* quickly caught on, first in the scientific communities in the 1970s and then in the computer-art industry in the mid 1980s.

The red circle shows an enlargement of the image. Notice how you can see actual pixels when you increase the magnification of an image. These sqaures of light are the building blocks of all digital photos.

PIXEL IS REALLY A PORTMANTEAU

OK, I admit that I didn't know what a *portmanteau* was at first… but it's such a cool concept (so let's start there). Taken from the French word for a type of suitcase, it was Lewis Carroll who invented the usage of the word in *Through the Looking-Glass, and What Alice Found There.* Humpty Dumpty says, "Well *slithy* means *lithe* and *slimy*… You see it's like a portmanteau—there are two meanings packed up into one word."

We are surrounded with these combo words. If you've ever visited Los Angeles, you may have noticed the smog (which is a combination of the words *smoke* and *fog*). Perhaps while there you logged on to a restaurant critic's Web log (or *blog*) to find a great place for breakfast-lunch (or *brunch*). Once you found the perfect spot, you might have called a friend on your cellular telephone (or *cellphone*) or sent her an electronic mail (or *email)* to get together. So, a pixel is really a portmanteau. Don't you feel smarter already?

A portmanteau of the nonverbal kind.

Digital cameras use card-based storage, like this compact flash card, to hold the captured pixels.

So What Are Megapixels?

When you shop for a digital camera, you are bombarded with talk of megapixels. Consumers are often misled about what megapixels are, and how many are needed. A *megapixel* is simply a unit of storage, whether internal or on a removable card. A megapixel is 1 million pixels, and is a term commonly used to describe how much data a digital camera can capture. As with your car, just because your tank can hold more gallons of gas doesn't mean it's more fuel-efficient or better than your co-worker's.

For example, if a camera can capture pictures at 2048×1536 pixels, it is referred to as having 3.1 megapixels ($2048 \times 1536 = 3,145,728$).

If you were to print that picture on paper at 300 PPI (pixels per inch), it would roughly be a 7" × 5" print. Professional photographers need more pixels than this, but a consumer may not. It all depends on how the pixels are meant to be displayed.

The more pixels you capture, the larger the image is (both in disk space and physical print size). Consumer usage such as email or inkjet prints are less demanding than professional usage such as billboards or magazines. Professionals need more mega-pixels than consumers, hence high-end cameras cost more since they are targeted at people who make money by taking pictures.

Understanding Resolution

OK, prepare to be confused (but hopefully not for long). There are a lot of terms used to describe the resolution of images. The problem is that many people (and companies) use the wrong terms, which leads to a lot of understandable confusion. Let's take a quick look at the most common terms and their accurate meanings.

Dots Per Inch (DPI)

The most common term used to describe image resolution is *dots per inch (DPI)*. While you'll hear it used for digital cameras and scanners, it is really only appropriate for printers. As a measurement of resolution, dots per inch is fairly straightforward.

It's only in evaluating printers that the term dots per inch (DPI) *makes sense.*

In a commercial printing environment, very high-resolution images are required.

To determine DPI, it is necessary to count how many dots can fit in a 1" × 1" area. A higher DPI can mean smoother photographs or line art. Consumer printers easily print 600 DPI or even higher, which can produce extremely good results. An increase in DPI can produce better-looking images. While you'll see (and hear) DPI used a lot… it solely refers to print and physical output.

VIDEO TRAINING
Setting Preferences

Pixels Per Inch (PPI)

When you view your images on a computer monitor, you are seeing pixels displayed on your screen. Computer monitors traditionally hold 72 pixels per inch (however, modern monitors have variable resolution settings). The standard measurement of resolution in Photoshop (and all computer programs) is *pixels per inch (PPI)*.

When you view a photograph on a computer monitor, you're looking at pixels.

A FIX FOR THOSE WITH LESS THAN PERFECT EYESIGHT

Working with a high-resolution monitor and having a hard time seeing your menus in Photoshop? Starting with Photoshop CS2, Adobe has given the user the option to change the size of the display text. Press Cmd+K (Ctrl+K) to open the General Preferences window. From the UI Font Size menu choose Medium or Large to give your eyes a break.

Detect Displays

Color LCD
640 x 480, Millions
640 x 480 (stretched), Millions
800 x 500, Millions
800 x 600, Millions
800 x 600 (stretched), Millions
1024 x 640, Millions
1024 x 768, Millions
1024 x 768 (stretched), Millions
1152 x 720, Millions
✓ 1440 x 900, Millions

Number of Recent Items ▶
Displays Preferences…

Samples Per Inch (SPI)

What about scanners? Manufacturers often tout the DPI capabilities of their scanner. This is inaccurate. Scanners don't use dots, they use samples. A *sample* is when the scanner captures part of the image. *Samples per inch (SPI)* is a measurement of how many samples are captured in the space of one inch. In general, an increase in sampling leads to a file that is truer to its analog original. However, there is a threshold: Once we pass

Modern computer monitors support various screen resolutions. Changing the monitor resolution results in a different amount of pixels per inch displayed on your monitor. Do not run Photoshop at a screen resolution smaller than 1024 x 768 or it will cause user interface problems.

a certain amount of information, our human senses (or electronic output devices) cannot tell the difference.

Consumer-level scanners can capture optical resolution ranging between 100 to 2400 SPI. Professional devices can go significantly higher.

Capturing a large number of samples is crucial if you need to enlarge an image. More samples per inch will translate into more information available as pixels, which can then be harnessed upon output when they are converted to dots in the printer. So if your scanner says DPI, it really means SPI… but you can see how the two are so closely related.

Lines Per Inch (LPI)

In professional printing environments, you'll most often hear of *lines per inch (LPI)*. This is from the traditional process where images with gradiated tones (such as photographs) are screened for printing to create a *halftone*. This was performed traditionally by laying film with dots printed on it over the film before exposing.

These days, the work of converting an image to lines is performed by an imagesetter. These dots are arranged in lines, and the LPI measurement refers to the number of lines per inch. An increase in LPI leads to smoother images. Table 1 shows the most common LPI settings for different output formats.

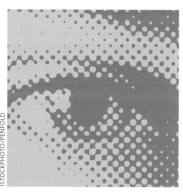

ISTOCKPHOTO/PENFOLD

This image has been converted to a halftone, as evident by the visible dot pattern.

Table 1   Common LPI Measurements

Output Method	Typical LPI
Screen printing	35–65
Laser printer (Matte paper)	50–90
Laser printer (Coated paper)	75–110
Newsprint	60–85
Offset printing (Uncoated paper)	85–133
Offset printing (Coated paper}	120–150+
High quality Offset printing	150–300

Image Mode

Within Photoshop, you need to choose from one of eight image modes when working with a document. The mode you pick will depend upon what you need to do with the image and how you intend to output it. The three most common modes are RGB, grayscale, and CMYK, but it's worth taking a quick look at all eight.

VIDEO TRAINING
Changing Image Modes

RGB Color

The most common mode for graphics in Photoshop is RGB mode. The RGB mode uses additive color theory to represent color (a 100% value of red, green, and blue light creates white light). Different intensity values of red (R), green (G), and blue (B) combine to form accurate colors. By mixing intensity values, virtually ever color can be accurately represented.

When working in Photoshop, most designers choose RGB mode for its wider range of available color (also known as *gamut*) and wide support for filters and adjustments. Additionally, computer monitors use RGB mode to display color and this is the native color space for onscreen display. Since you'll be processing images on a computer most often, it is easier to work in the same color space as your monitor.

CMYK Color

Professional printing uses a four-color process to simulate color. The four inks are cyan (C), magenta (M), yellow (Y), and black (K, for *key*). The CMYK color space uses the subtractive color model to re-create color. Subtractive color explains the theory of how ink or dye absorbs specific wavelengths of light and reflects others. The object's color is based on which part of the light spectrum is not absorbed. While print designers use CMYK mode for professional printing, they will work in RGB mode throughout the design stage. CMYK mode has a smaller color gamut, so CMYK conversion is saved until the last stage of image preparation.

Grayscale

A grayscale image uses different shades of gray to represent image details. For an 8-bit image, this is represented by 256 levels of gray (see "Bit Depth" later in this chapter). Likewise, a 16-bit image would show 65,536 levels of gray (a substantial improvement, but it requires an output device that can utilize the data). Grayscale mode can be greatly impacted by printer conditions, as the amount of ink coverage can vary, and this will impact how dark the image will print. For example, many newspaper images look washed out in Photoshop, but fine when the ink prints on the highly absorbent newsprint.

Duotone

The duotone can really be a monotone, duotone, tritone, or quadtone. Grayscale images that use a single-colored ink are called *monotones*. *Duotones, tritones,* or *quadtones* are a grayscale image printed with two, three, or four inks, respectively. Using both black and gray ink to represent the tonal values can allow duotones to create better-printed grayscales.

The most popular form of duotone is the sepia-tone image (often seen in historical prints). In modern times, a designer may use a duotone for style purposes, or to save money by using fewer inks.

Bitmap

A bitmap image is an image that uses only one of two color values—black or white (no gray)—to represent the pixel data. These 1-bit images have a very small file size. In order to create a bitmap, you first must convert the image to an 8-bit grayscale formula, and then convert to the bitmap color mode.

Do not confuse bitmap image mode with a bitmap image, which is another name for *raster* (or pixel-based) images. Additionally, there is the BMP file format, which is a standard Windows file format that dates back to the earliest version of Windows. Neither of these two usages means the same thing. An image in the bitmap color mode is simply using only black and white to represent image data.

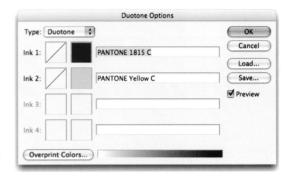

Indexed Color

Indexed color mode severely limits the number of colors used to represent the image. In indexed color mode, 256 colors are available. In order to reduce file sizes (and download times) some Web designers use fewer colors in their graphics. They will turn to specialized formats like GIF and PNG-8. While this mode reduces file size, it also visibly lowers the quality of the image. Indexed color mode works well for illustrations or logos, but not so well for photos on the Internet. Instead of converting the image to Indexed Color mode via the Image menu, you can access this mode by using the Save for Web command (File > Save for Web). This will convert the GIF or PNG-8 to indexed color but leave the original image at a higher quality image mode.

Lab Color

L*a*b* color is the most complete color mode used to describe the colors visible to the human eye. The three parameters of color are L for luminance of the color, a represents the color's position between red and green, and b represents its position between yellow and blue.

The Lab color mode was created to serve as a device-independent, absolute model to be used for a reference. Lab mode is most commonly used in Photoshop to work with Photo CD images. Lab attempts to simulate the full gamut of color, however, it is a three-dimensional model and it can't be represented properly within Photoshop. Hence the * after the L, a, and b to signify that it is a derivative model. Lab images can only be printed on Postscript Level 2 and Level 3 printers, for all others, they must first be converted to CMYK mode.

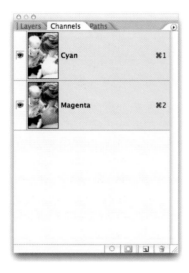

Multichannel

Multichannel mode is a highly specialized mode used for complex separations for professional printing. You may never need to use it. Photoshop automatically converts to multichannel mode when you delete a channel from an RGB or CMYK image. The color onscreen is no longer accurate because Photoshop cannot describe it. This is sometimes done for an effect, or as part of the image repair process if one channel did not capture properly (such as from a malfunctioning digital camera). Most likely, you'll never want to work in multichannel mode.

Bit Depth

Besides resolution (the number of pixels) and color mode (the way colors are processed) there is one other variable that affects image quality. Bit depth measures how much color is available for display or printing of each pixel. A greater bit depth means each pixel contains more information for describing the color. A pixel with a bit depth of 1 can display the pixel as either black or white. The most common bit depth is 8-bit mode, which has a possible value of 256 intensity levels per color

channel. However, depending on the version of Photoshop you are working with, you can access 8, 16, or 32 bits per channel. It's important to note, though, that larger bit depth can limit image adjustment commands.

Time to Move On

There's a lot more ground to cover, but we'll explore the topics discussed here and others in greater depth in each chapter. Hopefully you feel a little bit more comfortable with the language used to describe images and color. With this knowledge, we can jump into Photoshop and start to move around its interface.

Photoshop's Interface

2

Photoshop's interface can be pretty intimidating. Among all those windows, tools, and menu commands it's pretty easy to get lost. However, you know it's worth it to master these components. Adobe Photoshop is by far the most-used image editor, and knowing how to harness its power unlocks a world of design opportunities. Working professionals use it for a variety of tasks, from enhancing magazine photos to designing Web animations, from creating television graphics to performing medical imaging.

Open the file One Way.psd from the Chapter 2 folder on the DVD-ROM included with this book. Many of the windows in Photoshop require an image to be open before they display any detail.

You can press the letter F to enter full-screen mode. This can be useful as it blocks out other images on your computer's desktop.

The most important thing is to learn the essential features you need right away, then gradually grow into the rest as needed. I frequently tell students of all levels that there are often three or more ways to do the same thing inside of Photoshop. This is because Adobe's software designers have tried their best to make the program intuitive (and we certainly don't all think the same way). Additionally, new features are often unveiled with product updates, yet the old features remain for those who resist change or prefer the older method.

Learning Photoshop is a very doable task, especially if you take a balanced and measured approach. At this point in my career, I have taught over 25,000 people how to get more from Adobe Photoshop. I have seen older professionals as well as young students grow into the program. In fact, I tell people that learning Photoshop is the best way to learn other Adobe programs such as Illustrator and After Effects, as well as diverse tasks like color correction for video or Web page design.

Understanding the Interface

So let's start with a quick tour of the Photoshop interface. Since many of these windows will be new to you, we'll tackle them in alphabetical order. The goal here is to get the "lay of the land" and just learn what each tool is used for. Throughout the rest of the book we'll dig much deeper into how (and when) to use these tools. However, in our learning process, we'll need to use tools before we've had a chance to go into them in depth, so a basic knowledge right away is very important.

Actions

Actions are among the least-used features of Photoshop—and the most powerful. Actions allow for visual scripting, which means you can record commands or adjustments that you need on one image, and play them back on other images. For example, you could record an action that adjusts the size of an image, runs an adjustment to lighten the image, then converts it to a TIFF file for commercial printing. Then you could play that series of commands back on another image or even batch process an entire folder of images (which can eliminate boring, repetitive work). Actions can be very useful for both design and production tasks.

So why don't more people use them? There are a few hitches when creating actions (they are *very* literal and record exactly what you do). Learning to use keyboard shortcuts in Actions allows the action to be more flexible and work on several images and situations. However, learning to harness Actions can save you hours of time on complex jobs. I speak from personal experience having used them in my video and multimedia company from the technology's inception; I have saved thousands of hours through the years. I'm such a fan of Actions that I cowrote the Video Actions that ship with Photoshop CS2.

While we'll explore Actions fully in Chapter 15, "Actions and Automation," let's whet your appetite by running a built-in action:

1. Create a new Photoshop document by choosing File > New. From the New document window, click the drop-down menu next to preset and choose 640 × 480. Click OK to create the new window.

2. Choose the Actions palette and make it active. If you can't find it, then choose Window > Actions.

VIDEO TRAINING
Actions Palette

3. Click the Actions palette submenu (the small triangle in the upper-right corner). In the flyout menu, scroll to the bottom of the list and choose Textures.

4. In the Actions window, expand the Textures folder by clicking the triangle to the left of the Textures set (the folder icon). The set's contents open up, revealing some built-in texture actions.

5. Select Green Slime, and then press the Play selection button at the bottom of the Actions palette (it looks like the play button on a DVD player). Photoshop will run through a series of commands and create a new texture. Run the action again for further variety.

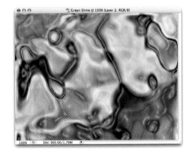

Animation
(Introduced in Photoshop CS2)

Photoshop has a companion program called ImageReady that began its life as a stand-alone Web graphics tool. Then with Photoshop 5.5 it got bundled in. The Animation window has always been a part of ImageReady. With the release of

Photoshop CS2, ImageReady development has virtually stopped and its features appear to be rolled into Photoshop.

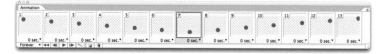

You can use the Animation window to create a frame-based animation (such as a banner ad for a Web site). We'll explore these techniques in greater depth later in the book.

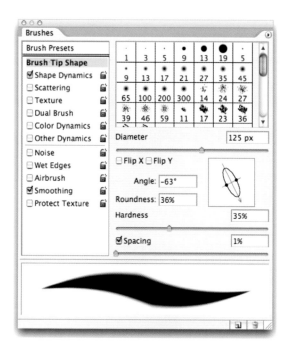

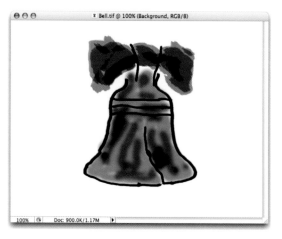

Brushes

You don't have to be a painter to appreciate the power of brushes in Photoshop. Brushes are a part of image touchup, masking, and design projects. Press F5 or choose Window > Brushes to view the Brushes palette.

Depending on the version of Photoshop you are using, the window may vary. What is important is to click the Brush Preset area and view the built-in brushes. Try your hand at using the brushes:

1. Create a new 640 × 480 document.

2. Press D to load the default colors of black and white.

3. Press B to select the Brush tool from the Toolbox.

4. Click the canvas and begin to paint with your mouse. I drew the Liberty Bell using a variety of brushes and shades of gray (access other colors or shades using the Swatches palette). Feel free to paint a different object or just doodle for practice.

5. Return to the Brushes palette and choose a different brush from the Brush Presets.

Continue to experiment. For more on brushes be sure to see Chapter 6, "Painting and Drawing Tools."

Channels

In the previous chapter we discussed different image modes that a computer graphic could occupy. In the Channels palette you can view the individual components of color. The brighter the area in the individual channel, the more presence there is for that color. Let's look at a simple example of an RGB graphic.

VIDEO TRAINING
Channels Palette

1. Choose File > Open and navigate to the Chapter 2 folder on the book's accompanying DVD-ROM.

2. Open the image called RGB Overlap.psd. You should see red, green, and blue circles overlapping one another. The overlap has also created new colors: red + green = yellow; blue + green = cyan; red + blue = magenta; and red + green + blue = white.

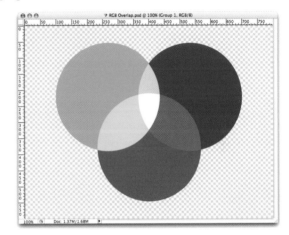

3. Activate the Channels palette; by default it is docked with the Layers palette (just click on its name and the window will switch to show you Channels). If you don't see it, choose Window > Channels.

4. Look at the individual channels; you'll see a definitive area for each color. Notice how the full circles are visible (and white) where there is 100% value of each channel.

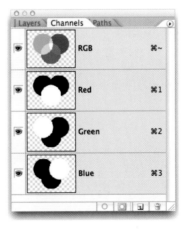

Fully understanding Channels unlocks a wealth of image-processing power. Harnessing color's individual components is difficult at first, but well worth the effort. We'll delve much deeper into Channels in Chapter 10, "Color Correction."

Character

While Photoshop began its life as an image editor (essentially a digital darkroom), it has greatly evolved over the years. Many people start and finish entire designs right inside of Photoshop. These include advertisements, posters, packaging, and DVD menus. A powerful text tool is essential and Photoshop has truly matured over the years. A close look at the Character palette will reveal complex control over the size, style, and positioning of individual characters within a word. The type tool is explained in significant depth in Chapter 12, "Using the Type Tool."

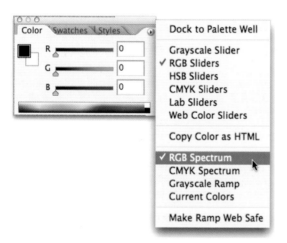

Color

Don't confuse the Color palette with the color mode of the document. The Color palette allows you to modify and select colors using six different color models. You can choose colors using RGB sliders, or the more intuitive Hue Saturation and Brightness (HSB) model. To adjust color, move the sliders for the corresponding value. Sliding the Red slider to the right increases the amount of red in the new color. Choosing colors is independent of image mode in that you can use a CMYK model for an RGB image. However, picking a color to use in a grayscale document will not introduce color into that image.

Spend some time exploring the Color palette and find a mode that works best for you. Clicking on a color swatch opens the powerful Color Picker, which unlocks a larger visual interface for exploring color, and enhances the use of the Eyedropper tool to sample color from a source image. We'll use color in several of our chapters and the Color palette and Color Picker are fairly easy to understand.

Histogram (Introduced in Photoshop CS)

While color-correcting or adjusting exposure, the histogram can be a great help. This graph illustrates how the pixels in the image are distributed across intensity levels. To read a histogram, start at the left edge, which shows the shadow regions. The middle shows the midtones (where most adjustments to an image are made), and to the right are the highlights. We'll cover image touchup and enhancement in Chapter 10. You may want to leave the Histogram palette open as you work, as it is an easy way to learn to read the graphical details of a digital image.

The Histogram palette has been set to Show All Channels view. You can choose this interface by clicking the triangle in the upper-right corner and choosing All Channels view. The top histogram is a composite histogram for the red, green, and blue channels combined; the next three show them individually.

History

The History palette will quickly become your best friend. It's here that Photoshop keeps a list of what you have done to the image since you opened it. By default, Photoshop keeps track of the last 20 steps performed on an image but you can modify this number. A higher number means more levels to Undo:

1. Press Cmd+K (Ctrl+K) to call up the Photoshop Preferences dialog box.

2. From the General pane, change History States to a higher number, such as 100.

3. Click OK.

Info

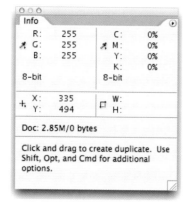

The Info palette is a useful place to find a plethora of information, even using the default options. However, by customizing the palette, you can make it truly useful:

1. Select the Info palette by choosing Window > Info or pressing F8.

2. From the Info palette submenu (the triangle in the upper-right corner) choose Palette Options.

3. The resulting dialog box has several options; I recommend the following choices for a new user:

   • Leave Mode set to Actual Color.

   • Set Second Color Readout to CMYK if you're doing print work or RGB color if you are preparing images to use on the Internet or in video exclusively.

   • Set Mouse Coordinates to Pixels.

- Enable the following choices under Status Information: Document Sizes, Document Profile, and Document Dimensions.

- The last option, Tool Tips, provides a detailed explanation for each tool you select from the Toolbox.

4. Click OK.

5. Leave the Info palette open as you work to get a clearer understanding of your tools and document.

Layer Comps (Introduced in Photoshop CS)

A Layer Comp is essentially a snapshot of a state of the Layers palette. New users may not be able to fully appreciate the power and flexibility that Layer Comps brings to a designer. Their usefulness comes from their ability to store multiple designs or options (also known as *comps*) within one document. You can record three kinds of layer options:

- **Layer visibility:** Whether a layer is visible or hidden.

- **Layer position:** Within the document.

- **Layer appearance:** Whether a layer style (such as a drop shadow or outer glow) is applied to the layer and the layer's blending mode.

We'll spend more time on Layer Comps in Chapter 8, "Compositing with Layers."

Layers

In Photoshop, a layer can contain artwork and transparency information. This allows you to combine (or composite) multiple images into a new piece (such as a postcard or advertisement). Originally, Photoshop did not have layers. You could open a picture to process it, but that was about it. However, over time the demands placed on Photoshop by its users led to its evolution. As Photoshop moved beyond a mere touchup tool, the flexibility of layers emerged to meet the demand. By isolating discrete elements to their own "layers," designers can make

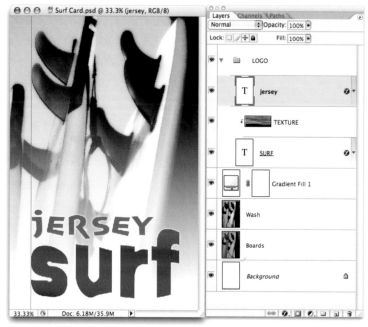

You can explore this layered file by opening Surf Card.psd in the Chapter 2 folder on the DVD-ROM.

several changes and freely experiment with their design.

Without sounding like a zealot, layers mean everything to a designer in Photoshop. You will spend much of this book (and your early career using Photoshop) getting comfortable with layers. With that said, *always* leave your Layers palette open while you work (press F7 to open); this is where most of the action takes place. The Layers palette is like the steering wheel of a car. We'll dig much deeper into layers in Chapter 7, "Layer Masking," and Chapter 8, "Compositing with Layers."

Navigator

While working with photos, you'll often need to zoom in to touch up an image. While it may sound cliché, it's easy to lose your perspective when working in Photoshop. When you zoom in to a pixel level for image touchup, you often won't be able to see the entire image onscreen. This is where the Navigator comes in handy:

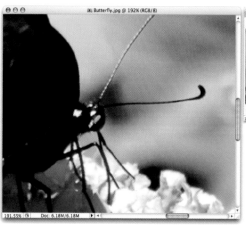

1. Open the photo Butterfly.jpg from the Chapter 2 folder on the DVD-ROM.

2. Select the Zoom tool from the Toolbox or press Z (the tool looks like a magnifying glass). Click multiple times near the butterfly's head to zoom in.

3. Call up the Navigator palette by choosing Window > Navigator.

4. You can now navigate within your photo:

   - Drag the red View Box around the thumbnail to pan within the image.

   - Resize the Navigator palette for a larger image preview.

   - Move the Zoom Slider to zoom in or out on the image.

   - Click the Zoom Out or Zoom In buttons to jump a uniform magnification.

VIDEO TRAINING 5
Navigator Palette

Options

The Options bar is essential, as it contains the majority of controls for the active tool. It consolidates the most used (and useful) options for the active tool and moves them up front for easy access. The Options bar is visible by default. It runs the length of your monitor and is docked directly below your menus. Be certain to keep the Options bar open, as you'll always need it. If you accidentally close it, you can bring it back by choosing Window > Options.

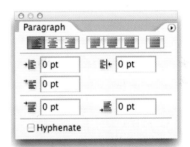

Paragraph

The Paragraph palette contains controls that impact Paragraph text. When using the Type tool, you can click and type, which creates Point Type. Or, for more control, you can click and drag to create a text block and have access to Paragraph Type. This will cause the text to have boundaries and wrap when it hits a margin. Within this text block, you can have a significant level of control on how your type is aligned and justified. For much more on text see Chapter 12.

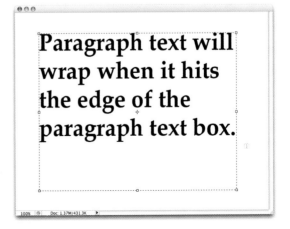

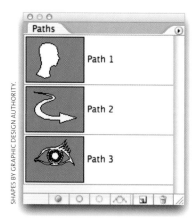

SHAPES BY GRAPHIC DESIGN AUTHORITY.

Paths

While Photoshop is known as a raster-editing tool (because of its several pixel-based functions), it does contain several vector tools as well. Vectors use lines that are defined by math equations; as such, they can be scaled indefinitely, and always remain crisp. Several of those vector tools can create paths, which are useful for complex selections. You can create a path with the Pen tool. By clicking around the image, anchor points are created, then Photoshop connects the dots with vector lines. Paths can also be created using the vector shape tools The Paths palette is where you can select which path you want to update. For more on complex selections, see Chapter 5, "Selection Tools and Techniques."

Toolbox

Your hands-on tools are all contained in the Photoshop Toolbox. Photoshop groups similar tools together. You can access these hidden tools by clicking and holding on a particular tool. Whenever you see a triangle in Photoshop, click it to open additional options.

The first keyboard shortcuts you'll want to master are those for the Toolbox. Frequently, the first letter of the tool is the keyboard shortcut. If you can't remember the shortcut, click the tool while holding down the Option (Alt) key to cycle through the available tools.

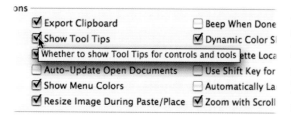

An alternative method is to press the keyboard shortcut multiple times while holding the Shift key (for example Shift+M will cycle between the Rectangular and Elliptical Marquee tools.) If you'd like to simplify things, then call up the Preferences dialog by pressing Cmd+K (Ctrl+K). Disable the Use Shift Key for Tool Switch option. You can now tap a shortcut key (such as G for Gradient Tool) and cycle through the tools contained in that tool's drawer. This speeds up your ability to switch tools. While you are in your General Preferences area, enable the Show Tool Tips feature to assist in learning common keyboard shortcuts.

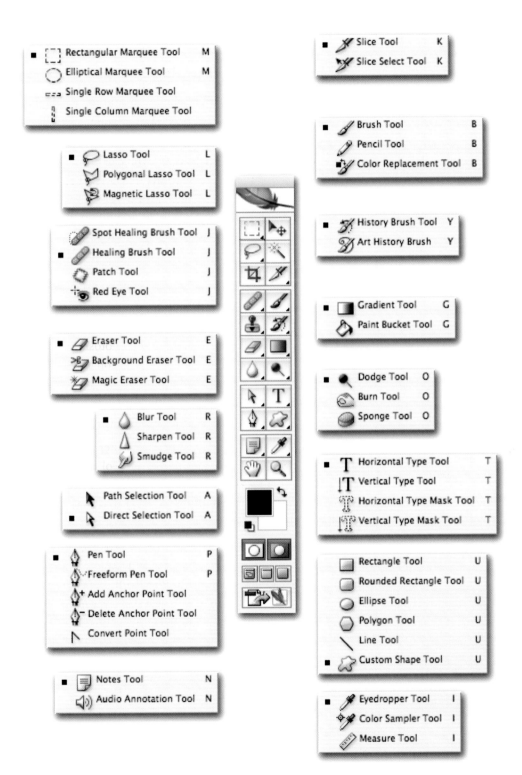

Rectangular Marquee Tool M
Elliptical Marquee Tool M
Single Row Marquee Tool
Single Column Marquee Tool

Lasso Tool L
Polygonal Lasso Tool L
Magnetic Lasso Tool L

Spot Healing Brush Tool J
Healing Brush Tool J
Patch Tool J
Red Eye Tool J

Eraser Tool E
Background Eraser Tool E
Magic Eraser Tool E

Blur Tool R
Sharpen Tool R
Smudge Tool R

Path Selection Tool A
Direct Selection Tool A

Pen Tool P
Freeform Pen Tool P
Add Anchor Point Tool
Delete Anchor Point Tool
Convert Point Tool

Notes Tool N
Audio Annotation Tool N

Slice Tool K
Slice Select Tool K

Brush Tool B
Pencil Tool B
Color Replacement Tool B

History Brush Tool Y
Art History Brush Y

Gradient Tool G
Paint Bucket Tool G

Dodge Tool O
Burn Tool O
Sponge Tool O

Horizontal Type Tool T
Vertical Type Tool T
Horizontal Type Mask Tool T
Vertical Type Mask Tool T

Rectangle Tool U
Rounded Rectangle Tool U
Ellipse Tool U
Polygon Tool U
Line Tool U
Custom Shape Tool U

Eyedropper Tool I
Color Sampler Tool I
Measure Tool I

The Tool Tips will teach you the proper name, as well as keyboard shortcut, for each tool.

There are many tools and each has multiple purposes (as well as strengths and weaknesses). Throughout this book, we'll address how to effectively use these tools. With patience, you'll get the most from Photoshop's powerful feature set.

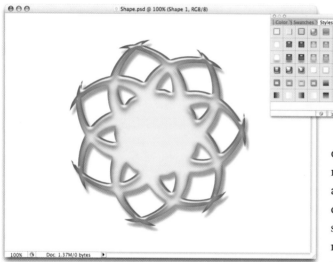

Styles

The Styles palette is where you can visually access Layer Styles. These are the combination of Layer effects (which can be applied singularly to create effects such as beveled edges, drop shadows, or glows). Effects are most useful in combination, however, and advanced photorealistic effects can be achieved. Photoshop ships with several built-in styles, and many more are available for download from Adobe's Web site (www.adobexchange.com) as well as many other Photoshop sites. Layer Styles are frequently used for text and image effects, but can also be harnessed for Web rollover effects for buttons. For more on Layer Styles, be sure to read Chapter 13, "Layer Styles."

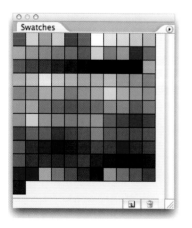

Swatches

The Swatches palette is like a painter's palette in that it holds several colors ready to use. There are several colors loaded by default , which are useful when painting or using filters that utilize those colors. If you click the palette's submenu, you'll discover many more swatch books to load for specialty purposes like Web browser colors, spot color printing, or thematic color swatches (such as a blue saturated range).

Tool Presets

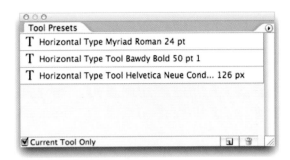

Tools in Photoshop are much like a socket wrench set. With little effort, you can quickly swap out a piece and have a different tool. For example, you can create a specialized brush then adjust its size, hardness, opacity, and color. Then, for a different task, you might choose to modify the brush again. Tool Presets enable a user to save tool setups to make it easier to jump back and forth between tools. We'll use Tool Presets in later chapters, and you can learn more about them in the Adobe Help Center.

Prevent Palette Popping

Many pro designers use two monitors (or a very large wide-screen monitor) to hold all of their design tools. For most users, though, infinite space is not a luxury. One of the biggest wastes of time is "palette popping." Many users open and close tools and palettes all day long–dragging windows all over the place, closing and opening the same windows over and over. Here are three solutions to avoid wasting time.

Temporary Banishment

If you want to hide your palettes, you can quickly toggle them off and on:

- Press the Tab key to hide all of your palettes.

- Press the Tab key again and they return.

- Press Shift + Tab to hide everything except the Options bar and Toolbox.

- To focus on only the active window, press the F key once to blank out all other images, or twice to darken the edges of your screen. Press F and Tab again to go back to standard screen mode with menus and tools.

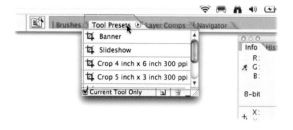

Sitting on a Dock

On the right side of the Options bar is the palette well. This is an empty space where palettes can be stored. When you drag palettes into the well, they are docked as drop-down menus. It's a good idea to put useful but rarely used tools like the Brushes palette and Navigator here.

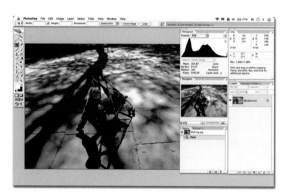

A Custom Workspace

You'll find the more you work with Photoshop, the more you'll want different tools for different situations. For example, you'll want Layer Styles and the Color Picker handy for text work, but will turn toward the Histogram and Brushes palette when doing image restoration.

You can save any combination and arrangement of windows that you want to reuse. Then you can access it in one click with Workspaces. Effectively, using Workspaces enables you to switch between different production tasks (such as image touchup and type work) with ease.

Plus, it is a way to customize the application and make it feel more welcoming to you. Let's try it out.

1. Open the windows you need, and arrange them into the desired positions.

2. To save the current workspace layout, choose Window > Workspace > Save Workspace.

3. Enter a unique name for the workspace, and click OK.

To activate a workspace, choose Window > Workspace, and select a workspace from the submenu. To update a workspace, resave it with the same name. To delete a workspace, choose Window > Workspace > Delete Workspace.

Acquiring Digital Images

3

While Photoshop is a great tool for a lot of tasks, most of them center around the sizing, manipulation, and processing of digital images. While their contents may vary, all digital images are essentially the same: They are composed of pixels that contain color and luminance information. Photoshop's powerful features will allow you to adjust those pixels to better match your needs.

While the destination may be the same, the path your digital images take to get inside of Photoshop will vary. Some may start out as digital images acquired with a still camera, while others may get loaded via a scanner. You may also find yourself turning to online resources to find specialized images. Let's take a look at the many ways to acquire your digital images.

Pixels in detail: When we zoom into the image at 1600% magnification, the pixels are very easy to see. You can open the photo Car in Mirror.tif from the Chapter 3 folder and use the Zoom tool (Z) to magnify the image.

Digital Cameras

This book will not teach you how to use your digital camera. There are many excellent books on that subject as well as classes offered. What we will address is how the pixels are converted, what file format you should choose to shoot your images, and how to transfer them to your computer.

Sensors in a digital camera acquire the image by converting light into pixel data.

The Bayer filter arrangement uses an arrangement of red, green, and blue pixels and is very common in digital cameras. There are more green pixels because the human eye is more sensitive to green information.

Digital Camera Technology

Shooting a photo digitally produces a less accurate image than scanning a photo shot on film and scanned with a flatbed scanner using a high SPI setting. This is because digital cameras capture data using photosensitive electronic sensors. These sensors record brightness levels on a per-pixel basis. However, these sensors usually are covered with a patterned color filter that has red, green, and blue areas. While the filter attempts to capture all detail that the lens sees, it is unable to due to its design.

The filter used is usually the Bayer filter arrangement, which contains two green pixels and one red and one blue. The Bayer filter uses more green because the human eye has increased sensitivity to green. This filter allows the image to record the brightness of a single primary color (red, green, or blue) as digital cameras work in the RGB color space. The RGB values combine using the additive color theory (which we briefly discussed in Chapter 1, "Digital Imaging Fundamentals") and form an image when viewed from a suitable distance.

Since not all traditional camera functions can be fully imitated by the computer sensors in a digital camera, the camera must interpolate the color information of neighboring pixels. This averaging produces an anti-aliased image, which can show visible softening. When anti-aliasing is present, hard edges are blended into one another. Sometimes this can be desirable (with low-resolution Internet graphics where you reduce file size by limiting color). Other times, anti-aliasing can produce an undesirable softness when you print an image. Depending on the colors in the original image, a digital camera may only capture as little as one-fourth of the color detail. For example, if you had a scene like a desert with a great detail of red, and little green or blue, the sensor would rely on the red areas of the filter (which only cover a fourth of the sensor face).

Am I saying to shoot film only? Of course not… I shoot both. What is important is to shoot for what you need; there are strengths and weakness to both film and digital (as well as several stylistic decisions as well). Ultimately, film captures a high-quality image that can be optically enlarged using the negative. However, digital can be more convenient and affordable as you get instant feedback on the images you have just taken, and you eliminate the time-consuming process and costs associated with developing the film. It is just important to note that you should shoot at a higher pixel count (which can be accomplished by telling the camera to shoot a high- or best-quality mode). You can always crop or shrink the image down for output or display, but you should avoid having to enlarge the image as this will create unwanted softness or pixelization (a visible blockiness) in the image.

Shooting JPEG vs. RAW

When digital cameras became commercially available, the memory cards used to store pictures were very expensive. Photographers could not afford multiple or high-capacity cards, so they wanted more images to fit on a single, smaller card. Many users also emailed their pictures to friends and family. Smaller file size enabled consumers who lacked an understanding of digital imaging to attach photos to email with minimum technical headaches. With these two scenarios in place, manufacturers turned to an Internet-friendly format, JPEG. It was a proven technology and one that was familiar to many users.

The Joint Photographic Experts Group (JPEG) format is extremely common as most hardware and software manufacturers have built support for it into their products. The JPEG format is also extremely efficient at compressing images, and it is a good format for continuous tone images, such as photos. A JPEG file looks for areas where pixel detail is repeated, such as the color white on every key of your computer keyboard. The file can then discard repeated information and tell the computer to repeat certain color values or data to re-create the image.

DSC_0177.jpg   DSC_0177.NEF

Many digital cameras allow you to shoot JPEG (left) and RAW (right) simultaneously. This is helpful for photographers who are in transition and learning how to switch to RAW as they have a JPEG safety around for ease of mind.

While JPEG is a good format for distributing images (due to their compatibility and small file size), it is not great for image acquisition or production. A JPEG file is lossy, as every time you modify it in Photoshop, and resave, additional compression is applied to the image. Over subsequent compressions, the image quality can noticeably deteriorate. This is similar to the act of making a photocopy of another photocopy: Additional image deterioration occurs with each processing step. The visible loss in image detail or accuracy is referred to as *compression artifacts*.

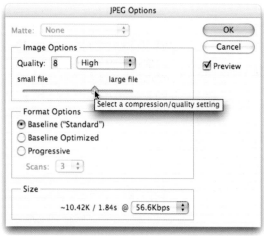

The JPEG Options box is present when you work with a JPEG in Photoshop. You can adjust the Quality slider to reduce file size. It is a good idea to leave Quality set to maximum if you are going to make changes to the image; this applies the least compression that could hurt the image's appearance.

So, if JPEG is so bad, why do so many people use it? Money and resistance to change are the simple answers. It's a lot cheaper to shoot JPEG images, as you don't need to buy as many memory cards. Additionally, even many pros have been slow to abandon JPEGs. Learning how to use new technology requires time, something that most people are short of these days.

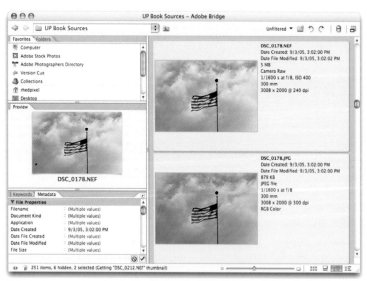

This shot was captured as both a Raw and a JPEG file when it was shot. The picture was taken with a Nikon D70, which can write both files to the memory card when shooting.

Newer digital cameras, generally the pro models, offer a newer format called raw. This newer format has several benefits over shooting to JPEG. The images are usually captured at a higher bit rate, which means that the pixels contain more information about the color values in the image. Most raw files have a depth of 12 bits (or 16 bits) per channel instead of the 8 used by JPEG. This raw format also has a greater tonal range, hence better exposure for shadows and highlights. This extra information will make your work in Photoshop easier as it adds greater flexibility and control in image adjustments and color correction. You should have less work to do as well, since the image captured more detail than a JPEG would have.

Raw files can be two to six times larger than JPEG files. This extra data is used to hold more image detail. This can reduce, or even eliminate, compression artifacts. However, that extra data can take longer for the files to write to the memory card.

The raw file captures the unprocessed data from the camera's image sensor. While your camera may contain settings for sharpness, exposure, or lighting conditions, the raw file stores that info as modifiable information, and captures the original (unmodified) data that came through your camera's sensors. Each manufacturer treats the format differently, using a proprietary format. Fortunately, Photoshop frequently updates its raw technology to support the newest cameras on the market. To find out if you can access a particular camera format from within Photoshop, visit Adobe's Web site (www.adobe.com/products/photoshop/cameraraw.html).

Workaround for Unsupported Cameras

If Photoshop does not support a particular raw format used by your camera, then turn to the software that shipped with the camera. The image can be converted into a TIFF image (a high-quality file with no compression), which Photoshop can open.

VIDEO TRAINING
Camera Raw Interface

Because the raw data is unprocessed, you must essentially "develop" the image data inside of Photoshop. You'll be presented with several choices when opening a raw image. You can choose to adjust several options related to the image, as well as the lens and lighting conditions. You can "tweak" the image after shooting it (as opposed to JPEG, which is limited to the settings you had when shooting).

The Adobe Camera RAW dialog box is a versatile environment for "developing" your pictures. The image Peppers. NEF is included on the DVD if you'd like to explore. Just choose File > Open and navigate to the file in the Chapter 3 folder.

IS DNG THE NEW RAW?

In 2004 Adobe released the Digital Negative Specification (DNG). The code and specifications have been made publicly available so manufacturers can build in support to their products. The goal was to replace several proprietary raw file formats with a universal format. Despite initial optimism, camera manufacturers have been very slow to adopt it (some even refusing). At this point, DNG files are a useful way to archive raw files and attach additional metadata. You can find out more at Adobe's site at www.adobe.com/products/dng/main.html.

The raw dialog box has continued to evolve since it was first introduced as a purchased add-on to Photoshop 7. Subsequent versions of Photoshop have continued to modify the user interface. To help you learn about these options, your safest bet is to read the many entries in the Adobe Help Center. Fortunately, the Camera RAW dialog box is fairly intuitive, especially once you understand the concepts of adjusting images. Once you have completed Chapter 10, "Color Correction," you should feel much more confident using the options in the Camera RAW dialog box.

TIP

Make Backup Copies

You may want to work with a copy of your transferred image, especially if you are just getting started in Photoshop. Many users will duplicate a folder of images and work with those. Others will burn a copy of the original images to a CD or DVD for backup. Preserving an original digital file is a good idea for future usage. If shooting raw, there is no need to duplicate the raw file. The modifications to the image are stored in a separate sidecar file in the folder with your images.

Acquiring Images from a Digital Camera

There are two major ways of downloading images from a digital camera. Which connection type you choose will depend upon your work environment and budget for additional hardware.

The first method involves plugging the camera directly into the computer. Many cameras ship with a connecting cable (generally USB). The advantage of this approach is that it doesn't require an extra hardware purchase. The primary disadvantages of this method are that it ties up the camera and it is hard on delicate ports built into the camera. If you break the USB port by constantly plugging and unplugging a camera, it can lead to an expensive service bill. The data port is interconnected with several other systems on the camera; a break at one end can result in problems in other areas.

A better option is to purchase a stand-alone memory card reader. There are many options available, so ask yourself a few questions and choose wisely:

1. Do you need only one card format, or do you need to read multiple formats?

2. Is read-only enough, or do you want to be able to erase and reformat cards while they are in the reader?

3. How fast do you want your files to transfer? Many card readers are USB 1, which can take a long time to transfer files. Look for USB 2 or FireWire for faster data rates. Laptop users with a PC card slot can purchase an effective card adapter for fast file transfers without tying up ports.

This card reader is designed for laptop users who have an open PC card slot.

NOTE

Transferring Files

The actual transfer of files is handled natively by your computer's operating system. You can use built-in tools (like iPhoto) to transfer files, or manually copy them to a folder on your computer.

Scanners

While it may come as a surprise to some of the people reading this book, not all cameras are digital. Shooting on film is still a very valid choice. Film offers greater flexibility for low-light situations, as well as offers some aesthetic options not afforded by digital. Many purists swear that shooting film adds richness in detail and color, as well as the introduction of subtle nuances like film grain, which cannot be replicated with a digital camera. Additionally, many pictures that you'll need to work with may exist on traditional media (such as prints) or as a negative. You'll need to use a scanner to turn these optical formats into digital formats.

Choosing a Scanner

If you are in a computer lab or work environment, your choice in scanners may have already been made for you. However, it is still important to understand the different types of scanners that are available to consumers.

TIP

Keep Your Images Organized on Your Computer

To manage your digital photo collection you have several options. Photoshop CS2 includes an application called Bridge that works efficiently to search and organize images. Additionally, I find that iPhoto works well for the Mac (and its bundled with most machines or part of the $49 iLife suite). You can also modify iPhoto's preferences so double-clicking a photo opens it in Photoshop. For PC users, be sure to check out Photoshop Album for its convenient cataloging abilities.

NOTE

LPI versus PPI

The general rule is to take your LPI requirement and multiply by two. Round up to the nearest large number and you have your PPI requirements.

Flatbed Scanners

The most common scanner type is a flatbed scanner. Photos are loaded, face down, on a piece of glass. The scanner then moves a charge-coupled device (CCD) across the image to capture/digitize the image. High-quality scans can greatly increase the amount of data that is captured. As such, be sure to look at high-speed scanner-to-computer connection options. For a modern computer, FireWire or USB 2 are the best options. Do not get too bogged down with scanner attachments. Unless you only occasionally need them, slide adapters and transparency adapters don't work as well as a dedicated specialized scanner. These options often just add to the cost of the scanner. Be sure though to pay close attention to the optical resolution of the scanner; this is the maximum size of the image before software interpolation to enlarge it. Most users doing intermediate-level work, or desktop publishing, find a scanner capable of 600 to 1200 SPI to be adequate. Remember, samples per inch can translate fairly well into pixels per inch. It is a good idea to have more pixels to start with, and size the image down for delivery.

COMMON PPI REQUIREMENTS FOR FINAL FILE

Output Method	Typical PPI
Onscreen	72–96
Screen Printing	100–150
Laser Printing	150–250
Newsprint	120–170
Offset Printing	250–300
High-Quality Offset Printing	300–600

TIP

Multifunction Units

Many people purchase all-in-one units to save space and money. These combo machines can offer scanning, printing, photocopy functions, and faxing abilities. Do not ignore these units, as they can be great space-savers. Do realize, though, that if part of the unit breaks, you may be faced with a higher replacement cost. Consider an extended warranty, especially if you are a heavy user.

Film/Slide Scanners

Specialized scanners load in slides or film negatives. These scanners use a tray to hold the material, and then a motor pulls the tray slowly across an optical sensor. This process is relatively slow due to the resolution needed. The scanner must capture a lot of data from a very small surface area in order to produce a usable image. These scanners are slightly more expensive than flatbed scanners, but are essential if you work with slides or negatives frequently.

Drum Scanners

When top image quality is a must, pros turn to drum scanners. These units are very expensive (starting at $5,000 and going up–significantly). This scanning technology is the oldest. It calls for the image to be mounted on a drum. This drum is then rotated in front of a photomultiplier tube. This tube is much more sensitive than the CCDs used in flatbed scanners. Drum scanners' primary advantage is resolution, and they should be used when you need to significantly enlarge a scanned image (such as museum archival pieces or for magazine output). Because the machines are expensive and very complex (as well as potentially destructive), users will often send images to a service bureau for drum scanning.

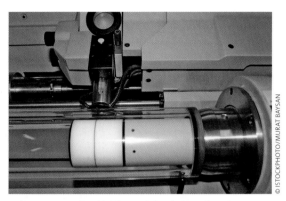

A drum scanner is a highly specialized piece of equipment. These machines are very expensive and are usually found only in high-end service bureau facilities.

What Size to Scan? Think in Pixels

People often get thrown when determining how big to scan. Too little information and the picture goes soft. Too much and you'll just slow the scanning down to a crawl. The answer is to know your intended output resolution as well as your device.

PURCHASING POWER

Shopping for a scanner can be a very confusing experience (which is usually made worse by the sales staff). Prices have plummeted in recent years as scanners have become more common. (Scanners used to cost so much that they would bundle in full copies of Photoshop to entice purchasers).

Be sure to keep the following in mind when looking to buy a scanner:

1. **Does the scanner connect to my computer using a fast interface such as USB 2 or FireWire?**
2. **What is the optical resolution of the scanner? For example, 3000 pixels are enough to print a 10-inch image at 300 DPI.**
3. **Does the scanner support my computer's operating system?**
4. **Does the scanner come with a TWAIN plug-in that will allow Photoshop to see the scanner for direct import of images?**
5. **Does the scanner offer special features such as Digital ICE or a descreen filter for improving image quality?**

For example, if you need to create a poster that is 20 inches wide and will be printed on a high-quality press requiring 300 PPI, use this calculation:

20 (inches) × 300 (PPI) × 1.25 (pad for flexibility) = 7500 pixels

TROUBLESHOOT YOUR SCANNER

Routinely check your manufacturer's Web site for new drivers. This software improves how well your scanner interfaces with Photoshop. The updates are generally free.

If your scanner malfunctions, power down your system and check your cable connections. When satisfied, power up the scanner first and restart your computer. If the problem is not fixed, check for new drivers.

Do not adjust the DPI (or PPI) settings of your scanner. Rather, crop the image after running a preview scan. You can then adjust the scanner's resolution by looking at the output size of the scanned file. As you adjust the output file size, the scanning software will automatically determine the appropriate settings for samples per inch. All scanners tell you just how many samples you are about to capture. Looking at these numbers gives you a truer sense of what you are really going to get. Total pixel count is much more important than DPI, especially when scanning images of various original sizes.

Scanner Operation

VIDEO TRAINING
Scan, Crop & Straighten

It is safe to say that every scanner model is a little different. Hardware manufacturers must write software that allows the scanner to interface with your computer. When choosing a scanner, be sure it works with your computer's operating system (always check the box or manufacturer's Web site carefully).

1. Before scanning an image, install the software and drivers needed by your scanner. These are usually included on a disc provided by the manufacturer or for download from its Web site.

2. Ensure that the scanner is lying flat, or you may get misregistered scans.

3. Place your photos on the scanner straight. Use the edges to help you maintain parallel edges on your photos. If you get crooked photos, try the new automation tool File > Automate > Crop and Straighten Photos (available in Photoshop CS or later). You'll find two Crop and Straighten demo files in the Chapter 3 folder.

4. Run a preview scan first to check image placement and details.

5. If your scanner allows you, set the white and black points before scanning. This is accomplished by making a preview scan, then using your scanner's software to identify a black and a white point in the image. You can then use Photoshop's color correction tools to adjust the white and black points as well as make additional color changes. Every scanning software program is different, so be sure to see the documentation included with the scanner or on the manufacturer's Web site.

6. Scan slightly higher than the quality you need; for example, scan at 300 SPI for newsprint, even though you may only deliver it at 170 PPI. The extra pixel information will allow you to zoom in for further corrections. It also gives you extra pixels in case you need to crop the image.

7. Save to formats such as TIFF (Tagged Image File Format, a standard in the print industry). This file is efficient for storage and supports Lossless compression to reduce file size. The Photoshop (PSD) format is great for layered files, but is not as efficient for single-layer files. Always save the appropriate file extension for your file type.

GOOD CLEAN FUN

There is no quick fix for dirt or grime on an image once it's in Photoshop. With this in mind, make sure your scanner and images are clean before you scan.

1. Make sure the scanner is clean. Use a gentle glass cleaner whenever smudges appear. Spray the cleaner on a soft cloth, and then wipe the scanner bed down. Let the scanner completely dry before placing photos on the glass.

2. Make sure your photos are clean before scanning. Never write on the back of photos, instead write on a Post-it note and temporarily adhere it to the back.

3. If scanning previously printed items (such as magazines, books, or inkjet prints) you will likely get a moiré pattern. This is manifested by visible dots and is caused by the scanner grid not lining up with the dot pattern of the original image. Try scanning at a higher resolution, and if that doesn't work, use the descreen filter in the scanning software. If this option is not available (or you can't rescan the picture), run Photoshop's Median filter at a low value (Filter > Noise > Median).

TIP

Capture More Than You Need

There's no need to overdo it, but I always recommend capturing two to three times more data then you will need. For example, if you are going to be outputting a Web graphic at 1024 × 768, you should capture at least 3000 × 2000 pixels to start. Having the extra pixel data will give you more details to work with when zooming in for touchup. It also allows for you to make decisions about cropping and reformatting.

If you scan an item that has been previously printed, you'll often see a moiré pattern. To fix this problem, your best option is to go back to the original source, or turn on the descreen option in your scanner's software.

Importing from CD/DVD

You will often find image collections available for sale on CD-ROM or DVD-ROM discs. While this is a great way to distribute images (cheap to manufacture and large-capacity discs that are cross-platform compatible) it is not a good way to work on images. You'll want to copy the images to your hard drive before you bring them into Photoshop. This will significantly increase the speed at which you can work on the images (hard drives transfer data faster than optical media drives). Additionally, you will be able to save your work in progress to your hard drive; you can't save to the CD or DVD.

© ISTOCKPHOTO/MAARTJE VAN CASPEL

Stock Photo Services

Professionals find it is often necessary to purchase images to complete their projects. Whether it's a shot of broccoli for a magazine layout, or the New York skyline for the cover of a DVD, stock photo services can help. But finding the right stock photo service is a balancing act. You must consider several factors when making a choice.

- **Cost:** There is a lot of competition out there, and photos are priced accordingly. Some services offer annual subscriptions, others charge per image. Be sure to keep your budget in mind when searching for needed photos.

- **Resolution:** Sites often charge more for higher-resolution images. Be sure to know how you'll use the image; Web site designers will pay less for an image than someone designing an annual report. That's because a Web image is lower resolution, while the report will be professionally printed and require higher-resolution images.

- **Exclusivity:** Does the image need to be yours and yours alone? Or is it OK that you might see the photo in someone else's project? Images that have their usage rights-managed cost more. A rights-managed image has restrictions placed on who can use the image for a certain time period. In contrast, a royalty-free image is purchased once and can be used as many times as the designer wishes.

- **Quality:** Expensive doesn't guarantee "better," but it does increase your chances. More expensive sites often have a better selection and image choices (the best photographers charge more, go figure). If you are on a budget, prepare to spend more time searching. There's a line often used in the professional creative community: "Good, Fast, Cheap… pick two." Seems appropriate here as well.

ROYALTY-FREE DOES NOT EQUAL FREE

Do not confuse *royalty-free* and *free*. A royalty-free image must still be purchased. This is how the photographer and distributor make money. Royalty-free images can be a big savings as you can eliminate model releases, talent charges, location fees, travel, and many other costs associated with a photo shoot. However, someone had to pay those charges in the first place, and selling their pictures is their livelihood. Remember to pay for what you use. It's the professionally responsible way, as well as the law.

Finding Stock Photos with Adobe Bridge

Starting with Photoshop CS2, a stock photo browser is built into Photoshop (via Bridge, the file browser). Please note: These images are targeted at professionals, and are often expensive.

1. Choose File > Browse to access Bridge.

2. Click the Adobe Stock Photo link under Favorites.

3. In the search field, type a keyword to search. Press return.

4. The corresponding images will load. You can then choose to Get Price & Keywords, download a Comp Image (low-quality preview) to show your client, or Add to Cart to purchase.

TIP

Don't Pay Twice

Here are two cost-saving tips when it comes to purchasing stock images.

- If downloading images, be sure to back them up to CDs or DVDs. Most stock image sources allow you to make a backup copy for your own use.

- If you are a student, check with your school library. Many have memberships to online image services. Your tuition or tax dollars have paid for these images, just be sure to check out any restrictions you may have.

THE FAIR-USE MYTH

A popular myth in academic cultures is *fair use*. The doctrine provides situations where copyright works can be used without paying. It places restrictions on:

For more on copyright and fair-use doctrine, visit www.copyright.gov.

1. **The purpose and character of the use, including whether such use is of a commercial nature or is for nonprofit educational purposes;**

2. **The nature of the copyrighted work;**

3. **The amount and substantiality of the portion used in relation to the copyrighted work as a whole; and**

4. **The effect of the use upon the potential market for or value of the copyrighted work.**

Students and teachers alike get caught up in exemption number one. It is true that in a classroom situation, you can use virtually any image you want for practice or class exercises. However, here is the problem: As soon as a student wants to start looking for a job and builds a portfolio, those images are being used for financial gain. If you are a student, you need to build work samples that help you get a job. Use images that you have the rights to (or have photographed yourself).

The other clause that is often seen as a loophole is number four. People often think that because their project was "small" or "personal" that damage cannot be claimed. It is relatively easy for a copyright holder to claim damages or lost revenue. While they may not go after you, why take the chance? As a content creator, you should respect the law and the welfare of your fellow designers and photographers.

Finding Stock Photos Online

Another way to find stock images is to turn to the power of the Internet. There are several sites available to choose from. Here are some that offer high-quality images. Be sure to compare prices and usage rights to ensure they work for your project.

- **istockphoto:** (pay per image) www.istockphoto.com
- **AbleStock:** (subscription based) www.ablestock.com
- **Photo Objects:** (subscription based) www.photoobjects.net
- **Photos.com:** (subscription based) www.photos.com
- **Comstock Images:** (pay per image) www.comstock.com
- **Thinkstock Images:** (pay per image) www.thinkstock.com
- **Stockbyte:** (pay per image) www.stockbyte.com

Public Domain Images

I'd say "The best things in life are free" but that wouldn't be accurate here. More appropriately, "Why pay twice?" The federal government has several agencies that document their work and make it available to the public. This work was paid for with tax dollars, and the people of the United States own the work. Fortunately, through the Internet, the U.S. government is willing to share a lot of it with the world.

Be sure to check out the following Web sites. They offer print-resolution images that you can use. Nearly every image is copyright-free, but you may be required to cite the source. Be sure to look at the terms of use posted on the site. Be sure to fully explore each site; you'll be surprised by the wealth (and diversity) of available images:

- **Center for Disease Control- Public Health:** http://phil.cdc.gov/phil/home.asp
- **CIA World Fact Book:** www.cia.gov/cia/publications/factbook

- **Creative Americans 1932–1964:** http://memory.loc.gov/ammem/vvhtml/vvhome.html
- **Images of American Political History:** http://teachpol.tcnj.edu/amer_pol_hist/_browse.htm
- **Library of Congress:** http://lcweb2.loc.gov/ammem/ammemhome.html
- **NASA Earth from Space:** http://earth.jsc.nasa.gov/sseop/efs/land
- **NASA Image Exchange:** http://nix.nasa.gov
- **NASA Visible Earth:** http://visibleearth.nasa.gov
- **National Park Service Digital Image Archive:** http://photo.itc.nps.gov/storage/images/index.html
- **NOAA Photo Library:** www.photolib.noaa.gov
- **U.S. Army Corps of Engineers Digital Visual Library:** http://images.usace.army.mil
- **U.S. Air Force Link:** www.af.mil/photos/index.asp
- **U.S. Antarctic Program:** http://photolibrary.usap.gov
- **U.S. Department of State:** www.state.gov/r/pa/ei/pix
- **U.S. Fish & Wildlife Services:** http://images.fws.gov
- **U.S. Government Image Portal:** www.firstgov.gov/Topics/Graphics.shtml
- **U.S. Navy:** www.news.navy.mil/view_galleries.asp
- **USDA Agricultural Research Service:** www.ars.usda.gov/is/graphics/photos
- **USDA:** www.usda.gov/oc/photo/opclibra.htm

Sizing Digital Images

4

Once you've acquired your digital images, you will need to size them for your project (as well as ultimate output). For many Photoshop users, such as photographers, this may be as straightforward as cropping and sizing. This chapter explores several techniques for sizing your images. We'll examine the concept of resampling, which addresses how the computer adds or subtracts information from a digital image while trying to retain detail and clarity.

Resolution Revisited

In Chapter 3, we looked closely at the process of acquiring digital images. If you skipped ahead or just skimmed that chapter, go back—a solid understanding of those concepts is required. Quite simply, you must be aware of the ability of your hardware to ingest information. Be sure to know what your scanner or digital camera is capable of.

In previous chapters, we also briefly discussed output requirements for different formats. The second part of the image-sizing puzzle is a clear understanding of output

This photo was scanned at two different resolutions. The image on the left was scanned at 300 SPI and the image on the right was scanned at 72 SPI. Examine the detailed enlargements to see the impact of different scanner settings.

**START OUT RIGHT:
DIGITAL CAMERAS**

If you are acquiring a digital image, then be sure to capture enough pixels. If you are trying to make a 5 × 7 inch print and need 300 DPI, then do the math before shooting. Take the inch size and multiply it by the print resolution. In this example: 5 × 300 = 1500, and 7 × 300 = 2100. Therefore, 1500 × 2100 = 3,150,000, which is about 3.1 megapixels. To allow for cropping, you may want to shoot at an even higher resolution.

requirements. What resolution does your printer need? Are you sending the image to a service provider such as a developer or commercial printer? There are a lot of choices you'll need to make, but they are based on where the image needs to end up. Do not make assumptions when starting a project. Know your destination, and you will know which path to take.

START OUT RIGHT: SCANNERS

If you know the LPI requirements of your output device, then it is relatively easy to determine the resolution you'll need. In general, you'll want a resolution that's 1.5 to 2 times the screen frequency you'll use to print. For example, if you need a 3 × 5 inch image at 150 LPI, then you'll want to use the following settings to scan.

- 150 LPI × 2 = 300 DPI

- 300 DPI × 3 inches = 900 total pixels needed

- 300 DPI × 5 inches = 1500 pixels needed

- Scan with a pixel dimension of 900 pixels × 1500 pixels

Remember: To allow room for cropping, you may want to scan at a higher pixel count. If you feel unclear on determining the right scanning resolution, be sure to revisit Chapter 3, "Acquiring Digital Images."

Resampling

The process of resampling allows you to change the pixel dimensions of your image. This will affect the display and print size of your image. This part of the resizing process is important for several reasons:

- Images will print faster when they are sized properly for your output device.

- Images will print clearer when you size them to a target size, then run a sharpening filter to enhance the edge detail.

- Images appear crisper when they are displayed at 100% on a computer screen (such as for a PowerPoint presentation).

The process of resampling is often identified based on whether you are scaling the image smaller (downsampling) or larger (upsampling):

- **Downsampling:** If you decrease the number of pixels in an image, you have downsampled the image. When you downsample an image, you are permanently discarding data. You can specify an interpolation method (discussed in the next section) to determine how pixels are deleted. Once an image has been downsampled and saved, you cannot restore the discarded data.

- **Upsampling:** If you increase the number of pixels in an image, you have upsampled the image. When upsampling, you are creating new pixels to expand the image. Again, you can specify an interpolation method to determine how pixels are added. When upsampling, you are adding information that did not previously exist. This will result in a loss of sharpness and detail.

Choose an Interpolation Method

When you resample an image, Photoshop creates new pixels. Those new pixels are created based on the neighboring pixels. How those new pixels are formed is determined by the interpolation method you specify. Photoshop offers up to five methods to resample your image (older versions, such as Photoshop 7 and earlier, offered only the first three).

Choose one of the following methods:

- **Nearest Neighbor**: This method is fast but not very precise. It is useful for resizing illustrations. However, it can produce jagged edges.

- **Bilinear:** This approach uses pixel-averaging. It is a balance of speed and quality, and produces medium-quality results.

- **Bicubic:** This method is slower but more precise than the first two (and more desirable). Photoshop spends more time examining surrounding pixels before interpolating new ones. The math at work is very complex, and will produce smoother results than Nearest Neighbor or Bilinear.

TIP

Avoiding Upsampling

You can avoid the need for upsampling by scanning or creating the image at a sufficiently high resolution. If you want to preview the effects of changing pixel dimensions onscreen or to print proofs at different resolutions, resample a duplicate of your file.

- **Bicubic Smoother:** This method is a refinement of Bicubic. It is specifically designed for upsampling (enlarging images).

- **Bicubic Sharper:** This method is also a refinement of Bicubic. It is useful for downsampling (shrinking images). It does a better job of maintaining sharpness than the other methods.

Setting the Default Method

Photoshop allows you to choose a default interpolation method. This will be used when you invoke a sizing command, such as the Free Transform or Image Size commands (more on both in the pages ahead). Choose the method that best matches your workflow.

1. Choose Edit > Preferences or press Cmd+K (Ctrl+K) to call up your Preferences dialog box.

2. From the Image Interpolation drop-down menu, choose your default method (I recommend Bicubic as the most flexible method).

3. Click OK.

Resizing an Image

If you have an image, it's probably not sized exactly how you need it. You have several options at your disposal. To change the size of an image, you can use the Image Size or Canvas Size menu commands. You can also use the Crop tool or Free Transform command to make an adjustment. You can use these choices individually or in combination to achieve the desired results.

Image Size

The Image Size command lets you permanently reassign the total pixel count, as well as resolution, for a particular image. This command can also be used to upsample or downsample an image. This is an easy way to size an image to a specific height or width. Let's put the command into action:

1. Open the file Weis_Altar.tif from the Chapter 4 folder.

2. Choose Image > Image Size.

   In the Image Size dialog box, you have several choices. You can choose to manipulate the pixel dimension of the image (measured in pixels or percent). You can also modify the print size, which is the size of the image when printed. You can modify the print size based on percent, inches, centimeters, millimeters, points, picas, or columns. The most common choices will be percent, inches, or centimeters, as these are easily understood by most users.

3. Set the Document Size to measure in inches. Specify a new height of 4 inches.

4. Be sure Resample Image is checked if you want to change the pixel dimensions. Choose the method to Resample Image that is most appropriate for your image. Bicubic is the most common method but you may have special circumstances. See "Choose an Interpolation Method" earlier in this chapter.

5. Leave the Constrain Proportions box checked, or you will introduce distortion. You generally want to keep the width and height constrained to the same ratio so the image resembles its original appearance.

6. Click OK.

This photo was resized from a height of 5.5 inches to 4 inches. The resolution of 300 pixels per inch did not change. The image on the right is smaller because it has fewer total pixels.

RETURN OF FOCUS

When upsampling an image, you may notice visible softening. The more you enlarge the image, the more noticeable it will be. Enlargements greater than 30% can be particularly problematic.

One approach to solving this issue is to sharpen the image.

Applying the Unsharp Mask filter to a resampled image can help refocus the image details. Photoshop CS2 (and later) includes the Smart Sharpen filter, which is technically superior to the Unsharp Mask filter. You can find out more on sharpening images in Chapter 11, "Repairing and Improving Photos."

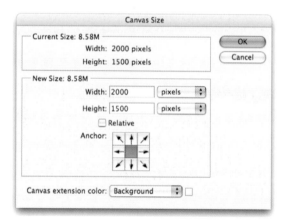

Canvas Size

The canvas size is your work area. When you create a new document you can specify the size of your canvas. When you scan a photo or import a digital image, the canvas size is set to the edge of the image. You may need to change the canvas size to crop or extend the canvas of your image to work on specific areas of the image. Let's try it out:

1. Open the file Beach.tif from the Chapter 4 folder.

2. Choose Image > Canvas Size.

When you launch the Canvas Size command, you will see the pixel dimensions of your current canvas. You can specify a new canvas size using a variety of measurements. Pixels is a useful measurement if creating screen graphics, while inches or centimeters is easier to understand for print work.

Let's place a uniform border around the image.

3. Check the Relative box. This disregards the numerical values of the current canvas size and allows you to specify a new amount to be added to the existing image.

4. Set the anchor point for the image to be centered. This will expand the border in all directions around the center of the current image.

5. Add a quarter-inch border on all sides. Type .25 inches into the Width and Height fields.

6. Specify a Canvas extension color. This is the color that Photoshop places around the image when you change the canvas size. You can choose to use the Foreground or Background colors that are loaded in the Toolbox. You can also use white, black, gray, or other… which can be any color you specify. In this case, choose white.

7. Click OK.

Crop Tool

The Crop tool allows you to change a viewer's perception of an image. You can choose to tighten the area of interest of an image, which allows you to deemphasize (or even eliminate) parts of a photo. This allows you to improve an image by better framing the subject.

By cropping this image, unnecessary portions of the background have been eliminated.

There are two ways to invoke cropping. The first method involves making a selection with the Rectangular Marquee tool, then choosing Image > Crop. While this works fine, it does not offer as much control as using the second method, the Crop tool. Let's put method two into action:

1. Open the image Riders.tif from the Chapter 4 folder.

2. Choose the Crop tool from the Toolbox or press the keyboard shortcut C.

3. With the Crop tool make a selection to crop the image. In this case, removing the rider on the far left (who is chopped off) will improve composition of the image. Additionally, reducing the headroom (space above the riders' heads) will also improve the image's appearance.

4. You can refine the crop selection after it is made. Click and hold on the crop selection border. You can pull the crop tighter, or expand it looser. Additionally, you can click the corner of the crop border to expand two sides at once.

5. Examine the crop. Make sure the Shield box in the Options bar is checked. This gives you a better idea of the area to be cropped.

6. When satisfied with the crop, press Return (Enter) or click the Commit button (check mark) in the Options bar. The shielded (darkened) areas will be cropped. To cancel, press the Esc key.

Cropping Keyboard Shortcuts

- To toggle the shielded area off, press the forward slash key (/).
- To hide the selection border (aka "marching ants"), press Cmd+H (Ctrl+H).

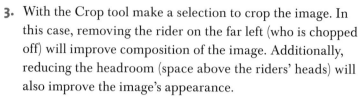

VIDEO TRAINING
Power Crop

Power crop

It is possible to crop and resize an image at the same time. I refer to this technique as a *power crop* and it is a huge timesaver. Before cropping, you can type the desired size of your final image into the Options bar. When you drag to crop the image, your box will constrain to the proper aspect ratio. This allows you to resize and crop in one step.

Let's crop an image to a 4-inch by 4-inch square at 200 PPI.

1. Open the file Ludwig_castle.tif.

2. In the Options bar, type 4 in (as in *inches*) into both the Width and Height fields.

3. In the resolution field, type in 200 and set it to pixels/inch.

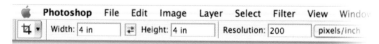

4. Drag to crop the image. Your crop selection is constrained to the shape you specified in the Options bar.

5. Click the Commit button or press Return (Enter). When finished cropping, you may want to press clear to reset the tool's default settings.

Nondestructive cropping

Cropping is very important, but it's also very permanent. When you crop an image, you are permanently discarding data. Nondestructive editing is a workaround that allows you to crop an image and keep the cropped pixels available for future use. Nondestructive editing provides you with flexibility throughout the design process. Let's put the technique to the test.

1. Open the image Flowers.tif from the Chapter 4 folder.

2. In order to crop nondestructively, you must "float" the *Background* layer. We'll explore layers in depth in Chapter 8, "Compositing with Layers." For now, convert the *Background* layer to a floating layer. Double-click the word *Background* in the Layers palette. Name the layer Flowers and click OK.

3. Select the Crop tool by pressing C.

4. Mark out the area to crop.

5. In the Options bar, change the Cropped Area to Hide (by default it is marked Delete).

TOOL PRESETS SAVE TIME

If you have a specific image size that you use often, then harness the power of Photoshop's Preset Manager. You can create tool presets that already have the values for a tool loaded.

1. Type in a desired size and resolution into the Options bar.

2. When the Crop tool is selected, you will see its icon in the upper-left corner of the Options bar. Click the triangle to lower the drop-down menu.

3. You'll see several preset sizes that Photoshop has stored.

4. Click the Create new tool preset icon in the drop-down menu (it looks like a pad of paper).

5. Photoshop stores the preset crop size in a temporary preferences file.

6. To permanently save cropping sizes, click the submenu icon in the drop-down menu (the small triangle in a circle). Choose Save Tool Presets, and save them in a desired location.

VIDEO TRAINING
Nondestructive Cropping

6. Click the Commit button or press Return (Enter).

7. Select the Move tool by pressing the keyboard shortcut V (as in *moVe*, the letter *M* is taken by the Marquee tool). Drag in the image and reposition it, the original pixels are still there. This will allow you to modify the crop in the future.

Perspective cropping

Some images will have visible distortion; this is often caused by the camera not being square with the subject. If the photographer was higher (or lower) than the image, or if the photo was taken at an angle, you will see distortion. In some cases, this distortion is part of the shot composition and is desirable. In others, the distortion can be distracting. Let's square off an image:

1. Open the file Window.tif from the Chapter 4 folder.

2. Select the Crop tool by pressing C.

VIDEO TRAINING
Perspective Cropping

3. Crop around the window in the photo as tight as you can to frame it.

4. In the Options bar, set the Crop to Delete and not Hide. Then check the box next to Perspective.

5. Drag the upper-right and upper-left corners in towards center. You are trying to line up the crop borders parallel to the edge of the window. The crop selection will no longer look rectangular.

6. Click the Commit button or press Return (Enter). The resulting image should appear as if the photo was squared and the camera was level.

Rotate Canvas Command

Your image may need to be rotated or flipped. This is often caused by loading your image upside down on the scanner, loading a slide backwards into a slide scanner, or turning the camera on its side when taking a portrait. You may also want to make a change to the image for compositional purposes.

The Rotate Canvas command offers several choices. You can choose to rotate the image 180° (half a rotation), 90° clockwise or counterclockwise, or an arbitrary amount (the user types in a number of degrees). Additionally, the entire canvas can be flipped (creating a mirrored image). You can choose to flip the canvas horizontally or vertically:

1. Open the image Canyon.jpg from the Chapter 4 folder.

2. Choose Image > Rotate Canvas 90° CCW (counter-clockwise). The image is now properly oriented.

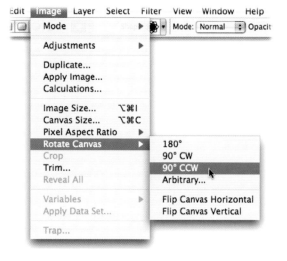

VIDEO TRAINING
Free Transform Command

Free Transform Command

The Free Transform command is another useful way to rotate and size an image. It works best when you have an object located on its own layer or if you have an active selection. We'll explore selections and layers in much greater detail in future chapters. For now, let's work with a simple layered image that has already been prepped.

1. Open the file Free_Transform_Basic.psd.

2. This image has two layers: a background, which is a gradient, and a vector shape layer. A vector layer is a special layer in Photoshop. It can be resized and transformed repeatedly with no degradation in quality. Vector layers use math to describe curves, and can be freely manipulated.

3. If it's not visible, call up the Layers palette from the Windows menu.

4. Select the Vector Shape layer so it is active.

5. Choose Edit > Free Transform or press Cmd+T (Ctrl+T).

You can access several controls for the Free Transform command by right-clicking/Control-clicking. Try the following transformations on the Vector Shape layer. You can press the Esc key to cancel the transformation or Return (Enter) to apply it.

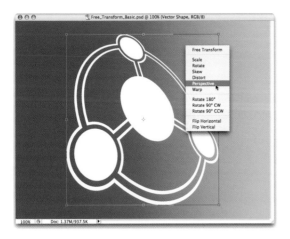

- **Scale:** You can scale by dragging a handle. Hold down the Shift key as you drag a corner handle to scale proportionately. Hold down the Option (Alt) key to scale in both directions simultaneously. To scale numerically, enter a value in the Options bar.

- **Rotate:** You can choose to rotate a preset amount by selecting Rotate 180°, Rotate 90° CW, or Rotate 90° CCW. To rotate freely by dragging, move your mouse outside the Free Transform box. It will become a curved, two-headed arrow. Hold down the Shift key while rotating to constrain the rotation to 15° increments. Additionally, you can rotate numerically by entering degrees in the rotation box in the Options bar.

- **Skew:** Skewing an image creates a sense of distortion, as if the image were leaning. To skew the image, hold down Cmd+Shift (Ctrl+Shift) and drag a side handle (not a corner handle). The cursor will change to a white arrowhead with a small double arrow.

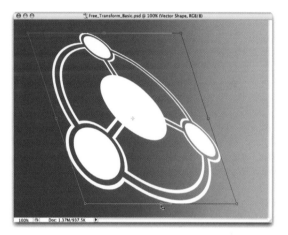

- **Distort:** If you want to distort an image freely, choose Distort. This allows you to move the corners of the image freely (a process also known as corner-pinning). This command can also be accessed by pressing Cmd (Ctrl) while dragging a corner point.

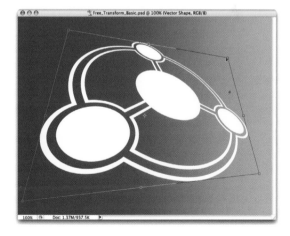

- **Perspective:** Transforming perspective creates the illusion that the image is being viewed from above or from the side. You can access this command by pressing Cmd+Option+Shift (Ctrl+Alt+Shift) or from the contextual menu. This is a useful command to fix perspective problems or to add perspective effects.

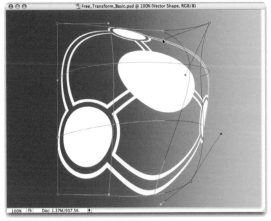

- **Warp:** The Warp command was first introduced in Photoshop CS2. It allows you to distort an image into a number of pre-defined shapes available in the Options bar (such as Arch, Flag, or Twist). By choosing Custom, several points can be freely dragged to distort the image as you see fit.

- **Flip Horizontal and Flip Vertical:** These simple commands let you flip an individual layer without having to flip the entire canvas.

The Free Transform command has one major benefit over choosing individual transform commands from the Image menu: Free Transform lets you apply transformations in one continuous operation, which cuts down on quality-loss for raster images.

For more practice, open the file Free_Transform_Additional.psd from the Chapter 4 folder. This will give you extra practice rotating, flipping, and positioning layers. Transform the images and create a basic layout that allows you to see all three images at the same time.

Open the file Free_Transform_Additional.psd. Using the Free Transform command, you can rotate, size, and flip the images to create a better layout.

USING SMART OBJECTS BEFORE TRANSFORMING

Adobe launched a new technology with Photoshop CS2 called Smart Objects. This powerful command allows you to embed raster or vector data into a layer. The layer can then be transformed indefinitely because the embedded data remains editable and scalable. You can convert one or more layers into a new Smart Object.

A Smart Object is simply one file embedded inside another. This can be very useful as Smart Objects allow greater flexibility. You can perform multiple nondestructive transforms (as long as you don't exceed the size of the original object).

VIDEO TRAINING
Smart Objects

1. Open the file Smart Object.psd from the Chapter 4 folder.

2. Select the layer City in the Layers palette.

3. Choose Layer > Smart Objects > Group into New Smart Object.

4. Invoke the Free Transform command and scale the image down very small. Apply the transformation.

5. Invoke the Free Transform command and scale the image up to its original size. Apply the transformation. You'll notice the image remains clear.

When you place a vector object into Photoshop (such as an Adobe Illustrator or EPS file), it will automatically come in as a Smart Object. Additionally, you can choose Layer > Smart Objects > Group into New Smart Object for raster-based layers.

PROFILE: STEVE UZZELL, PHOTOGRAPHER

Steve Uzzell began his career in 1972 on the photographic staff of *National Geographic*, then set out on his own in 1975. While he started as a traditional photographer, he has learned to embrace modern tools.

"There is *no* part or aspect of my job that is not impacted by digital tools—*none!*" said Uzzell. "From the beginning of every project to its end—from estimating to final image delivery to invoicing—every aspect of my daily life uses digital tools."

Uzzell is proof that the committed professional can learn digital tools and that the quest for knowledge has rewards. He's won numerous awards and has photographed two books: *Maryland* (Graphic Arts Press, 1983) and *The View From Sterling Bluff* (Longstreet Press, 1989).

Photoshop has given Uzzell greater flexibility than he had in the past. "It has completely replaced the analog (wet) lab. There used to be a need for me to use retouchers as well, and now I do it myself," said Uzzell. "Many of the effects I used to do in-camera I now do in Photoshop—for example, knock a sky down to bring a foreground forward, or double exposures, add warming or cooling tints, soft focus, etc."

While learning Photoshop is a challenge, Uzzell offers advice on where photographers and photography students should focus. "Photoshop is the image file processing/ manipulation software of choice for the industry," he said. "Not only is it used for raw file processing, but for conversion of raw files to DNG for archive purposes, and all file-manipulation purposes past raw and DNG."

For traditional photographers sitting on the fence or resisting new technology, Uzzell offers this advice: "If they want to be digital photographers, then they have to learn Photoshop by any and every means available. I'm 58, and have *never* studied as hard to learn anything else. That is how important the knowledge of Photoshop is to my continued success and how pervasive the knowledge of it needs to be to even start your job.

For students, Uzzell stresses balancing digital knowledge with traditional skills. He admits that he is often puzzled by the number of up-and-coming photographers who lack important skills.

"Learn Photoshop, certainly, but don't forget the basics. Regardless of what industry or business path you follow, you will need to be able to communicate—writing and speaking—preferably in more than one language. A frightening number of applicants (to be my assistant) cannot write or spell beyond a very elementary school level. They have considerable difficulty speaking accurately as well. Both are nonnegotiable skills—you have *got* to have them both."

For more information on Steve and to see his extensive online portfolio, visit www.steveuzzell.com.

Selection Tools and Techniques

5

If you want to really get things done in Photoshop, you have to be good at making selections. Perhaps you want to remove an object from a picture or maybe change the sky to the right shade of blue? Maybe the sweater in your advertisement needs to be blue instead of red or you'd like to duplicate some of the background crowd so your photo doesn't look so empty. In each of these cases, you're going to need an accurate selection.

Why? While you may be able to look at a digital image and clearly recognize that it's a picture of two brown bears lying on a rock ledge, your computer just sees a bunch of pixels. A little human intervention is necessary to distinguish which part of the image you want to manipulate or process. While this means extra effort, it also means that much of digital imaging requires human intervention (which means jobs for designers and artists). Accurate selections are important, and there are several techniques you can employ to get them just right.

While your eye can easily distinguish two bears in this photo, Photoshop just recognizes pixels. It will take some human intervention to make an accurate selection of the bears.

Some are easier than others, and some are more accurate. Knowing several techniques will let you make an accurate selection no matter what your source image looks like.

Basic Selection Tools

There are three categories of tools in Photoshop's Toolbox that you can use to create a basic selection: Marquee tools, Lasso tools, and the Magic Wand. While these three are very useful, many users forget that they are only starting points. Learning to use them is important, but again, it's just the beginning.

Marquee Tools

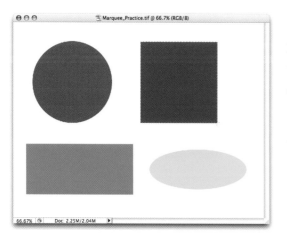

The Marquee tools allow you to click and drag to define a selection. The keyboard shortcut for selecting the Marquee tool is the letter M. To toggle between the next Rectangular and Elliptical Marquee tool, press Shift+M.

- **Rectangular Marquee tool:** Use this tool to make a rectangular selection. Press the Shift key to draw a square.

- **Elliptical Marquee tool:** Use this tool to make an elliptical selection. Press the Shift key to draw a circle.

- **Single Row or Single Column Marquee tool:** Creates a selection that is 1 pixel wide in the shape of a row or column. To be honest, these two tools are not used very often, which is why Adobe did not assign the keyboard shortcut M to trigger them.

Putting the Marquees into Action

Let's give the Rectangular and Elliptical Marquee tools a try:

1. Open the file Marquee_Practice.tif from the Chapter 5 folder on the DVD-ROM.

2. Select the four objects using both the Elliptical and Rectangular Marquee tools. Remember to use the Shift key to constrain proportions for the square and circle shapes.

A FASTER TOOLBOX

There are a few ways to access tools from the Toolbox:

- **You can click the tool icon.**

- **To access nested tools (ones that share the same well), click and hold the mouse button on the tool icon.**

- **You can press the letter shortcut key. Hovering over the Toolbox icon will teach you the shortcut keys when the tool tip pops up.**

- **To switch to a nested tool, hold down the Shift key and press the tool's shortcut key.**

- **If the Shift key is an extra step you'd rather not use, modify your user preferences. Press Cmd+K (Ctrl+K)) to call up your Preferences screen. Uncheck the box next to Use Shift Key for Tool switch.**

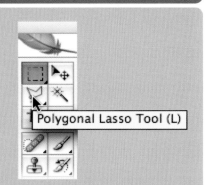

Selection Options for Marquee Tools

When using the Marquee tools, several options are available to you in the Options bar. These modifiers can improve or alter your selection.

The first four icons specify the kind of selection:

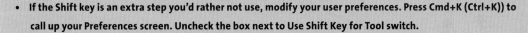

- **New Selection:** Create a new selection.

- **Add To Selection:** After you create one selection, you can click this button so subsequent selections are combined with the existing selection. You can also hold down the Shift key to add to a selection.

- **Subtract From Selection:** After you create one selection, you can click this button so subsequent selections are subtracted with the existing selection. You can also hold down the Option (Alt) key to subtract from a selection.

- **Intersect With Selection:** This option requires you to make a first selection. When you draw a second selection, Photoshop will create a new selection where the two selections overlap.

These options modify the selection tool, and must be chosen *before* making a selection:

- **Feather:** A normal selection has a crisp edge. Feathering a selection creates a gradual blend at the selection's edges. Think of it as the difference between a line drawn with a pencil and one drawn with a felt-tip marker. Feathered selections are useful when you want to extract objects.

- **Anti-alias:** When working with the Elliptical Marquee tool, you can check Anti-alias. This will create a smoother edge for curved lines (especially if your image is at a low-resolution).

- **Style:** For the Rectangular Marquee tool and Elliptical Marquee tool, you can choose from three styles in the Options bar:

  - **Normal:** This is the default option. Click to draw your marquee freehand.

  - **Fixed Aspect Ratio:** You can set a width-to-height ratio. For example, to draw a marquee three times as wide as it is high, enter 3 for the width and 1 for the height.

  - **Fixed Size:** You can specify an exact size for the marquee's height and width. You can enter the value in pixels (px), inches (in), or centimeters (cm).

Moving a Selection

There are a few ways to reposition a selection:

- While drawing a selection (with the mouse button still depressed) you can hold the space bar down and move the selection.

- With an active selection, move the tool's cursor inside the selection border (marching ants). The icon will change to a triangle with a marquee border; you can now click inside and drag the selection to move it.

- To modify a selection with controls similar to the Free Transform command, choose Select > Transform Selection. All of the options available to the Free Transform command can be applied to the selection border. For more on Free Transform, see Chapter 4, "Sizing Digital Images."

Selection Lassos

The Lasso tools allow you to draw freeform segments to create a selection border. The Lasso tools are most often used to create a rough selection (which can then be refined using techniques such as Quick Mask mode; see the section "Quick Mask Mode" later in this chapter). The keyboard shortcut for selecting the Lasso tool is the letter L. To select the next Lasso tool, press Shift+L.

- **Lasso tool:** Use this tool to make a freehand selection. You must return to your starting point to close the selection loop.

- **Polygonal Lasso tool:** Use this tool to draw straight-edged segments for a selection border. With every click, a part of the segment is drawn. Continue clicking to set endpoints for additional segments. Click your starting point to close the loop and create an active selection. To constrain to 45-degree angles, hold down the Shift key while drawing.

- **Magnetic Lasso tool:** When you use the Magnetic Lasso tool, Photoshop attempts to snap the border to the edges of the image. If the anchor point doesn't snap accurately, click once.

TIP

Deleting Selection Segments

In the middle of making a selection with the Polygonal or Magnetic Lassos, you can press the Delete key to remove segments. Press and hold once, then release and press subsequent times to remove segments (one per click).

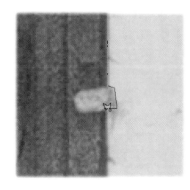

Putting the Lassos into Action

Let's give these tools a try:

1. Open the file Latin.tif.

2. Use the Polygonal and Magnetic Lasso tools to select the sign. Make multiple attempts at practicing the selection.

Selection Options for Lasso Tools

When using the Lasso tools, several options are available to you in the Options bar. These can improve or alter your selection. These modifiers are very similar to those for Marquee Tools, so we'll just briefly mention them.

The first four icons specify the kind of selection:

- **New Selection**
- **Add To Selection**
- **Subtract From Selection**
- **Intersect With Selection**
- **Feather:** This option creates a softer edge on your selection.
- **Anti-alias:** This option creates a smoother edge for curved lines.

Magnetic Lasso Options

The Magnetic Lasso has a few additional options that mainly deal with its snapping behavior:

- **Width:** The width specifies how wide an area the Magnetic Lasso looks at when trying to detect edges. If you'd like to see the width area visually, activate the Caps Lock key before making a selection.

- **Edge Contrast:** This value (measured in percent) determines the lasso's sensitivity to edges in the image. Higher values detect high contrast edges, while lower values detect lower-contrast edges.

  On an image with well-defined edges, you should use a higher width and edge contrast setting. For an image with soft edges, use a lower setting for both width and edge contrast.

- **Frequency:** The rate at which Photoshop adds anchor points is based on the Frequency setting. Anchor points are the point at which the lasso attaches, so you can move the selection border in another direction. You can enter a value between 0 and 100. Higher values add more anchor points to your selection border.

- **Stylus Pressure:** Click the Stylus Pressure button if you have a tablet connected. This option allows you to use the pressure of the pen to affect edge width.

Magic Wand Tool

The Magic Wand Tool allows you to click an area of color, and Photoshop will create a selection based on adjacent pixels and your tolerance setting. The Magic Wand Tool works reasonably well on photos with large areas of similar color. It's important to note, though, that it pales in comparison to the capabilities of the Select > Color Range Command (see the section "Color Range Command" later in this chapter).

Selection Options for the Magic Wand Tool

When using the Magic Wand tool, several options are available to you in the Options bar. These modifiers can improve or alter your selection. These modifiers are very similar to those for Marquee and Lasso tools, so we'll cover them in brief.

The first four icons specify the kind of selection

- **New Selection**
- **Add To Selection**
- **Subtract From Selection**
- **Intersect With Selection**

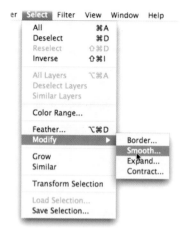

VIDEO TRAINING
Modify Selection

COMMANDS TO MODIFY A SELECTION

There are several menu commands you can use to adjust an existing selection. These can all be found on the Select menu or by choosing Select > Modify:

- **FEATHER:** The Feather command blurs the edge of the selection. While this creates a loss of detail at the edges, it can be very useful to create a blending transition (such as when extracting an object with a soft edge, like fabric or hair). The feather becomes apparent when you move, copy, or fill the selection. If you feather the edges too much, you might lose the selection border (marching ants), which is only visible above a 50% threshold.

- **BORDER:** If you have an existing selection, you can use the Border command. You can enter a value between 1 and 200 pixels. A new selection that frames the existing selection will be created.

- **SMOOTH:** The Smooth command simplifies selection by adding more pixels to the selection to make it less jagged.

- **EXPAND:** The Expand command allows you to add pixels in an outward fashion to the selection. The border will get wider based on the number of pixels you add.

- **CONTRACT:** The Contract command works the opposite of the Expand command. Specify the amount of pixels that you want the selection to decrease.

- **GROW:** The Grow command selects adjacent pixels that fall within a certain tolerance range. To modify the range, adjust the tolerance settings of the Magic Wand tool (see the next section).

- **SIMILAR:** The Similar command also selects pixels based on the tolerance settings of the Magic Wand tool. The pixels do not need to be adjacent, however.

- **TRANSFORM SELECTION:** The Transform Selection command allows you to modify an existing selection. Invoking it gives you controls similar to the Free Transform command (see Chapter 4 for more on the Free Transform command).

The remaining settings allow you to refine your selection parameters:

- **Tolerance:** This setting determines how similar the pixels must be to your initial click in order to be selected. You can enter a value in pixels, ranging from 0 to 255. A higher value selects a broader range of colors.

- **Anti-alias:** This creates a smoother edge when you click.

- **Contiguous:** When Contiguous is checked, only adjacent areas with the same colors are selected. If unchecked, all pixels in the entire image that use the same colors will be selected.

- **Sample All Layers:** If you have a multilayered document and you want to select colors on all layers, check this box.

Putting the Magic Wand into Action

Let's try out the Magic Wand Tool:

1. Open the file Sky.tif from the Chapter 5 folder.

2. Select the Magic Wand Tool by pressing W for *wand.*

3. Check the Contiguous box to better limit the selection. If unchecked, it is likely that some of the jacket will accidentally be selected.

4. Set the tolerance to 30 and check the Anti-alias box.

5. Click the sky in the upper-left corner to make an initial selection.

6. Part of the sky will be selected. Hold down the Shift key and click another area of the sky to add to the selection. Repeat as needed until the entire sky is selected.

A BETTER WAND

The Magic Wand Tool works best if you turn on the pixel-averaging option. But where is it? It doesn't appear in the Options bar when the Magic Wand Tool is selected. Instead you must select the Eyedropper tool. Then in the Options bar you can change the Sample Size to a 5 by 5 Average. The Magic Wand Tool (as well as a few other tools) will then become less sensitive to erroneous clicks.

Additional Selection Commands

There are a few more Selection commands that can be found under the Select menu. For a sense of completion, let's take a quick look:

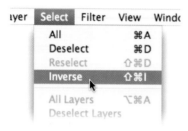

- **All:** Pretty obvious… this command selects everything on the active layer or in your flattened document. The keyboard shortcut is Cmd+A (Ctrl+A) when the canvas window is selected.

- **Deselect:** This command removes the active selection. You may need to do this when finished altering your selection to avoid accidentally modifying your image.

- **Reselect:** This command is truly useful as it allows you to reactivate the last selection in your document. It only works with selections made since you've last opened the document.

- **Inverse:** The concept of inverse is very important. It is often far easier to select what you don't want, then inverse the selection to get what you do want.

Let's try out the concept of Inverse, as well as some of the other commands:

1. Open the file wave.tif from the Chapter 5 folder.

2. Select the Magic Wand tool by pressing the W key.

3. Set the Tolerance to 30 and check the Anti-alias and Contiguous boxes.

4. Click the sky to make an initial selection.

5. Hold down the Shift key and click in another area of the sky to capture more.

6. When most of the sky is active, choose Select > Grow. If needed, repeat the command.

7. Choose Select > Inverse to capture the waves.

Intermediate Selection Techniques

Simply put, don't stop now! Most Photoshop users develop an over-dependence on the Magic Wand tool. While the basic selection techniques are important, they are not necessarily the best solution.

Color Range Command

If you liked the Magic Wand tool, then prepare to love the Color Range command. The Color Range command allows you to select a specified color within the document. You can then easily add to the selection to refine it. All of its speed and power is complemented by a very intuitive user interface.

Let's try out the Color Range command:

1. Open the file Flowers.tif from the Chapter 5 folder.

2. Choose Select > Color Range to launch the Color Range command.

3. With the eyedropper, click the Orange flowers. You'll see an initial selection created in the dialog window.

4. Hold down the Shift key and click more of the orange flowers to build a larger selection.

5. Adjust the Fuzziness slider to your preference.

6. If too much is selected, you can hold down the Option (Alt) key to subtract from the selection.

7. When you're satisfied, click OK.

8. Soften the selection further by choosing Select > Feather and enter a value of 5 pixels.

9. Let's use the selection to make an isolated image adjustment. Choose Layer > New Adjustment Layer > Hue/Saturation.

10. Adjust the Hue slider to change the colors of the flowers (try a value of -37 to make the flowers redder. Adjust the saturation to your preference.

11. Click OK.

Quick Mask Mode

VIDEO TRAINING
Quick Mask Mode

The Quick Mask Mode can be a bit time-consuming, but its accuracy and flexibility make it worth using. The primary advantage of editing your selection as a mask is that you can use almost any Photoshop tool or filter to modify the mask. You can create a rough selection using a basic tool like the Magnetic Lasso, and then refine it with other tools such as the Brush or Blur tools.

Let's give Quick Mask a try:

1. Open the file Pump.tif from the Chapter 5 folder. We are going to create an accurate selection around the water pump.

2. Select the Polygonal Lasso tool from the Toolbox.

3. If you're working on a Macintosh, press F to enter full-screen mode; this will block out your other documents and desktop, thus making it easier to focus on this image.

4. Make an accurate selection around the pump, but don't worry about perfection. Treat it as if you were cutting out the image with a pair of scissors. Remember, you must return to the starting point with the Lasso tool and click to close the loop.

5. Click the Quick Mask icon (near the bottom of the Toolbox) or press Q. The shielded (tinted) areas will become the area outside the active selection when you exit Quick Mask Mode.

6. The default Quick Mask color is red set to 50%. In this case, another color may be more helpful. Double-click the Quick Mask icon to call up the Quick Mask Options window. Change the color to blue and set the opacity to 75%. You may want to revisit this window when masking to adjust your settings to improve visibility.

7. Select the Brush tool from the Toolbox or press B. We will paint the mask in, using brushes. However, we must first "fix" the Brush tool, so it's more accurate.

8. Press Cmd+K (Ctrl+K) to call up your Preferences menu. Choose the Display & Cursors category from the drop-down menu on the top of the window. Under the Painting Cursors area, click Normal Brush Tip (this will show you the size of your brush before clicking). While in your preferences, change the Other Cursors to Precise.

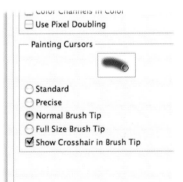

9. Call up the Navigator window. This useful palette makes it easy to zoom in and pan around. The slider will change your magnification level; the red box indicates your work area.

10. Zoom in to high magnification level (between 200–300%). This will make it easier to paint in the rest of your selection.

11. Check your Brush options in the Options bar and Toolbox. Black will add to your mask; white will subtract from it.

    • Pressing the D key will load the default black and white values.

    • You can quickly adjust the size of your brush from the keyboard as well. Press the right bracket (]) to enlarge the brush or the left bracket ([) to reduce the size of the brush.

    • You can soften your brush if you want a feathered edge. Shift+] makes the brush harder, and Shift +[makes the brush softer.

12. Click and paint in the remaining areas of the mask.

    • Use smaller brushes to paint in tiny areas.

    • Use larger brushes to paint in big areas.

    • Use the keyboard shortcuts so you can quickly change the size of your brush as needed.

    • If you have a long, straight run (like an edge), you can click once with a brush. Hold down the Shift key and click again further away. Photoshop will "connect the dots." This is the fastest way to fill in the mask.

    • If you paint too close to the image, you can fix it. Press X to toggle from black to white. Painting with white will subtract from the mask (the color overlay is removed from areas painted with white). Painting with gray creates a semitransparent area, which is useful for feathering edges. (Semitransparent areas may not appear to be selected when you exit Quick Mask Mode, but they are.)

13. To pan around your image, you can move the spacebar red box in the Navigator. Alternately, hold down the spacebar and drag around in the document window.

14. If you want to soften the edge of the Quick Mask, use the Smudge or Blur tools. The Smudge tool set to Darken mode works very well.

15. Continue to paint in the mask. For an image of this complexity, this may take 5–20 minutes, but professional work takes time.

16. When finished, press Q to exit Quick Mask Mode. You should now have an active selection.

17. Let's test the selection by making an image adjustment. Choose Layer > New Adjustment Layer > Hue/Saturation. Pull the Hue slider left or right to see the color of the pump change. Pull the Saturation slider left to reduce the intensity of the color change. Click OK when you are done with the adjustment to apply it. Because you had an active selection, the adjustment is constrained to only the selected areas.

18. Let's make one more adjustment. Reload the selection by choosing Select > Reselect. Then reverse it by choosing Select > Inverse.

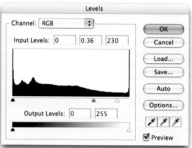

19. We'll now reduce the exposure of the grass. Choose Layer > New Adjustment Layer > Levels. Move the middle (gray) input slider. Notice how the image got darker? You have adjusted the gamma or midtones of the image and changed its exposure. Click OK to apply the Levels change.

20. You may now notice a slight red fringe around the pump. This is easy to fix. In the Layers palette, click the black and white mask icon (which looks like a silhouette of the pump) for the Hue Saturation adjustment layer.

21. We're now going to use a Filter to perform a specialized image processing command (in this case soften the mask). Choose Filter > Blur > Gaussian Blur, and enter a low value like 3 pixels. (This softens the edge of the mask.)

22. Press Cmd+L (Ctrl+L) to invoke the Levels command. Levels is used to adjust the balance between light and dark areas in an image (or mask). Moving the middle (gray) slider will allow you to gently adjust the mask. When satisfied, click OK.

Was that easy? Probably not, but with time and practice it gets significantly easier, so don't give up. Accurate selections are extremely important as you begin to combine multiple images or need to make specialized image adjustments such as color correction. If you'd like some more images to practice with, look in the folder called Quick Mask Practice in the Chapter 5 folder.

SAVING AND RELOADING SELECTIONS

If you'd like to save your selection for later use, you need to create a channel (see the section "Using a Channel" later in this chapter). With an active selection made, choose Select > Save Selection. Name the selection and click OK. This will save the selection as an alpha channel. Alpha channels are simply saved selections that can be reloaded at a later time. They are also stored with your document when you close the file (unlike a Quick Mask, which is discarded when you close the file). We'll cover channels in greater depth in Chapter 7, "Layer Masking."

Using a Path

You can use the Pen tool to create paths. Many users swear by the Pen tool, but be warned: It's not the easiest tool to use. The Pen tool allows you to click around the image, adding anchor points. Photoshop then connects those points with vector lines, which can be adjusted or resized. Those users coming to Photoshop from Adobe Illustrator may find the Pen tool relatively easy to use.

VIDEO TRAINING
Using a Path

Let's give the Pen tool a try:

1. Open the file Orange_Flower.psd from the Chapter 5 folder.

2. Choose the Pen tool from the Toolbox or press the keyboard shortcut P.

3. Choose the following options from the Options bar:

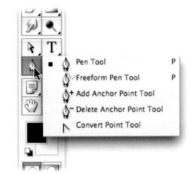

   • Choose Shape Layer from the first three buttons. This will put a solid color over your image and make it easier to see if you are accurately tracing the object.

   • Select Auto Add/Delete so anchor points will automatically be added when you click a line segment. Likewise, Photoshop will automatically delete an anchor point when you click it with the Pen tool.

   • Click the inverted arrow next to the shape buttons in the Options bar to access the submenu. Choose the Rubber Band option, which will make it easier to preview path segments while drawing.

4. Position the Pen tool in the lower-left corner of the flower and click. An initial anchor point is added.

5. You'll now need to draw curved paths. When you click to add a new point, keep the mouse button depressed. You can drag to create the curve.

   - Drag towards the curve for the first point. Drag in the opposite direction for the second point.

   - Dragging both direction points in the same direction will create an "S"-shaped curve.

   - Try to minimize the number of anchor points added. Move forward along the object and pull to form the curve.

6. When you reach the end of your path, you can click to close the shape. As with the Polygonal Lasso tool, you must click your starting point to close the path.

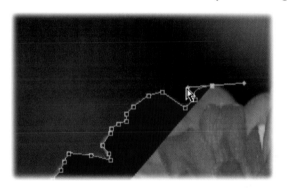

7. To end an open path, Cmd-click (Ctrl-click) away from the path.

8. You can adjust the path by using the Direct Selection tool (A). This will allow you to click an anchor point, or handle, and adjust the position or shape.

9. When satisfied, you can Cmd-click (Ctrl-click) on the path's thumbnail in the Layers palette. You will see the "marching ants," which indicate an active selection has been made.

And that is how paths work. Either you found that enjoyable (and if so, keep practicing—it will get easier), or you disliked it. Because paths are vector, they don't have to be part of your Photoshop workflow. There are other techniques (such as Quick Mask Mode) that may seem easier to you.

Advanced Selection Techniques

The next two selection techniques are advanced (in that they utilize channels). Remember, channels represent the components of color. The brighter the area in the individual channel, the more coverage there is for that color. By harnessing the black and white details of one (or more) channel you can create a mask. These two techniques won't be appropriate to use every time (they are image dependent), but they are pretty easy to try out and should be part of your skill set.

Using a Channel

In many images, there is often high contrast between the different elements. For example, a person framed by a bright blue sky may clearly stand out, since there are a lot of red values in skin and a lot of blue in the sky. You can make a quick decision whether the channel selection technique will work by looking at the Channels palette. Look for a single channel that is high contrast. It doesn't need to be perfect; you can use the Paintbrush to touch it up.

Let's use the channel selection techniques to select and modify a logo on the side of a building:

1. Open the image Hotel.tif from the Chapter 5 folder.

2. Open the Channels palette. Go to the Channels palette submenu (the triangle in the upper-right corner). Choose Palette Options and set the thumbnail to the largest size.

3. In the Channels palette, click on the word *Red* to view just the red channel. Examine the channel for contrast detail. Repeat for the green and blue channels. Look for the channel with the cleanest separation of the motel's name. The blue channel should appear the cleanest.

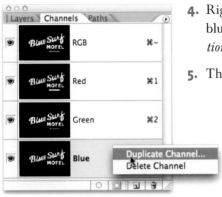

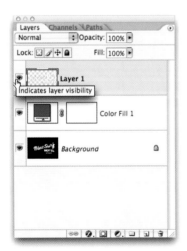

4. Right-click (Ctrl-click with a single-button mouse) on the blue channel and choose Duplicate Channel. Name it *Selection* and click OK to create a new (alpha) channel.

5. The new channel should be automatically selected.

6. Press Cmd+L (Ctrl+L) to invoke a Levels adjustment. This will allow you to adjust contrast on the mask. Make sure the Preview box is checked.

7. Move the Black Input Levels slider to the right to increase contrast in the black areas.

8. Move the White Input Levels slider to the left to increase contrast in the white areas.

9. Move the middle (gray) slider to the right to touch up the spotty areas.

10. Click OK to apply the adjustment to the channel.

11. To soften the edges of the channel, choose Filter > Blur > Gaussian Blur. Apply the filter with a value of 2 or 3 pixels to soften the edge.

12. To load the selection Cmd-click (Ctrl-click) the Selection channel. This will create an active selection.

13. Since we want to work with the image data (in this case the sign) we need to select and enable the RGB channels. Click the visibility icon next to the RGB channels to enable them. Turn the Selection channel off by clicking the visibility icon. You should still have an active selection.

14. Switch back to the Layers palette and click the *Background* layer to activate it.

15. Press Cmd+C (Ctrl+C) to copy the text to your clipboard.

16. Since we are done with the current selection, choose Select > Deselect or press Cmd + D (Ctrl+D) to disable the active selection.

17. Choose Layer > New Fill Layer > Solid Color then click OK.

18. From the Color Picker, choose a highly saturated color and click OK.

19. Choose Edit > Paste or press Cmd+V (Ctrl+V) to paste your clipboard contents. The text from your clipboard should be added above the solid color layer.

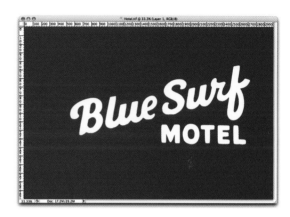

20. If you then want to clean up the text, you can reload the selection by choosing Select > Reselect.

21. Choose Edit > Fill and select White at 100%. Click OK to apply the fill.

Calculations Command

You can use the Calculations command to create a new selection based on the details in an image's channels. This technique is a hit-or-miss, as it won't work with every image. But when it succeeds, it's a big success. The Calculations command works well when there is high contrast between the subject and the background. You'll want to look at each channel independently until you find ones with highest contrast. Depending on the source photo, you will generate anything from a perfect selection to a great start.

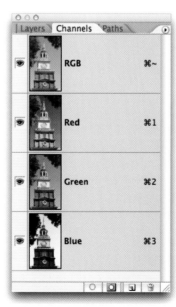

VIDEO TRAINING
16
Calculations Command

Let's put the Calculations command into action to create an active selection and a saved alpha channel:

1. Open the file Independence Hall.tif from the Chapter 5 folder.

2. Bring up the Channels palette (Windows > Channels) and look for the highest contrasting channels. Because you want to remove the background, look for the contrast between foreground and background. The blue channel should stand out the most.

The name *Calculations* can be scary, as math is not the most popular subject for many people. But don't worry; the computer will do all of the calculations for you as it combines two channels to create a new selection.

3. Choose Image > Calculations and make sure the Preview box is checked. We'll now combine two of the color channels to create a new alpha channel. An alpha channel is simply a saved selection. You can Cmd-click (Ctrl-click) it to turn it into an active selection.

4. In the Source 1 area, set the Channel to Blue.

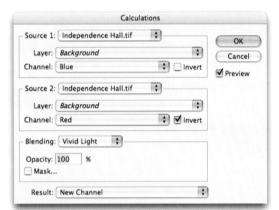

5. In the Source 2 area, we'll experiment to find the right combination. The red channel is a good place to start, as it looks very different than the blue channel. It's also a good idea to experiment by clicking the Invert button to reverse the channel. Calculations is all about trial and error, but since it works so well, taking a little time to experiment is worth it.

6. Combine the red and blue channels by using Blending. From the drop-down list, try different Blending modes. Blending modes control how two different images or channels blend together placed on their color and luminance values (for more on blending modes see Chapter 9, "Using Blending Modes." Different source images will need different modes. Experiment by clicking through each mode on the list. You may also want to try unchecking the Invert box when working with other images. In the Independence Hall image, the blue and red (inverted) channels combine most effectively using the Vivid Light Blending mode. This will create a new channel that has clean separation between the building and sky.

7. Click OK to create a new channel. The channel, called Alpha 1, should be selected in the Channels palette. Photoshop turned the RGB channels off for now.

8. Choose the Brush tool and set the foreground color to white.

9. Paint over the trees so the sky becomes pure white.

10. Run a Levels adjustment on the channel to adjust the contrast between black and white. Choose Image > Adjust > Levels or press Cmd+L (Ctrl+L). Move the Black Input slider to the right to darken the gray areas to black. Move the White Input slider to the left to brighten the whites in the image. Move the Gray (gamma) slider to the right to close up gray areas.

11. Click the OK button to apply the Levels adjustment.

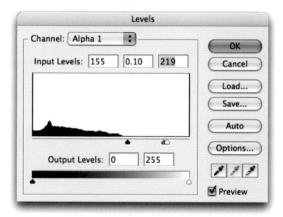

12. Zoom in to 100% magnification to look for gaps in the alpha channel. You should see a few in the tower. With your Paintbrush set to black, paint out the spotting.

13. Cmd-click (Ctrl-click) on the alpha channel thumbnail to load the selection. You will need to choose Select > Inverse to choose Independence Hall.

14. Click the visibility icon next to the RGB composite channel.

Look closely at the selection; it should be pretty impressive. You could now copy the image and add it to a different composite image, or run a filter or image processing command on the building. With a little bit of experimentation, a perfect alpha channel can be generated and turned into a layer mask (as we'll try in Chapter 7, "Layer Masking"). Calculations isn't a solution all the time, but it's worth a try when you have high-contrast channels.

Advice on Selections

There is no single technique that is ideal for making the perfect selections. Every image is unique and will require you to analyze it. Knowing multiple techniques is *very* important, as it expands your options. Get comfortable with all of the techniques in this chapter and be sure to practice. Practice really does make perfect.

Painting and Drawing Tools

6

Photoshop has a very rich set of painting and drawing tools. These tools have been in Photoshop since its first release, yet they have evolved greatly over time. The painting and drawing tools have many uses. To name a few:

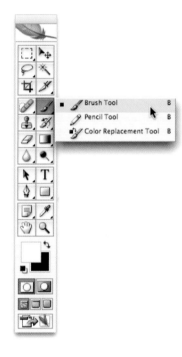

- Fine artists can paint entire works into Photoshop with its realistic painting system. Using software can be an affordable alternative to traditional methods, which require more space and supplies.

- Comic book colorists can use Photoshop to paint the color into the inked drawings.

- FX designers can create background paintings for movie special effects work. In fact, the cocreator of Photoshop, John Knoll, is a lead visual effects supervisor at Industrial Light and Magic, the group behind the *Star Wars* franchise and many other well-known films.

- Commercial photographers can touch up and enhance photos using digital tools instead of a traditional airbrush. Nearly every photo you see in a fashion or entertainment magazine has undergone some digital touchup in Photoshop to paint out imperfections.

These tools appear simple at first, and in fact they are. After all, the technology behind a paintbrush is pretty straightforward. It's the skill of the user holding the tool that determines results. A thorough understanding of the painting and drawing tools can come in handy while working in many areas of Photoshop. Whether you use Photoshop for image touch-up or to create original images from scratch, be certain to master these tools.

Working with Color

Working with painting and drawing tools requires you to use color. Photoshop offers several flexible ways to choose colors. You can sample a color from an open image, choose a color from a library, or mix a new color by entering numerical values. Which method you use will depend on a mixture of personal choice and the job at hand. Let's explore the different options.

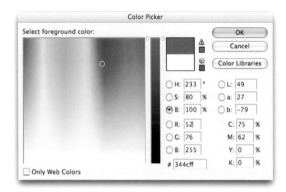

Adobe Color Picker

The Adobe Color Picker is a consistent way to choose colors while using any Adobe software program. Both Macintosh and Windows systems have their own color pickers, but its best to stick with the standardized Adobe Color Picker as it is more full-featured and cross-platform.

You can choose a color from a spectrum or numerically. Use the Adobe Color Picker to set the foreground color, background color, and text color. Additionally, you can use the colors for gradients, filters, or layer styles.

Double-click a color swatch (such as in the Toolbox) to open the Color Picker. In the Adobe Color Picker, you can select colors based on:

- Hue Saturation Brightness (HSB)
- Red Green Blue (RGB)
- Lab color
- Cyan Magenta Yellow Key (or Black) (CMYK)

Color Libraries

In some cases, designers need to access specific colors—those that come from a particular color and brand of ink. This is most often to match colors used by a specific company. For example, McDonald's always uses the same red on all of its printed materials. This helps create a specific look or identity by branding based on color.

A designer can keep color consistent by specifying Pantone colors. The Pantone Matching
System (PMS) is the most widely accepted
color standard in the printing industry (www.
pantone.com). Each color is assigned a PMS
number, which corresponds to specific ink or
mixing standard, thus ensuring that a client
will get consistent printing results. Accessing
Pantone colors within Photoshop is easy:

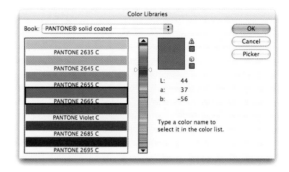

1. Activate the Adobe Color Picker by double-clicking the
    foreground or background color swatch.

2. Click the Color Libraries (or Custom) button. The Color
    Libraries window opens.

3. From the Book menu, you must choose among several
    options. Always ask your clients for specific color informa-
    tion. You can quickly jump to a specific color by typing in
    its number.

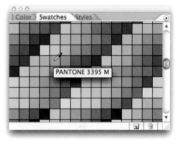

4. When you have a color selected, click OK.

5. Photoshop loads the closest equivalent color into your color
    picker. Essentially, the Pantone color will be simulated as
    accurately as possible by an RGB or CMYK equivalent.

*Color Libraries can also be loaded as
color swatches. Just click the submenu
(triangle) in the upper-right corner
of the Swatches palette. Choose the
library you need from the pop-up list.*

6. If you need to have the exact color for printing, you will
    need to make a spot color channel.

Creating Spot Color Channels

While most jobs use a four-color process to simulate colors, you
may need to use a special printing technique called spot colors.
Spot color channels are specialty channels used by a printer to
overprint special inks on top of your image. You can create a
new spot channel based on a selection.

**VIDEO
TRAINING**
Spot Color Channels

1. Open the file Postcard.tif from the Chapter 6 folder on
    the DVD-ROM. This layered TIFF file has been mostly
    prepped for printing at a commercial printer (note that it's
    in cmyk mode). One of the last steps is to specify the spot
    color ink for the type.

2. Choose Window > Channels to display the Channels palette.

3. Select the layer Surf - PMS 8883 C. Cmd-click (Ctrl-click) on the layer's thumbnail to create an active selection.

4. Switch to the Channels palette. Cmd-click (Ctrl-click) on the New Channel button in the Channels palette.

5. If you made a selection, that area is filled with the currently specified spot color. If you want to modify the color, click the swatch next to the word *Color*.

6. Enter a name for the spot color channel. If you've chosen a custom color, the channel automatically takes the name of that color.

7. Set Solidity to 100%. This will simulate the spot color within your Photoshop file.

8. Click OK to create the spot color channel.

Eyedropper Tool

The Eyedropper tool lets you sample colors from an open document. This can be a useful way to choose colors that work well with an image. Let's try out the tool:

1. Open the file Ludwig7.tif from the Chapter 6 folder.

2. Select the Eyedropper tool from the Toolbox or press the keyboard shortcut I.

3. Adjust the sample size in the Options bar:

Using the Eyedropper tool, you can sample the color of the castle's bricks. This can be useful for painting as well as color correction. For example, you can check the color details of the bricks on two different shots of the castle. You could then adjust color to make the images better match. For more on adjusting color, see Chapter 10, "Color Correction and Enhancement."

- **Point Sample:** This reads the value of a single pixel. It is very sensitive to clicking as you can have slight variation in color at the pixel level. For example, if you clicked on a blue sky, adjacent pixels could vary from each other.

- **3 by 3 Average:** This reads the average value of a 3×3 pixel area. This is a more accurate method for selecting a color using the Eyedropper tool.

- **5 by 5 Average:** This method reads the average value of a 5×5 pixel area. It creates a more representative color sample.

4. Click the brick area to set the Foreground Color.

5. Option-click (Alt-click) the sky area to set the Background Color.

Color Palette

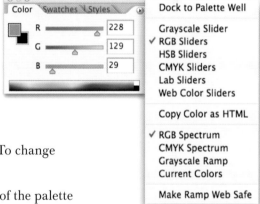

The Color palette is another way to access color without having to load the Adobe Color Picker. The Color palette shows you the values for the Foreground and Background colors. You can quickly mix or pick new colors from within the palette.

- You can adjust the sliders to mix a new color. To change color models, click the palette's submenu.

- You can click the spectrum across the bottom of the palette to pick a new color.

The Color palette may display two alerts when you select a color:

- An exclamation point inside a triangle means the color cannot be printed using CMYK printing.

- A cube means the color is not Web-safe for color graphics viewed on a monitor set to 256 colors.

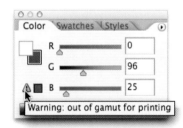

Swatches

The Swatches palette holds color presets. You can quickly access frequently used colors by clicking their thumbnails. You can load preset swatches by clicking the Swatches palette submenu (top-right arrow). Additionally, Table 6.1 shows several important shortcuts when working with the Swatches palette.

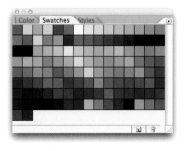

Table 6.1   Keyboard Shortcuts for the Swatches Palette

Result	Macintosh	Windows
Create new swatch from foreground color	Click empty area of palette	Click empty area of palette
Select foreground color	Click swatch	Click swatch
Select background color	Cmd-click swatch	Ctrl-click swatch
Delete color swatch	Option-click swatch	Alt-click swatch

Painting Tools

Several tools are available for painting inside of Photoshop. While these tools have subtle differences, they have one important thing in common: use of Photoshop's dynamic brush engine. Before we explore the unique tools, let's discuss how to control your brushes.

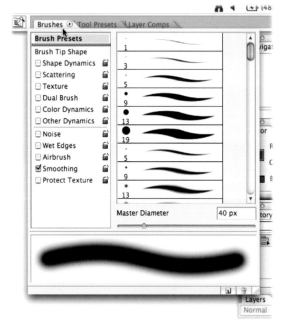

Brushes Palette

The Brushes palette contains several options. Most of these will be well beyond what you'll need to get started. We'll cover the options in brief, but be sure to return to this palette as you grow in skill and confidence.

Brush Presets

Photoshop has several brush presets to get you started right away. These presets are accessed from the Brushes palette; several are loaded and more are in storage. Let's check them out.

1. Create a new document. Since this is for practice and we won't be printing the file, choose the 800 × 600 preset from the New Document dialog box.

2. Press D to load the default colors of black and white.

3. Select the standard Brush tool by pressing B.

4. Click the Brushes palette tab (by default it is docked in the palette well in the Options bar).

5. Click the words *Brush Presets.* Photoshop will show you a list and thumbnails of several brush styles.

6. Scroll through the list and pick a style to try.

7. Draw a stroke in your blank document to see the brush preset in action.

8. Repeat using different presets and create strokes to get familiar with your options.

9. Click the Brushes palette submenu (the triangle in the upper-right corner) and load a new Brush library.

10. Experiment with these brushes.

11. Load additional presets and continue to get familiar with your many options.

VIDEO TRAINING
Creating Custom Brushes

12. When done, you can restore the default set of brushes. Click the palette's submenu and choose Reset Brushes.

CREATING CUSTOM SAMPLED BRUSHES

You can use an image to create a custom brush. This can be a scan that you input or a stroke that you draw using other brushes. Let's give it a try:

1. Open the file Brushes to Sample.tif from the Chapter 6 folder.

2. Select the first brush shape with the Rectangular Marquee tool. You can sample an image in size up to 2500 pixels × 2500 pixels.

3. Choose Edit > Define Brush Preset.

4. Give the brush a name, and click OK. The brush is loaded into the set you currently have loaded in the Brushes palette.

5. Activate the new brush and paint in a new document to try it out. You may want to adjust the Spacing option to taste.

6. Repeat for the other three brush shapes.

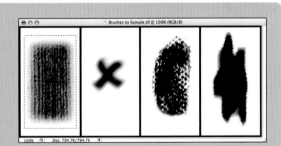

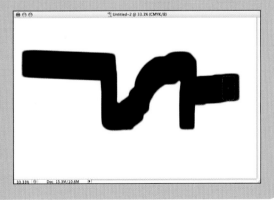

Brush Tip Shape

While the brush presets are readily available and very diverse, they won't cover all your needs. Fortunately Photoshop offers a flexible interface for customizing existing brushes as well as creating new ones.

1. Make sure you have the Brush tool selected.

2. Bring the Brushes palette forward and make it active.

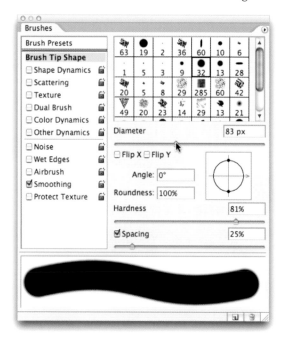

3. Choose a brush preset (from the thumbnail icons) that you'd like to modify. You can see the changes in the preview area, or click your test canvas to try the brush out.

You can modify the following brush tip shape options in the Brushes palette:

- **Diameter:** Controls the size of the selected brush. You can enter a value in pixels (px) or drag the slider to a new size.

- **Use Sample Size:** Resets the brush to its original diameter. If the brush was created by sampling pixels (such as part of a photo or a scanned stroke), you can use the sample size.

- **Flip X:** Changes the direction of a brush by flipping it on its X axis (essentially making a mirrored image). This is useful if the brush is asymmetrical.

- **Flip Y:** Flips the brush on its Y axis.

- **Angle:** Specifies the angle of a brush. This works well for sampled or elliptical brushes. You can type in a number of degrees or visually change the angle of the brush by dragging the arrow in the brush preview interface. You can use angled brushes to create a chiseled stroke.

- **Roundness:** Specifies the ratio between the short and long axes. A value of 100% results in a rounder brush, whereas 0% creates a linear brush. Elliptical shapes can be used to create natural-looking strokes.

- **Hardness:** Creates brushes with soft edges. This can be useful to create more natural-looking strokes. You can adjust between 0% (very soft) and 100% (no feathering). You cannot adjust hardness for sampled brushes.

- **Spacing:** Controls the distance between brush marks when you create a stroke. You can adjust spacing using the slider or type in a number. If you uncheck the box, the speed of your cursor will determine spacing.

Shape Dynamics

To create a more natural brush, you should adjust the Shape Dynamics of the brush. This can create natural variances that make the brush more realistic. The Shape Dynamics option adjusts the currently selected brush; therefore, be sure to choose one from the Brush Presets or Brush Tip Shapes area.

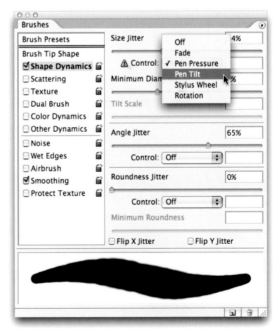

- **Size Jitter and Control:** This option specifies how much variety Photoshop places in the size of the brush. You can specify a total size of jitter in percentage. Additionally, you can specify how to control the jitter from the Control pop-up menu:

  - **Off:** This option places no control over the size variance of brush marks. The jitter is random.

  - **Fade:** If you want the brush to taper off (like it ran out of ink or paint) then choose Fade. The brush will get smaller based on a specified number of steps. Each step is one mark of the brush tip. If you specify 15, the brush will fade out in 15 steps.

IMAGE COURTESY WACOM

- **Pen Pressure, Pen Tilt, Stylus Wheel, or Rotation:** Some Photoshop users unlock more features by hooking up a stylus and graphics tablet. The most popular manufacturer of tablets is Wacom (www.wacom.com). These options let you tie jitter to different features of the pen.

- **Minimum Diameter:** This option sets a limit on how much variation in scale can be introduced in the brush. An option of 0% lets the brush shrink to a diameter of 0, whereas 25% would let the brush range from full size to a quarter of its starting width.

- **Tilt Scale:** This option ties the amount of scale to the tilt of the pen (or stylus). You must have a graphics tablet attached to utilize this feature.

- **Angle Jitter and Control:** You can specify how much variety in the angle of the brush can occur. A larger number creates more variety. The control area ties the jitter to your pen.

- **Roundness Jitter and Control:** You can introduce jitter into the roundness of the brush. Additionally, you can control the jitter with a pen.

- **Minimum Roundness:** This option limits the amount of jitter.

Scattering

Enabling Scattering can add variation to the placement of strokes. This can simulate splattering or wilder strokes. There are a few options to work with:

- **Scatter and Control:** You can distribute brush strokes from the center of the click. The Both Axes option distributes strokes radially. When the option is unchecked, the strokes are distributed perpendicular to the stroke path.

- **Count:** This option specifies the quantity of brush marks applied at each spacing interval. This option works in conjunction with the Spacing option from Brush Tip Shape.

- **Count Jitter and Control:** You can specify how much variety there is in the number of brush marks for each spacing interval. A high value will put more brush marks into the stroke. These are controlled in the same way as Shape jitter.

Texture

You can enable the Texture option to introduce a pattern into your strokes. This can help simulate canvas in your texture. Click the pattern sample to choose from one of the loaded patterns. Click the triangle menu to open the pattern picker to choose from the loaded textures. If you'd like to load additional textures, click the submenu in the pattern picker to load a built-in texture library. You can adjust several other options in the window and examine their effects in the preview area.

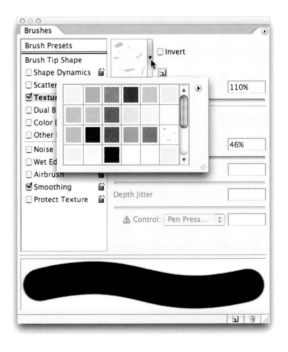

Dual Brush

What's better than one brush? Two, of course. By using a dual brush, you can use two brush tips to create a more dynamic brush. When selected, you'll have the option of choosing from a thumbnail list of presets for the second brush. You'll also see several options to modify the brush tip. You can modify the diameter of the second brush as well as specifying spacing and scatter amounts.

Color Dynamics

By now you might be thinking, "Those brushes are pretty dynamic, what else can Photoshop change?" Well, color, of course. When you check Color Dynamics, you can enable several options that will produce subtle (or dynamic) variations in color.

- **Foreground/Background Jitter and Control:** This option allows the brush to utilize both the foreground and background colors that you have loaded. This can create a nice variation in color by loading lighter and darker shades of one color as your foreground and background color swatches.

- **Hue Jitter:** Hue jitter allows you to specify how much variety of color can be introduced. Low values create a small change in color and higher values create greater variety.

- **Saturation Jitter:** This option introduces variation in the intensity of the selected color.

- **Brightness Jitter:** This option adds variety in brightness. A low value creates very little change in the brightness of the color. A higher value creates greater variations.

This butterfly was drawn with Color Dynamics enabled. Notice the subtle variations of color within the stroke.

Other Dynamics

The Other Dynamics section offers additional styles of jitter that can be added.

- **Opacity Jitter and Control:** You can add variety to the brush so the opacity varies throughout the stroke. You can tie the opacity variation to a pen and tablet for greater control.

- **Flow Jitter and Control:** Flow affects how paint flows through the brush. A larger number means more paint flows through. The default value is 100%, which creates even strokes. A lower value causes less ink to be applied with each stroke.

Other brush options

A few Other options can affect your active brush. These are either enabled (checked) or disabled (unchecked); they have no modifiable properties.

- **Noise:** This option places additional grain into the brush tip. It works well with soft-tip brushes.

- **Wet Edges:** This option causes the paint to appear darker at the edge of the stroke. It simulates the effect of painting with watercolors.

- **Airbrush:** This option allows you to simulate a traditional airbrush (a device that uses pressurized air to spray paint out of a nozzle). The airbrush applies gradual tones and allows the paint to build up. You can also access this option by clicking the Airbrush option in the Options bar.

- **Smoothing:** This option produces better curves in your brush strokes when painting.

- **Protect Texture:** If you are using Texture in your brush strokes, this is a good option to enable. It keeps the pattern and scale consistent when switching between textured brushes. This will make your strokes more consistent.

Table 6.2 shows the frequently used Brushes palette keyboard shortcuts.

Table 6.2   Shortcut Keys for Using the Brushes Palette

Desired Result	Macintosh	Windows
Decrease/increase brush size	[or]	[or]
Decrease/increase brush softness/hardness in 25% increments	Shift + [or Shift +]	Shift + [or Shift +]
Select previous/next brush size	, (comma) or . (period)	, (comma) or . (period)
Display precise crosshair for brushes	Caps Lock	Caps Lock
Delete brush	Option-click brush	Alt-click brush
Rename brush	Double-click brush	Double-click brush
Toggle Airbrush option	Shift + Option + P	Shift + Alt + P

Brush Tool

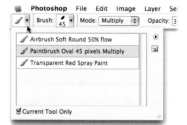

After all this talk of brushes, there are still a few important things to say about the Brush tool. Be sure to look in the Options bar for important brush controls. From left to right, these options are the most useful controls for brushes.

- **Tool Presets:** You can save a frequently used brush configuration for convenient access.

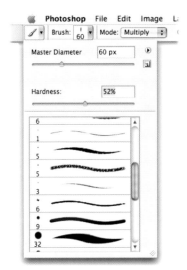

- **Brush Preset Picker:** This area is a greatly reduced Brushes palette. You can access thumbnails of the loaded brushes, as well as adjust diameter and hardness.

- **Mode:** The Mode menu lets you change the blending mode of your painted strokes. Blending modes attempt to simulate real-world interactions between two elements. For example, Multiply allows the strokes to build up, much like a magic marker. You'll find much more on blending modes in Chapter 9, "Using Blending Modes."

- **Opacity:** This option affects the opacity of your strokes.

- **Flow:** This option reduces the amount of paint flowing to the brush.

- **Airbrush button:** This button enables the Airbrush.

- **Brushes Palette button:** This button toggles visibility on the Brushes palette. Click it and it will open the Brushes palette, which gives you greater control over the brush shape and dynamics.

Pencil Tool

The Pencil tool is similar to the Brush tool. It shares many of the same options and controls. The fundamental difference is that it can only be used to create hard-edged strokes. While there is a Hardness setting available, it does nothing to change the stroke.

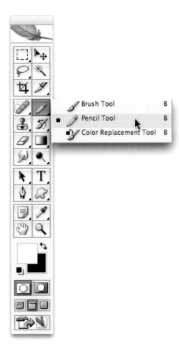

There is one unique option for the Pencil tool: Auto Erase. Enabling it via the Options bar will tell the Pencil tool to erase previously drawn strokes if you draw over them a second time.

Color Replacement Tool

The Color Replacement tool can replace a selected color with a new, user-specified color. This tool was first introduced with Photoshop CS, and was originally positioned as a way to remove "red eye" from photos. Photoshop CS2 added a new Red Eye tool specifically for that purpose, yet the Color Replacement tool remains somewhat useful. Let's try it out:

1. Open the file Balloons.tif from the Chapter 6 folder.

2. Select the Color Replacement tool from the Toolbox. It is nested with the regular Brush tool's well

3. Choose a soft brush tip from the Options bar. Leave the blending mode set to Color.

4. Select one of the three Sampling options:

   • **Continuous:** This option updates with each drag of the brush.

   • **Once:** In this mode, you must make an initial click. Photoshop will replace the targeted color only in areas that closely match the initial click.

   • **Background Swatch:** This mode requires you to change the background color swatch. You can do this by choosing the Eyedropper (I) and Option-clicking (Alt-clicking) on a color in your document. Photoshop will then replace only areas containing the current background color.

   For this image, let's use the Once option.

5. You can place additional color replacement limits using alternatives in the Options bar:

   • **Discontiguous:** This option replaces the sampled color in all places that it occurs in the whole image.

   • **Contiguous:** This option requires that colors are contiguous to, or touching, the color immediately under the pointer.

   • **Find Edges:** This option attempts to replace color while preserving the sharpness in the detail of the edges.

   For this image, let's use the Discontiguous option so we can get the widest range of colors.

6. Enter tolerance as a percentage (between 0 to 100%). Lower values require the colors to be very similar to the pixels you click. Higher values have a greater tolerance and will modify more colors. For this image, we'll go towards the middle of the road with a setting of 40%.

7. Check the Anti-alias box to reduce any fringe in the color-corrected regions.

8. Pick a foreground color to replace the unwanted color. For this image, we'll change the orange balloons and make them blue.

9. Zoom into the image near the orange balloon near the top of the image.

10. Click and start to paint; be careful not to get too close to the edges.

11. Some spotting may occur, so you'll need to click in the center of any spotting and paint additional strokes.

12. When you complete the first balloon, move on to the additional orange balloons and paint them in as well.

ALTERNATIVE COLOR REPLACEMENT

While the Color Replacement tool is effective, using it can be a bit time-consuming. An effective alternative is to use the Select > Color Range Command. For more practice you can try it out on the Balloons. tif image as well. This command allows you to select a color, then add additional colors to the selection. For more on this useful tool, be sure to see Chapter 5, "Selection Tools and Techniques."

History Brush Tool

The History Brush is easy to use, but a little hard to understand at first. Essentially, it allows you to paint backwards in time. This can be very useful as it enables you to combine the current state of an image with an earlier state. For example, you can process an image with a stylizing filter, then restore part of the image to its original state.

The History Brush is directly tied to your History palette. This useful window shows you each action you have taken on an image. You can then move backwards through your undos by clicking them. By default you have 20 levels of undo, but you can change this by increasing the number of History States in your general preferences.

Let's put the History palette and History Brush into action:

1. Call up your History palette, so it is active (Window > History).

2. Open the file Hannah.tif from the Chapter 6 folder.

3. Use the Select > Color Range Command to select the sandy beach area. When you have most of the beach selected, click OK to make a selection.

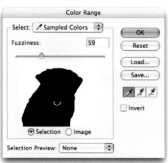

4. We are now going to run a Brush Stroke filter to stylize part of the image. Filters can be used to create special effects in an image. (For more on filters, see Chapter 14, "Filters"). Choose Filter > Brush Strokes > Sumi-e. Adjust the sliders to taste. Click OK to apply the filter.

5. Choose Select > Inverse to select the dog in the photo.

6. Most of the image is selected; you can select the stray area by using the Lasso tool and holding down the Shift key to add to the selection.

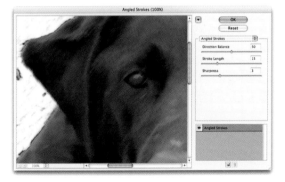

7. Choose Filter > Brush Strokes > Angled Strokes. The default settings are fine for this purpose (but feel free to adjust as needed). Click OK to apply the filter.

8. Choose Select > Deselect to clear the active selection.

9. Examine the image and the History palette. The image looks more like a painting at this point, but some key areas (like the eyes and mouth) are too heavily stylized. The History palette shows you all of the actions you have performed on the open image.

10. Look at the top of the History palette; you will see a Snapshot for the document. It was automatically created when the document was first opened. The brush icon next to it indicates that it has been set as the source for the History Brush.

11. Choose the History Brush from the Toolbox or press Y. Be sure to not choose the Art History Brush.

12. Select a soft-edged brush, sized approximately 30 pixels.

13. Zoom in on the eye area. Paint in the eyeball to restore the original detail of the eye.

14. Hold down the Spacebar to access the Pan tool. Pan around the image to access the other eye. Restore the second eye.

15. Pan down to the mouth area and paint back the original detail.

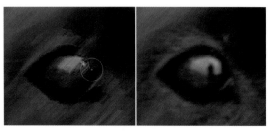

The History Brush can be used to paint back original details after running an image-processing command (such as a filter). This can restore parts of the image that improve its appearance.

The History Brush can be very useful when either filtering an image or performing color correction tasks. It allows you to selectively paint back in time to restore lost or important details.

Art History Brush Tool

Officially, the Art History Brush tool can be used to create stylized paintings. Unofficially, it doesn't work very well. The Art History Brush tool is very similar in setup to the regular History Brush. It requires you to select a snapshot to paint from.

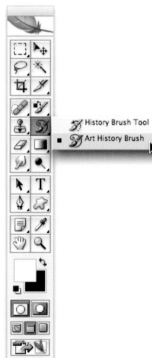

1. If you'd like to try this tool out, open the image Peacock.tif from the Chapter 6 folder.

2. In the History palette, choose a Snapshot or History State to use.

3. Select the Art History Brush tool from the Toolbox.

4. Select a small, soft brush from the Brush Presets picker.

5. Choose a method from the Style menu. The tight methods work better than the loose ones.

6. Set the area number to a low value. This reduces the number of strokes and gives you better control over the tool.

7. For Tolerance, enter a low value to constrain the strokes to a tighter area.

8. Drag in the image to paint.

What you should see could be loosely called "impressionistic." Chances are this tool won't become part of your regular workflow.

Paint Bucket Tool

The Paint Bucket tool allows you to quickly fill an area of adjacent pixels with a new color. The command is quick, but not extremely accurate. The Paint Bucket tool works similarly to the Magic Wand tool, but instead of creating a selection, it fills with a color. The Paint Bucket tool works well if you have an easy to select area, but not well on complex images.

Let's try it out:

1. Open the file Helmet.tif from the Chapter 6 folder.

2. Select the Paint Bucket (G) tool from the Toolbox.

3. Load purple as your foreground color.

4. Set the Tolerance setting to 90. A high tolerance fills more pixels within a broader range on the first click.

5. To make a smoother selection, make sure the Anti-aliased box is checked.

6. Click with the Paint Bucket tool on the red helmet. The colors will change, but it will look flat and unnatural.

7. Choose Edit > Undo and go back to before using the Paint Bucket.

8. In the Options bar, change the Paint Bucket's blending mode to Color. This will paint with the color you've selected, but blend it with the existing luminance and saturation values.

Using blending modes can make paint-ing tools more useful. In this case, the Paint Bucket tool was set to use Color mode, and it created a gentle shifting of the color in the helmet.

Working with Gradients

A gradient is a gradual blend between two or more colors. You can use gradients to cre-ate a photo-realistic backdrop or to draw in areas like a blown-out sky. The Gradient tool is extremely flexible and offers the versatile Gradient Editor for creating custom gradi-ents. Before we utilize the Gradient tool, let's explore how gradients are formed.

Gradient Editor

All gradients are edited using the Gradient Editor (which becomes available when you ac-tivate the Gradient tool). To access it, click the thumbnail of the gradient in the Options bar.

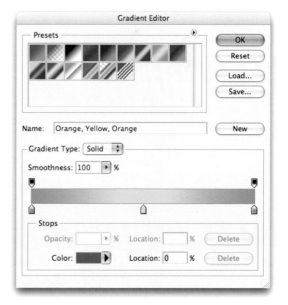

- **Presets:** You have several preset gradients to choose from and you can browse them by thumbnail. Additionally, you can load other gradients by clicking the palette's submenu.

- **Name:** Giving each gradient a name can make them easier to sort through.

- **Type:** The two major categories of gradi-ents are Solid and Noise. Solid gradients use color and opacity stops, with gradual blends in between. Noise gradients con-tain randomly distributed colors within a user-specified range. Each has a unique interface.

Solid Editor

Solid gradients blend from one color to another, providing a traditional gradient type.

- **Smoothness:** This option controls the rate at which the colors blend. You can set it to be gradual or steep. The larger the number, the more Photoshop optimizes the appearance of the blend.

- **Opacity stops:** A gradient can contain blends between opacity values. To add a stop, click in an empty area on the top of the gradient spectrum. To adjust a stop, click it, and then modify the opacity field.

- **Color stops:** A simple gradient contains only two colors. However, you may want to use a more complex gradient in your project. You can click below the gradient to add another color stop. Double-click a stop to edit its color with the Adobe Color Picker.

- **Stop Editor:** Selected gradient stops can be adjusted numerically. You can edit the opacity, color, and location (0–100%, read left to right.)

- **Midpoint:** Between stops are midpoints. By default, the midpoint is halfway between two stops. You can adjust the midpoint to shift the balance of the gradient.

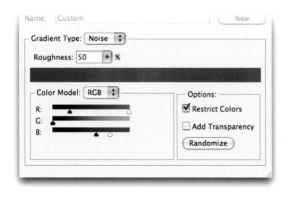

Noise Editor

Noise gradients use a specified range of color to create noise. These gradients do not blend smoothly between colors, but rather create a new gradient each time the Randomize button is clicked.

- **Roughness:** Noise gradients use a roughness setting to determine how many different colors are used to create noise.

- **Color Model:** You can choose between three models: Red-Green-Blue, Hue-Saturation-Brightness, or Lab.

- **Color Range sliders:** Adjust the range of colors available to the gradient. Bring the black and white sliders closer together to limit the amount of color present in the noise gradient.

- **Options:** You can choose to further restrict colors as well as introduce random transparency. To create a new gradient, click the Randomize button. Every time you click, a new gradient will be generated.

- **New button:** To add a gradient to the Presets window, type a name into the name field then click the New button. This new gradient is not yet permanently saved, but stored temporarily in the Preferences file. You must click the Save button and navigate to your Presets folder (inside the Photoshop application folder). Be sure to append the file name with .grd to inform Photoshop that it is a gradient set.

Gradient Tool

You can use the Gradient tool to manually draw a gradient on a layer. To access the Gradient tool, select it from the Toolbox, or press G. The Paint Bucket shares the same well as the Gradient tool, so if you don't find the Gradient tool, press Shift+G to cycle through your tools.

The Gradient tool can use any gradient you create in the Gradient Editor or from the Presets menu. To select a gradient, you can choose from available ones in the Options bar. You can also load preset libraries or manually load gradients by accessing the palette's submenu.

You must choose one of these five methods to build your gradient:

- **Linear Gradient (A):** This gradient blends from the starting point to the ending point in a straight line.

- **Radial Gradient (B):** This gradient blends from the starting point to the ending point in a circular pattern.

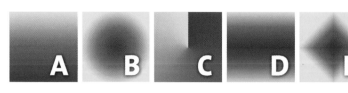

- **Angle Gradient (C):** This gradient blends in a counterclockwise sweep from the starting point.

- **Reflected Gradient (D):** This gradient blends symmetrically on both sides of the starting point.

- **Diamond Gradient (E):** This gradient blends in a diamond-shaped pattern outward from the starting point.

You have a few available options to further modify the gradient:

- You can specify a blending mode to affect how the gradient is applied to the layer. (For more on blending modes, see Chapter 9.)

- To reverse the direction of colors in the gradient, check the Reverse box.

- To create a visually smoother blend by adding noise, check the Dither box.

- To use a gradient's built-in transparency, check the Transparency box.

Let's use the Gradient tool to fix a common problem, a washed out sky:

1. Open the file Cliff.tif from the Chapter 6 folder.

2. Use the Select > Color Range Command to create an active selection in the sky area. Adjust Fuzziness to get a gentle selection.

3. Load a dark blue as your foreground color and a lighter blue as your background color.

4. Choose the Gradient tool and select a Linear Gradient.

5. Select the Foreground to Background gradient from your preset list (it's the first one).

6. Click at the top of the sky and drag down towards the rocks.

The sky should look more natural now with greater variation in colors.

GRADIENT MAPS OFFER UNIQUE COLOR

Gradient Maps are another way to harness the power of gradients to enhance an image. The Gradient Map can be applied as an adjustment layer or image adjustment command (stick with the adjustment layer for greater flexibility). You can create a new Gradient Map by choosing Layer > New Adjustment Layer > Gradient Map.

The Gradient Map will map a new gradient to the grayscale range of an image. A two-color gradient produces a nice duotone effect. Shadows map to one of the color stops of the gradient fill; highlights map to the other. The midtones map to the gradations in between. A multicolored gradient or noise gradient can add interesting colors to an image. This is an effective technique for colorizing textures or photos.

Open the file GradientMapDemo.psd to see Gradient Maps in action. Turn on each map one at a time to see their effect. By using blending modes in conjunction with the Gradient Map, you can get a more pleasant effect.

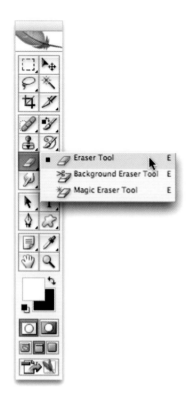

Eraser Tools

Photoshop offers three kinds of Eraser tools to complement your drawing tools. While these tools have a purpose, you should quickly move beyond them as they often produce crude edges in the erased area that lower the quality of your project.

The three options are

- **Eraser tool:** This tool will delete pixels as you drag over them. On a layer they are replaced with transparency. On a *Background,* the pixels are replaced with your background color. To use, just drag through the area you want to erase.

- **Background Eraser tool:** This tool is designed to help erase the background from an image. The difference between foreground and background in the image must be very clear and high contrast. This tool is significantly less flexible than the technique of layer masking, which we'll cover in Chapter 7, "Layer Masking."

- **Magic Eraser tool:** This tool is most similar to the Paint Bucket tool in that it attempts to select and modify similar pixels under your click point. Instead of filling those pixels with a color, however, the Magic Eraser tool deletes them.

From years of personal experience, I strongly suggest avoiding the Eraser tools. These three tools are relatively primitive in their approach to selecting pixels for deletion. Additionally, the erasers are permanent—the discarded pixels are gone for good. It bears repeating: If you have anything beyond a basic image that you need to extract from its background, the answer is layer masking, which will be covered in depth in Chapter 7.

Drawing Tools

While Photoshop is best known as a pixel-based (or raster) program, it does have a respectable set of vector drawing tools. Vector graphics are made up of mathematically defined lines and curves. Vector graphics are resolution-independent, as they can be scaled and repositioned with no loss of quality. Vector graphics are a good choice for creating shapes (such as rectangles, circles, or polygons) within your Photoshop document. The added benefit to using the drawing tools is that you can then scale the shapes and modify the design while still maintaining a crisp image.

Choosing the Right Drawing Tool

Photoshop offers six shape tools. They can be used to create vector shapes, vector paths (which can be used to make a selection), or raster shapes. The following list explains how to change how the shape tools work:

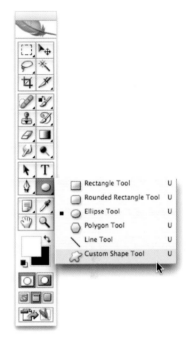

- **Rectangle tool:** The Rectangle tool draws rectangles; if you hold down the Shift key, it draws squares.

- **Rounded Rectangle tool:** The Rounded Rectangle tool is well suited for drawing buttons for Web sites. Adjust the Radius setting to modify the amount of curvature.

- **Ellipse tool:** The Ellipse tool draws ellipses; if you hold down the Shift key, it draws circles.

- **Polygon tool:** The Polygon tool creates polygons. The fewest number of sides a polygon can have is three (which is a triangle). The most complex polygon you can create is a hectagon (a 100-sided figure). Enter the number of sides in the Options bar. Additionally, the Polygon tool can be used to create stars by clicking the Geometry Options button in the Options bar.

- **Line tool:** The Line tool draws lines. Specify a thickness in the Options bar. The line can be between 1 and 1000 pixels in width. You can also choose to add arrowheads by clicking the Geometry Options button in the Options bar.

- **Custom Shape tool:** The Custom Shape tool is *very* versatile. There are several shapes built into Photoshop. These can be extremely useful during the design process. To view your loaded shapes, click the drop-down Custom Shape Picker. Additional shapes can be loaded by clicking the submenu of the Custom Shape Picker. Choose from the built-in libraries or load more.

Loading Custom Shapes

Thousands of free shapes are available to download for Photoshop. An Internet search using the keywords "Photoshop," "Free," and "Custom Shapes" returns plenty of great results. You can choose to load these custom shapes temporarily, or add them to your preset list.

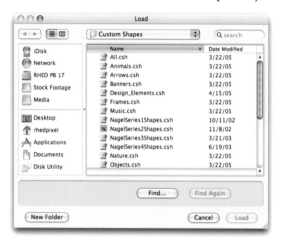

Temporary Load

1. From the Custom Shape Picker, click the submenu.

2. Choose Load Shapes.

3. Navigate to the desired shape library (it should end in the extension .csh).

4. Select the shape and click OK.

5. You can choose to Replace the current shapes or Append the new shapes to the end of the old list.

Load Into Presets

1. Navigate to your Photoshop application folder.

2. Open the Presets folder.

3. Open the Custom Shapes folder.

4. Copy the custom shapes files into the Custom Shapes folder. Be sure the shapes are not compressed (such as a .sit or .zip file).

5. Restart Photoshop; the presets will be loaded into the submenu of the Custom Shape Picker.

Drawing Shapes

Using the Shape tools is very similar to using the Marquee tools. In fact, the same shortcut keys apply: Holding down the Option (Alt) key after you start drawing will cause the shape to draw from the center of the initial click, whereas holding down the Shift key constrains the width and height to preserve a constant ratio.

CREATING CUSTOM SHAPES

You can create your own custom shapes and save them for future use:

1. Create your own shape with the Pen tool or paste one into Photo-shop from Adobe Illustrator.

2. Select the Paths palette, and select a path. It can be a vector mask from a shape layer, a work path, or a saved path.

3. Choose Edit > Define Custom Shape.

4. Enter a descriptive name for the new custom shape in the Shape Name dialog box. The new shape now appears in the Shape pop-up palette, which can be quickly accessed from the Options bar.

5. If you'd like to permanently save the shape by adding it to a library, choose Save Shapes from the submenu of the Shapes pop-up palette.

Let's try using the Shape tools:

1. Create a new RGB document sized 1024 × 768 pixels. Fill the Background Contents to Transparent. Name the document Playing Card.

2. Select the Rounded Rectangular Shape tool. Set the Radius to 10 pixels.

3. In the Options bar, choose to create a Shape Layer and set the fill to White.

4. Click and draw a rectangle in the shape of a playing card.

5. Choose the Custom Shape tool. Open the Custom Shape Picker and select the Heart shape. If it is not visible, choose Reset Shapes to load the default set.

6. In the Options bar, set the fill color to red.

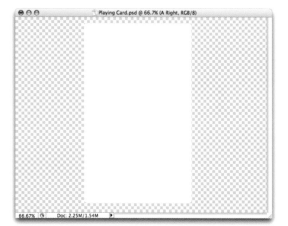

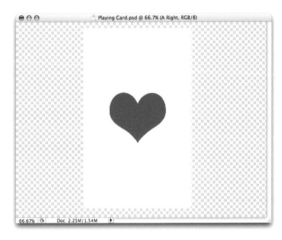

7. Draw a large heart in the center of the card.

8. Use the Alignment tools to center the heart in the middle of the card. Under Photoshop CS2 (or later) select both layers. Activate the Move tool and choose the Horizontal and Vertical Alignment buttons in the Options bar.

9. Draw a heart icon near the upper-left corner of the card. Leave room for a letter A (for *Ace*).

10. Press Cmd+J (Ctrl+J) to duplicate the current heart layer. Move it to the lower-right corner. Invoke the Free Transform command and rotate the heart 180°.

11. Press T to select the Type tool. In the Options bar choose a font such as New York or Palatino. Set the style to Bold, the size to 100 pt, and the color to Red.

12. Click in the upper-left corner and add the letter A.

13. Press Cmd+J (Ctrl+J) to duplicate the current "A" layer. Move it to the lower-right corner. Invoke the Free Transform command and rotate the A 180°.

If you'd like to look at the completed project, open the file Playing Card.psd and check it out.

THREE KINDS OF SHAPES

You can use the Shape tools
to create shapes in three
different ways:

- **SHAPE LAYERS:** This option creates a shape on a separate layer.
  A shape layer has a fill layer that defines the color and a linked
  vector mask that defines the shape.

- **PATHS:** This option draws a work path on the current layer. This
  path can then be used to make a selection. It can also be used to
  create a vector mask or it can be filled or stroked. Paths appear in
  the Paths palette.

- **FILL PIXELS:** This option paints directly on the active layer. It makes
  the Shape tools perform like Paint tools. In this mode you are creating raster, not vector, graphics.

Felix Nelson is a busy man. As the creative director of the National Association of Photoshop Professionals he has to oversee the direction and production of conference materials and four magazines. All are created for a tough audience, which is filled with professional photographers and designers who have to be inspired and impressed by his work. Nelson turns to Photoshop for its power and flexibility.

"Almost every project we work on involves Photoshop," said Nelson. "Everything from promotional posters, direct mail campaigns, product brochures, and magazine layouts to logo designs, video production, and Web design. It all uses Photoshop to some extent."

Nelson's ability to harness this power for diverse projects comes from his thorough knowledge of the program.

"When I'm illustrating, I rely on one specific set of features. When I create a poster design, it's another skill set. Logo design involves yet another set of features and software," said Nelson. "I would say learn what each tool is capable of. Know what they can and can't do."

While traditional tools still exist, Nelson has found that Photoshop has replaced many of them. Its flexibility is a huge time-saver that lets him bring his ideas to life and speeds up the creative process.

"When I first started in the graphics field, most of my time was spent creating mock-ups for various projects. This meant illustrating images [usually marker or pencil renderings] and placing all headlines and body copy [using Letraset press-on type or hand lettering]," said Nelson. "It was a pretty messy undertaking. I've inhaled tons of Spray Mount and rubber cement fumes, not to mention the multi-burns and cuts from waxers and Xacto knives. Photoshop allows me to create digital mock-ups that match the final printed version perfectly, in a fraction of the time."

Nelson offers advice to those studying Photoshop. He strongly suggests mastering shortcuts and techniques that make a designer faster. While the Photoshop skill sets needed for Web designers are dramatically different than those for an illustrator, both can benefit from increased productivity.

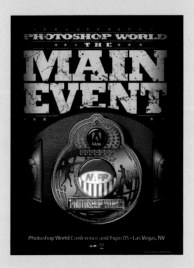

"A few years ago I had a designer create a cover for one of our publications. It was amazing. The concept, the attention to detail, and the execution were spectacular. Since they were doing this pro bono [free], I just had to know how long it took them to create it," said Nelson. "I found out they spent 80 hours designing the cover. We generally spend 8 to 10 hours on an average cover. So the old saying 'time is money' certainly applies in this case."

Nelson stresses that mastering Photoshop is a gateway to opportunity. If students apply themselves, there are several jobs and projects out there.

"It never ceases to amaze me how wide open the graphics field is. Just walk into any store and take a look around. Every

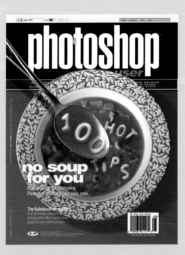

sign, display, sales sheet, brochure, package design, CD/DVD cover, commercials, video... all of these things involve graphic design of some kind," said Nelson. "I simply love the broad spectrum of projects I get to work on. It definitely keeps you on your toes,creatively speaking."

Layer Masking

When working in Photoshop, you'll often need to combine multiple images together into a new composite image. Those original images, however, may have backgrounds or objects that you no longer want. This is where Layer Masks come in. Far superior to erasing pixels, Layer Masks allow you to hide (or mask) part of a layer using powerful painting and selection tools. The more you work on combining multiple images, the more you'll find yourself using masks.

The mask is the black-and-white area attached to the layer thumbnail. It contains all of the transparency information that the layer needs to isolate the flower from the background.

Layer Mask Essentials

In this chapter, we'll revisit several techniques we harnessed in Chapter 5, "Selection Tools and Techniques." This is because masks generally start as a selection, which is then attached to a layer. The mask can be refined, adding to it with black or subtracting with white. Learning to create and modify masks is important—and a skill that becomes significantly easier with a little practice.

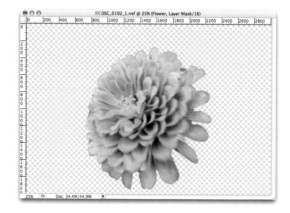

Adding Layer Masks

The best way to learn about Layer Masks is to jump right in and create one. We'll start with an easy image, but one that will help illustrate the important concepts. Let's get started:

1. Open the file Sundial.tif from the Chapter 7 folder on the DVD-ROM.

2. Convert the *Background* layer into a floating layer by double-clicking its name in the Layers palette. Name the layer Sundial.

3. Select the Polygonal Lasso from the Toolbox.

4. Make a rough selection around the octagon-shaped platter and the metal sundial bar. Be accurate, but not obsessed with making a perfect selection.

5. When you close the selection, by returning to the starting point, it will become active. You should see the "marching ants" encircling the sundial.

6. Click the Add layer mask button to add a mask to the layer.

7. To make it easier to see the edges of the border, place a solid color layer behind the Sundial layer. Choose Layer > New Fill Layer > Solid Color. Choose a color that is not in the image, such as green.

8. Drag the fill layer below the Sundial layer in the Layers palette.

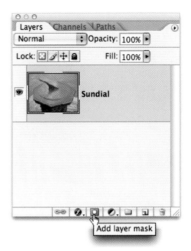

9. Depending on the accuracy of your initial selection, your mask may be usable as-is. If needed, you can quickly touch it up using the Brush tool.

10. Click the Layer Mask thumbnail to select it.

11. Activate the Brush tool by pressing B or choosing it from the Toolbox.

12. Press D to load the default colors of black and white. Black will add to a mask and create transparency, white will subtract from the mask. Using gray or blurring will create a softer edge.

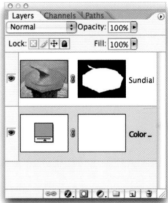

13. Zoom in to better see your edges. You can use the Zoom tool or the Navigator to get a better look at your edges.

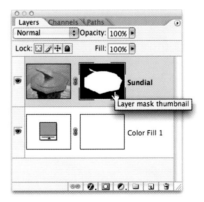

14. Paint with a soft-edged brush to refine the mask. If you add too much to the mask, press X to toggle the mask colors. Remember, painting with black will add to the mask (hence removing or masking the image).

15. You can improve the edges of the mask by using the Blur tool (R) or the Smudge tool (R) on the edges. You can stop tweaking when you are satisfied with your results.

Disabling Layer Masks

The primary benefit of masks is their flexibility. In the previous section we explored that flexibility by adding and subtracting to a mask. This flexibility can also carry forward with the ability to temporarily disable a mask. This can be useful if you want to check your progress, or if you need to restore the original image to use on another project:

1. Work with the Sundial image from the previous exercise or open the file Sundial_Masked.tif from the Chapter 7 folder.

2. Select the Layers palette so it is active.

3. Shift-click the Layer Mask thumbnail to disable it. Alternately, you can right-click the mask's thumbnail to access more options.

4. To re-enable the mask, Shift-click its thumbnail again.

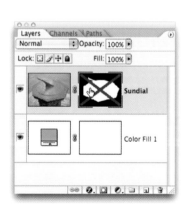

Shift-clicking a Layer Mask's thumbnail will temporarily disable the mask.

Deleting Layer Masks

After going through the effort of creating a mask, you are unlikely to want to permanently discard it. But if you change your mind and are certain you want to delete it, doing so is easy:

1. Work with the Sundial image from the previous exercise or open the file Sundial_Masked.tif from the Chapter 7 folder.

2. Select the Layers palette so it is active.

3. Click the Layer Mask thumbnail. Drag it to the trash icon in the Layers palette.

4. A dialog window appears asking you to decide what to do with the mask:

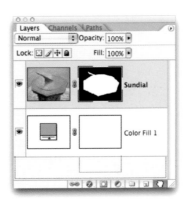

- **Delete:** This will discard the mask and restore the image to its premasked state.

- **Cancel:** This allows you to cancel the command and return the image to its masked state.

- **Apply:** This permanently applies the mask and deletes the pixels that were originally masked.

5. Click Apply to permanently apply the mask.

Using Vector Masks

Most users choose to work with the raster-based Layer Masks discussed earlier in this chapter. These raster-based masks tend to be the easiest to work with and allow the most flexibility in editing due to the wide variety of tools you can use to modify the mask. However, some users prefer to work with vector tools like the Pen tool or the Shape tools because of personal preference (or more experience with programs like Adobe Illustrator). There are several ways to add a Vector Mask:

- After you've added a raster Layer Mask, click the Add Mask button in the Layers palette to add a second mask that is vector-based.

- To add a Vector Mask initially, Cmd-click (Ctrl-click) the Add Mask button when adding the first mask.

- To add a new (empty) vector mask, you can choose Layer > Vector Mask > Reveal All.

- To hide an entire layer, choose Layer > Vector Mask > Hide All.

Mask Creation Strategies

There are many different approaches to creating Layer Masks. The approach you should take will vary based on your source image. Let's try four different images and techniques to refine our Layer Masking ability.

Using a Gradient as a Mask

When designing, you may need to gradually blend the edges of an image. This can be easily accomplished by combining a Layer Mask and a Gradient. Let's give it a try:

1. Open the file Desert.tif from the Chapter 7 folder.

2. Duplicate the *Background* layer by pressing Cmd+J (Ctrl+J).

3. Select the top layer and choose Image > Adjustments > Desaturate.

4. With the topmost layer active, click the Add layer mask button at the bottom of the Layers palette. A new, empty Layer Mask is added to the layer.

5. Press G to select the Gradient tool.

6. Press D to load the default colors of black and white.

7. From the Options bar, choose the black-to-white gradient. If it's not available, choose Reset Gradients from the Gradient Picker's submenu.

8. With the Layer Mask selected, click and drag to create a new linear gradient going from top to bottom.

9. The new Layer Mask will create a gradual blend from the grayscale version to the colored version.

This technique can also be used on one layer to create a gradual fade to transparency, or to another layer.

Using a Channel

Oftentimes, a channel will get you very close to having a perfect Layer Mask. This technique works particularly well when the subject is against a high-contrast back-

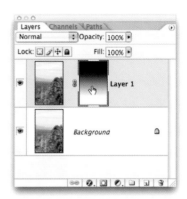

The gradient mask allows the image to blend between the grayscale and color image.

ground (such as a sky or a wall), and it works very well with fine details like hair. The image can be masked so it is ready for integration into a composite image. For example, a masked image could be used to add palm trees to a different photo. Let's give it a try:

1. Open the file Palm_Tree.jpg from the Chapter 7 folder. This image was shot against a night sky using a flash.

2. Switch to the Channels palette and examine the red, green, and blue channels. Look for one with high contrast from the background. While all three channels are fairly high-contrast, the green channel stands out the most.

3. Duplicate the green channel by dragging it onto the New Channel icon at the bottom of the Channels palette (it looks like a pad of paper).

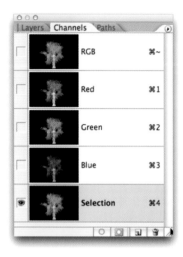

4. Rename the new channel Selection, by double-clicking its name.

5. With the Selection channel selected, press Cmd+L (Ctrl+L) to invoke a Levels adjustment. Levels is a powerful command that allows you to adjust the gamma (gray) point as well as the black and white points.

6. Move the black slider to the right, setting the Input Level to around 60. The black in the channel should get crisper.

7. Move the white slider to the left, setting the Input Level to around 100. The gray areas in the channel should switch to pure white.

8. Move the middle (gray) slider to refine any gray spots in the channel. A value of 2.25 should be approximately correct.

9. Cmd-click (Ctrl-click) on the Selection channel's thumbnail to load the selection.

10. Turn off the visibility for the RGB channels by clicking the RGB composite channel's visibility icon. Turn off visibility for the Selection channel.

11. Switch to the Layers palette.

12. Turn the *Background* layer into a floating layer by double-clicking its name in the Layers palette. Name the layer Palm Tree.

13. Click the Add layer mask button at the bottom of the Layers palette.

VIDEO TRAINING
Alpha Channel

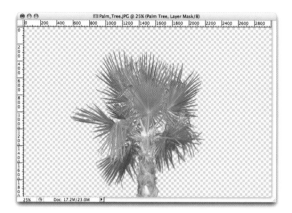

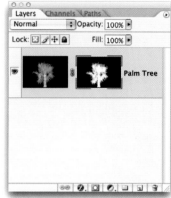

Using the Color Range Command

Sometimes, a color (or range of colors) will be very present in your image. These colors can be used to quickly create an accurate Layer Mask. Even if the color cannot be used to select the object entirely, you can always harness the Brush tool to clean up stray areas.

1. Open the file Bees_and_Flower.jpg from the Chapter 7 folder.

2. Turn the *Background* layer into a floating layer by double-clicking its name in the Layers palette. Name the layer Bees and Flower.

3. Choose Select > Color Range to make a selection based on a range of colors.

4. With the Eyedropper, click within the yellow area of the flower to make an initial selection. Hold down the Shift key and drag through other areas of the flower to add to the selection.

5. Leave the Fuzziness set to a low value (like 30). When most of the flower is selected, click OK to create an active selection.

6. Click the Add layer mask button for the layer. The petals will show well, but parts of the flower will be missing.

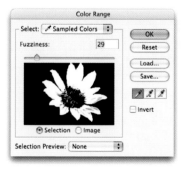

7. Add a solid color layer to make it easier to see your edges. Choose Layer > New Fill Layer > Solid Color. A purple layer will help things stand out nicely. Click OK and drag the solid layer below the masked flower.

8. Examine the masked layer closely. You will need to paint in part of the center of the flower. Additionally, some of the petals contain unwanted transparency. You may also have some leaves or stems that bled through. We can fix all of these problems quickly using the Brush tool.

9. Press D to load the default colors of black and white.

10. Select the Layer Mask attached to the Bees and Flower layer.

11. Press B to activate the Brush tool. Adjust the size of the brush and its hardness settings so you have a smaller brush with a gentle edge (an 80-pixel brush with a hardness of 75% is a good place to start).

12. Paint in spotted or missing areas with white. You can remove any unwanted areas by painting with black.

13. When finished, you can save the image as a layered file such as a TIFF or PSD format-ted file.

Using Calculations

We explored the Calculations command to create an advanced selection in Chapter 5. This command uses channel data to create a new alpha channel. We can then refine the channel to create an accurate selection. We can also take this one step further to make a high-quality Layer Mask. Let's give it a try:

1. Turn the *Background* layer into a floating layer by double-clicking its name in the Layers palette. Name the layer Lamp.

2. Open the file Lamp.tif from the Chapter 7 folder.

3. Call up the Channels palette and closely examine the channels for a high contrast between the lamp and the background. While all three channels have great contrast between the sky and the lamp, only the blue channel has some contrast between the building and the lamp.

4. Invoke the Calculations command by choosing Image > Calculations.

5. Since the other two channels do not contain much contrast, we'll use only the blue channel. Set both Source 1 and Source 2 to the blue channel.

6. Experiment with different blending modes so you get clearer separation between the lamp and all other elements. In this case, the Vivid Light mode works best to create a new channel. Click OK.

Compare the different channels to identify the one (or two) with highest contrast.

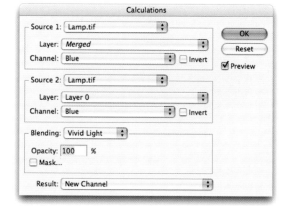

7. The new channel will need a little touch-up. We can get most of the way there with a Levels adjustment. Press Cmd+L (Ctrl+L) to invoke the Levels dialog box.

8. Adjust the black, white, and gray points to improve the matte. The results will be closer, but not complete. Click OK when satisfied.

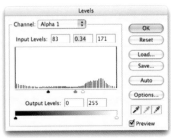

9. With your Brush tool, paint out the buildings with white.

10. With the Brush tool, paint in the gaps in the lamp with black.

11. We need to reverse the channel so the area we want to discard is black. Press Cmd+I (Ctrl+I) to invert the channel.

12. Soften the selection by blurring it. Choose Filter > Blur > Gaussian Blur; set it to a value of 5 pixels and click OK.

13. Load the channel as a selection by Cmd-clicking (Ctrl-clicking) the channel's thumbnail.

14. Switch to the Layers palette and click the Lamp layer.

15. Click the Add layer mask button to apply a mask to the selected layer.

Refining Masks

So by now, you should be feeling more comfortable making Layer Masks. However, there's always room for improvement (at least where masks are concerned). Let's take a look at three ways to refine or adjust a mask.

Choking a Mask with Levels

While we've used Levels to adjust a channel to create a mask, we can also turn to the flexible command to refine a mask after it has been created. By moving the gray slider, you can expand or contract an existing mask. Let's give it a try:

1. Open the file Cactus.tif from the Chapter 7 folder.

2. Select the layer's mask.

3. Soften the mask slightly by running a Gaussian Blur (Filter > Blur > Gaussian Blur). A low value like 1 or 2 is enough to feather the mask around the spikes of the cactus. Click OK.

4. Run a Levels adjustment by pressing Cmd+L (Ctrl+L).

5. Move the gray (middle) slider to adjust the gamma. To the right will contract the mask, to the left will expand it. Experiment with adjusting the mask to improve the border around the cactus spines.

6. Click OK when you are satisfied.

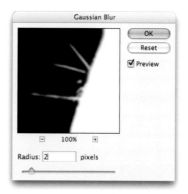

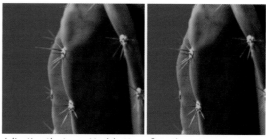

Adjusting the Layer Mask better refines the transparent areas. Look closely at the edges of the image and the spines on the cactus. The ones on the right are more clearly defined.

Maximum and Minimum

Photoshop offers two specialty filters for refining masks. Lumped into the amorphous "Other" category, most users miss the Minimum and Maximum filters. Both are useful for modifying a mask as they can expand or contract.

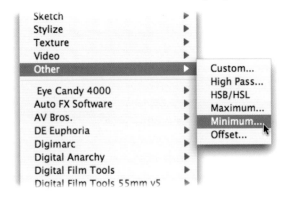

- **Maximum:** The Maximum filter applies a choke, which spreads the white areas and chokes the black areas. This filter will grow a Layer Mask outward, which is useful if the matte is hiding too much of the image.

- **Minimum:** The Minimum filter applies a spread, which expands the black areas and shrinks the white areas. This filter will shrink a Layer Mask and contract it inward. This is useful if the matte has a fringe around the outside edge.

1. Open the file Flower.psd from the Chapter 7 folder. Notice how there is a thin black border around the flower.

2. Select the Layer Mask's thumbnail.

3. Choose Filter > Other > Minimum to contract the mask. A value of 5–7 pixels should be enough to contract the edge to remove the border. Click OK when satisfied.

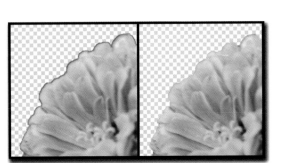

The Minimum filter modified the Layer Mask by contracting it. The minor adjustment removed the dark edge.

Using Smudge and Blur

Sometimes a mask is close to being ready, but needs a little touch-up. What better way to do this than to paint? By using the Blur and Smudge tools you can polish problem edges.

- **Blur:** Choose the Blur tool to soften a hard edge that looks unnatural. Just be sure the mask is selected before blurring.

- **Smudge (Lighten):** Choose the Smudge tool and set its mode to Lighten in the Options bar. This is useful for gently expanding the matte. Leave the Strength set to a low value to make gentle changes.

- **Smudge (Darken):**
Choose the Smudge tool and set its mode to Darken in the Options bar. This is useful for gently contracting the matte. Leave the Strength set to a low value to make gentle changes.

Open the file Lion_Mask. tif to try out the Smudge and Blur tools.

Adjusting Content Within a Mask

By default, Layer Masks are linked to their respective layers. Applying a transformation (such as a Free Transform command) will affect a layer and its Layer Mask. However, there are times when you won't want this default behavior. Sometimes it is useful to adjust the contents of a masked layer without repositioning the mask. Let's give it a try:

1. Open the file Monitor.psd from the Chapter 7 folder. While the Layer Mask is accurate, too much of the layer's content is obscured.

2. Click the chain icon between the layer thumbnail and Layer Mask icons for the Content layer. You can now manipulate the layer Content or its mask independently.

3. Select the Content layer's thumbnail to modify the visible pixels of the layer.

4. Press Cmd+T (Ctrl+T) to invoke the Free Transform command. Scale the Content layer smaller and rotate it slightly to better match the angle of the monitor. Click the Commit button to apply the transformation.

Advice on Masks

Layer Masking and Advanced Selections go hand-in-hand. The more you practice one, the easier both will get. New users often lapse and are drawn back to features like the Eraser tools or the Extract command. While these may seem easier, in the long run they are not. Learn to work like a professional and you'll achieve professional results.

Compositing with Layers

8

When Photoshop debuted, it did not have layers. In fact, its original purpose was to touch up frames of motion picture and photography film. It was, as its name implied, a photo shop. The purpose was a digital darkroom where photos could be enhanced, color-corrected, and even repaired. Over time, however, people wanted to do more inside of Photoshop, including print advertisements and television broadcast graphics. As people expected Photoshop to do more, Adobe responded with the introduction of layers.

What Are Layers?

In traditional cel animation, the artists would paint their animations onto clear sheets of acetate. These clear sheets would often contain a single character or element. They could then be laid together with sheets containing other characters and backgrounds to create a composited scene.

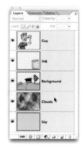

Layers work the same way. Each layer can contain discrete elements of your design. You then combine these to create the finished product. Layers can contain photos, text, logos, shapes, and even textures. There are lots of ways to create and manage layers, but it all comes back to having an organized design. Every layer should have a clear, descriptive name to make your design work easier.

Why You Need Layers

If you plan to create complex designs in Photoshop, then layers are a must for a few reasons:

- **Easy modification:** Layers make it easier to modify your design. Separate elements can be easily accessed and edited.

- **Easy manipulation:** If you are using Photoshop to create Web or video animation as well as multimedia elements like slides or DVD menus, individual elements can be animated, highlighted, or revealed.

- **Interface with other programs:** Many other software programs rely on Photoshop layers as a content creation tool since they lack the drawing and painting tools of Photoshop. Through support of the layered Photoshop format, they allow their software to cleanly interface with the best-selling image-editing tool.

Dissecting a Composite Image

When designers need to create complex screen graphics, they usually turn to Photoshop. Its combination of flexible compositing tools, color correction and grading tools, and flexible type engine make it an ideal choice.

Let's create a composite image by building up its layers. To begin this exercise, open Ch08_Composite.psd on the book's DVD-ROM. This composite image is a mock-up of a promotional graphic to be used in a PowerPoint presentation. We'll build this graphic up to examine its layers.

1. When you first open this document, all you will see is a black screen. This is because most of the layers are not visible. We will need to activate them in the Layers palette. Make sure you can see the Layers palette (if you can't, press F7 to toggle it on). We'll begin turning on the visibility icons (eye icon) from the bottom up by clicking in the column next to the layer's thumbnail. The first layer of our

TIP

Preserve Your Layers

You should always keep a layered file, as it will come in very handy for future changes and distribution.

composition is called the *Background* and it has a locked icon. The background is locked initially because it is treated as the canvas or paper that the rest of the image is built upon. Technically, the background is not a layer. If you want to turn it into a layer (so you could use a layer mask, for example), you need to double-click its name and rename it.

2. Turn on the next layer by enabling the visibility icon Painted texture. This, as its name implies, is a photo of real paint on a canvas, and it serves as the starting point for our design. If you look closely in the upper-right corner of the Layers palette, you'll see that this layer has been set to 60% opacity. This was to reduce the intensity of the painted texture, which is caused by it mixing with the black background layer.

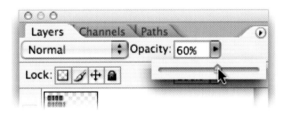

3. Turn on the next layer, Keyboard, to reveal another feature of layers, blending modes. In the top-left corner of the Layers palette, you'll see that this layer uses the Luminosity blending mode as well as an Opacity setting of 40%. Blending modes are covered in depth in Chapter 9, "Using Blending Modes," but essentially they cause layers to mix based on properties like color and lightness. In this case we used a blending mode to create a subtle, but themed, background image.

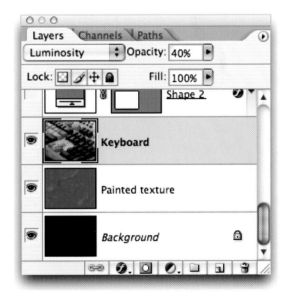

4. Click the visibility icon for the next four layers: Shape 2, Camera, Shape 1, and Edit. Here we are using three more features of the Layers palette.

- **Shape layers:** The Shape layers were created using the Rounded Rectangle Tool (U) and were created as Vector Shapes by choosing that style from the Options bar. The benefit is that vectors can be resized indefinitely with no quality loss.

- **Layer Styles:** The Shape layers also have a stroke and a bevel applied to them using Layer Styles. (For more on layer styles, see Chapter 13, "Layer Styles"). Layer Styles can be accessed by selecting a layer, then clicking on the *f* icon at the bottom of the Layers palette.

- **Clipping Mask:** Photos were trapped inside the vector shapes by using a Clipping Mask. A Clipping Mask acts much like a cookie cutter, by trimming the edges of a layer based on what's beneath it. Simply place one object above another and choose Layer > Create Clipping Mask. Older versions of Photoshop call this command Group with Previous. More on Clipping Masks later in this chapter

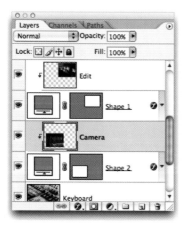

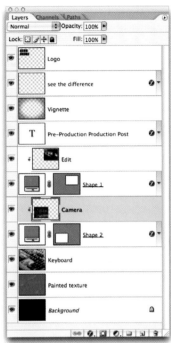

5. Click the visibility icon for the remaining four layers. Here you will see a text layer, which was added with the Vertical Type tool (for more on type, see Chapter 12, "Using the Type Tool"). You'll also find two logos, which were originally Adobe Illustrator files that were opened inside of Photoshop. The last layer, Vignette, provides a focal point for the image. It was created by filling a layer with black, then making a selection with the Elliptical Marquee tool (with a large feather), and pressing Delete. Vignettes are often used in TV commercials and feature films, and they draw the viewer's eye toward the center of the image.

Creating Layers

Creating a new layer is easy… in several ways!
You can click the Create New Layer icon
(looks like a notepad) at the bottom of the
Layers palette. If menus are your thing, choose Layer > New >
Layer or press Shift+Cmd+N (Shift+Ctrl+N). Additionally,
you can drag layers up or down the layer stack or from one
document to another, if you are so inclined.

You can also move layers or reorder them to change your image. Table 1 shows a few keyboard shortcuts for just this purpose.

Table 1 Layer Mobility

Keyboard Shortcut	Layer Movement
Cmd+[(Ctrl+[)	Move current layer down one position
Cmd+] (Ctrl+])	Move current layer up one position
Shift+Cmd+[(Shift+Ctrl+[)	Move current layer to bottom of Layers palette
Shift+Cmd+] (Shift+Ctrl+])	Move current layer to top of Layers palette

Duplicating Layers

When you need to duplicate a layer, you have a few choices. You can choose Layer > Duplicate Layer or right-click (Ctrl-click) the layer's name in the Layers palette and choose Duplicate Layer. Another method is to drag one layer onto the Create New Layer button at the bottom of the Layers palette. My favorite, though, is Cmd+J (Ctrl+J)–think *jump*–to create a copy of a layer immediately above itself.

Deleting Layers

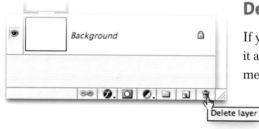

If you decide you don't need a layer, you should throw it away. This will reduce the size of your file, which means it'll take up less disk space and require less memory to work with. To throw away layers, drag them into the trash can at the bottom of the Layers palette. You can also right-click/Ctrl-click a layer's name to throw it away or choose Layer > Delete > Layer. Starting with Photoshop CS2, you don't have to throw layers away one at a time. Just Cmd+click (Ctrl+click) on multiple layers, then delete with one of the above methods.

Fill Layers

Besides layers that you create or import, Photoshop allows you to create specialty Fill Layers. These layers allow you to quickly create graphical content for your designs. These can be accessed by choosing Layer > New Fill Layer and the choosing Solid Color, Gradient, or Pattern (alternatively, click the black and white half circle on the bottom of the Layers palette). Create a new document (sized 1024 × 768) and try out these new layers:

JUMP IT UP

You can press Cmd+J (Ctrl+J) to duplicate (or jump) the current layer to a copy above. With a selection made, Cmd+J (Ctrl+J) will jump only the selection and create a copy above. Adding the Shift key to the Jump command will cut the selection and place it on its own layer above its previous position.

- **Solid Color:** Choose Layer > New Fill Layer > Solid Color. Pick from any color using the Color Picker or Color Libraries. To edit the color layer, just double-click its thumbnail in the Layers palette.

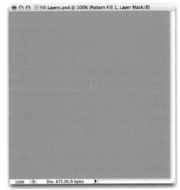

- **Gradient:** Choose Layer > New Fill Layer > Gradient. A *gradient* is a gradual blend between two or more colors. Gradients can be used as backgrounds, or blended over an image to perform the same function as a camera filter. Photoshop supports five types of gradients: Linear, Radial, Angle, Reflected, and Diamond. You can double-click the gradient in the Gradient Fill window to launch the Gradient Editor. Within the editor you can modify the gradient, or click the submenu to load addition gradient presets. For more on gradients, be sure to read Chapter 6, "Painting and Drawing Tools."

- **Pattern:** Choose Layer > New Fill Layer > Pattern. Photoshop comes with a variety of seamless patterns built in. These can be accessed from the Pattern Fill window. To choose a different pattern, click the drop-down menu to see the active patterns. To load even more patterns, click the triangular submenu on the right edge of the drop-down palette.

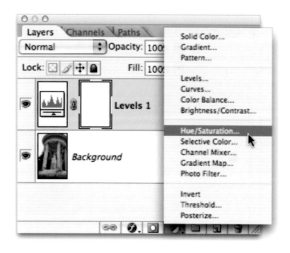

Adjustment Layers

While clicking through your Layers menu, you likely noticed Adjustment Layers (from Levels to Posterize). These important layers are for image enhancement and color correction. They offer a nondestructive way to fix image problems. These special layers can contain one of 12 image manipulations. Unlike normal image adjustments, these can be enabled or disabled as well as modified with no loss in image quality. For now, be patient—we'll tackle these in depth in Chapter 10, "Color Correction."

Working with Multiple Layers

VIDEO TRAINING
Layer Organization

As Photoshop has continued to evolve, so has its ability to offer powerful layer management. When creating complex designs, such as Web site mock-ups or print advertisements, it is important to maintain control over your design. This includes naming all of your layers, as well as creating relationships or linking between them. Depending on which version of Photoshop you are using, you may find slight differences in layer behavior.

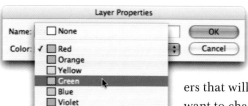

To get some practice, open Ch08_Layer_Organization.psd from the book's DVD. This file contains several color-coded layers that we will manipulate (the color coding identifies layers that will interact with each other). In the future, you might want to change the color of layers in your own documents to better organize them. To change the label color of a layer, just press Option+double-click (Alt+double-click) on a layer (except for its name).

Selecting Multiple Layers

One of the first skills to learn is how to select multiple layers. Select both the Right Foot and Left Foot layers (which are color-coded red) in the Ch08_Layer _Organization.psd using one of the following methods:

- **Photoshop CS2 or later:** You can click multiple layers to select them. Hold down the Shift key and click to select multiple contiguous layers or use the Cmd (Ctrl) key to select noncontiguous layers.

- **Photoshop CS or earlier:** You will need to highlight the first layer, then click in the link column (adjacent to the visibility column) for the other layers you want to select. Technically, you can only select one layer at a time, but through linking, other layers can be adjusted along with your main selection.

Linking Layers

Linking layers creates a family relationship. When one of the family members moves, the others move along with it (same goes for scale and rotation). You would choose to link two layers together in order to create a relationship of particular elements needing to react to one another. For example, if you had a logo and text that you wanted to scale together (at the same time), you'd link them together. Go ahead and link the Right Foot to its companion Left Foot using one of the following methods:

- **Photoshop CS2 or later:** You can click multiple layers to select them using the techniques mentioned in the preceding section. When all layers that belong together are active, click the link button (chain icon) at the bottom of the Layers palette.

- **Photoshop CS or earlier:** You will need to select the first layer, then click in the link column next to other layers you want to select.

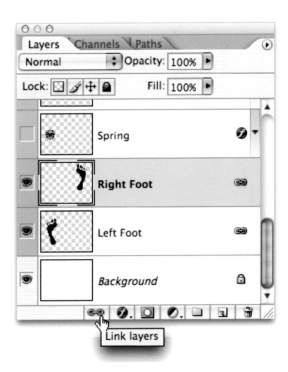

Link layers

Aligning Layers

A design can look sloppy if the designer relies solely on his or her eyes for a precise layout. Alignment is the process of causing multiple objects to rest on a straight line. This line is usually determined by one of the edges of the selected objects. This is useful to create a professional-looking design where the objects appear precise and organized. Let's align the two layers we are working with:

1. Select both the Right Foot and Left Foot layers.

2. Pick the Move tool by pressing V or clicking in the upper-right corner of the Toolbox.

3. In the Options bar you will notice alignment options. Hover your pointer over each to familiarize yourself with their names.

4. Select the object that you want to use as a reference point for the alignment. In this case let's use Left Foot.

5. Click the Align bottom edges button. You'll notice the feet shapes are aligned along their bottom edge.

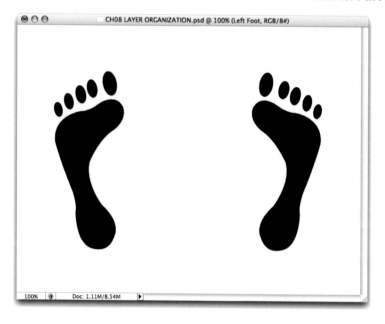

Distributing Layers

Distribution places an identical amount of space between multiple objects. This can be an important step in creating a professional-looking design. Distribution is similar to Alignment in how it is accessed. However, the intent is slightly different. You will need three or more objects in order to distribute them. Let's distribute a few layers:

1. Turn off the visibility icons for all layers except *Background,* Spring, Summer, Fall, and Winter. Click the eye icon to make a layer invisible.

2. Select Spring, Summer, Fall, and Winter layers.

3. Choose the Move tool by pressing V or clicking in the upper-right corner of the Toolbox.

4. In the Options bar you will notice distribution options (to the right of the alignment options). Roll over each to familiarize yourself with their names.

5. Click the Distribute horizontal centers button to spread the images apart evenly.

6. Click the Align bottom edges button. Your image will now be evenly aligned and distributed.

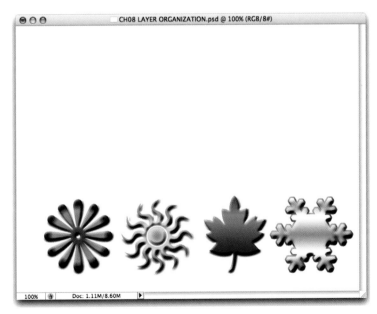

Grouping Layers (Layer Sets)

Sometimes you will want to take several layers and treat them as if they were one layer. This is useful for aligning a design composed of multiple images or just general cleanup for organizational purposes. The process of nondestructively joining layers is called *grouping*. A permanent technique is called *merging* (see "Merging Layers" later in this chapter), but that is pretty decisive. Instead, let's group these layers together so they still retain their individual identity, yet behave as a group:

- **Photoshop CS2 or later:**

  1. Select Spring, Summer, Fall, and Winter layers using the Cmd-click (Ctrl-click) technique.

  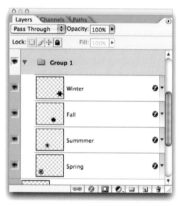

  2. Press Cmd+G (Ctrl+G) or choose Layer > Group to place these layers into a new group (which looks like a folder). If you'd like to name the group, double-click the folder's name in the Layers palette.

  3. You can now move these elements together. For example, select both the *Background* and Group 1, then use the horizontal center and vertical center alignment commands to center these icons on the page.

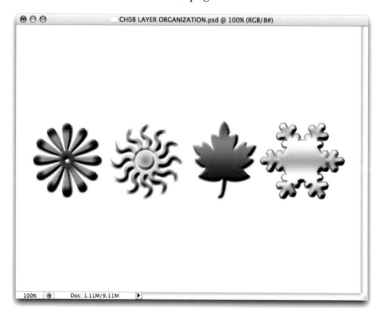

- **Photoshop CS or earlier:** Select the first layer, then click in the link column next to other layers you want to select.

    1. Select Spring, Summer, Fall, and Winter layers using the link technique. Make sure no other layers are linked to these four.

    2. From the Layers palette submenu (triangle in upper-right corner) choose New Set From Linked.

    3. You can now move these elements together. For example, select the *Background* and link it to Group 1, then use the horizontal center and vertical center alignment commands to center these icons on the page

Locking Layers

Sometimes you need to protect yourself from your own worst enemy (you). Photoshop gives you the option to lock properties of a layer to prevent accidental modification. Just click the icons next to the word *Lock* in the Layers palette. You can lock three separate properties (or a combination of the three):

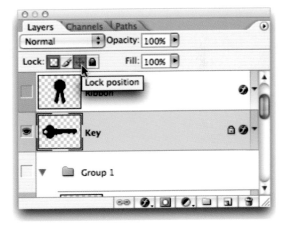

- **Lock transparent pixels:** The grid icon locks all transparent areas of an image, but you can still modify any data that was on the layer prior to locking.

- **Lock image pixels:** The paintbrush icon locks all image pixels in the layer.

- **Lock position:** The arrow icon prevents accidentally moving a layer out of alignment or changing its position.

- **Lock all:** The padlock icon locks all three properties in one click.

Let's try locking a layer:

1. Turn off the visibility icons for all layers except *Background* and Key.

2. Select the Key layer.

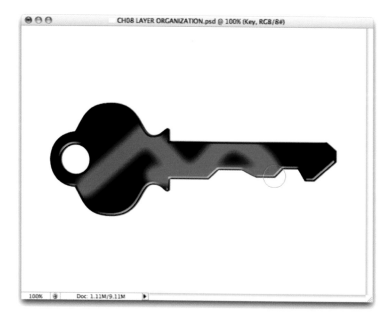

3. In the upper-left corner of the Layers palette, click the Lock transparent pixels and Lock position icons.

4. Press B to select the Brush tool.

5. Double-click the foreground swatch and load a color of your choice.

6. Paint on the Key layer. Notice that the paint stays "inside the lines."

7. Choose the Move tool (V) and try to move the layer. (A dialog box should pop up telling you no.)

Clipping Mask (Group with Previous)

Sometimes you'll want to place the contents of one layer inside those of another. Designers often use this technique to fill text with a pattern or to constrain a photo to fit inside a shape. The concept is called a Clipping Mask (older versions call it Group with Previous) and it's fairly easy and flexible. All you need to do is place the content layer above the container layer (the one you want to "fill") and choose Layer > Create Clipping Mask.

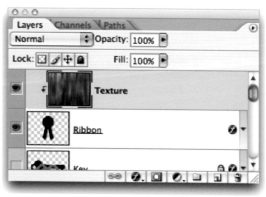

1. Turn off the visibility icons for all layers except *Background*, Ribbon, and Texture.

2. Select the Texture layer.

3. Choose Layer > Create Clipping Mask or press Cmd+Option+G (Ctrl+Alt+G). In the Layers palette, you'll see that the layer indents and fills the opaque areas in the Ribbon layer below. Notice that the layer style applied to the layer is still visible.

4. Choose Layer > Release Clipping Mask or press Cmd+Option+G (Ctrl+Alt+G) to toggle the mask on and off.

Merging Layers

Sometimes, you'll want to permanently merge layers together to commit a design. This can be useful to reduce file size, or to improve compatibility when importing a layered Photoshop document (PSD) file into another application (such as Apple Final Cut Pro or Adobe After Effects). This process is destructive (in that it is permanently joins the layers, which limits future changes). To merge layers, use one of the following methods:

- **Photoshop CS2 or later:** Select two or more layers by Cmd-clicking (Ctrl-clicking) on their names in the Layers palette. For practice, select the Texture and Ribbon layers. Then Choose Layer > Merge Layers or press Cmd+E (Ctrl+E).

- **Photoshop CS or earlier:** Select the first layer, then click in the link column next to the other layers you want to select. For practice, select the Texture and Ribbon layers. Then choose Layer > Merge Linked or press Cmd+E (Ctrl+E).

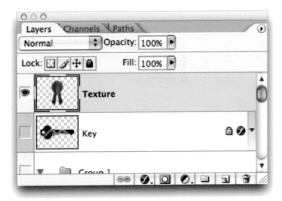

In this document, the Texture and Ribbon layers are joined into one new layer. Photoshop kept the name of the top layer. You can double-click the name field and rename the layer.

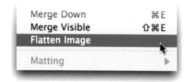

Flattening an Image

If you want to merge all of your visible layers and discard all layers with visibility disabled, you would choose Layer > Flatten Image. However, flattening an image is a permanent change. You work hard for those layers—*keep them!* Here are some alternatives to flattening that will preserve future flexibility:

- Save a copy of your image in a flattened format. By choosing File > Save As (with the As a Copy box checked) or File > Save for Web, you can save another version of your image.

- If you need a flattened copy to paste in another document (or within your current document), use the Copy Merged command. Select an active, visible layer, then choose Select > All. You can copy all visible items to your clipboard as a single layer by then choosing Edit > Copy Merged or by pressing Shift+Cmd+C (Shift+Ctrl+C).

TIP

Flattening Images

Remember, flattening is permanent. Be 100% positive before you discard your layers permanently. Saving a flattened copy is usually a better idea.

Creating a Panorama

By using layers, you can take several photos from one location and merge them together to create a large panoramic photo.

Many people take an assortment of photos of a subject with the camera handheld. Pros know it's better to use a tripod and slightly move the camera to create overlap. There are even specialized tripod heads that can be bought from companies like Kaidan (www.kaidan.com) that make the leveling and rotation much more precise.

Let's try piecing some photos together. If you are using Photoshop CS or later, use the Photomerge option. If not, place all three images into a larger document and manually line them up.

1. Choose File > Automate > Photomerge. Photomerge is a specialized "mini-application" inside of Photoshop that assists in combining multiple images into a single photo.

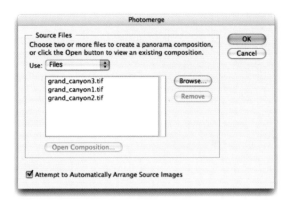

2. Click the Browse button and navigate to the Chapter 8 folder on the book's DVD-ROM.

3. Choose grand_canyon1.tif, grand_canyon2.tif, and grand_canyon3.tif.

4. Check the box next to Attempt to Automatically Arrange Source Images.

5. Click OK and be patient… each image has to open.

6. In the next dialog box, be sure to click Keep as Layers. You may also choose to click the Perspective radio button for a clearer view of the blending.

7. With the Select Image tool (A) you can grab individual panels and move them around for a better match.

8. Click OK to build the panoramic image. Photoshop will attempt to assemble the panorama based on your work in the dialog box. Since layers are preserved, however, you can still tweak the position of individual layers.

9. Nudge any layers with the Move tool if your alignment is off.

10. Choose Layer > Flatten Image.

11. Crop the image to a clean rectangular shape using the Crop tool (C).

12. There are a few visible seams… this is what the Healing Brush was made for! Select the Healing Brush (it looks like a bandage) by pressing J. The Healing Brush is a great way to remove blemishes or seams from an image. Option-click (Alt-click) on a similar surface where you need to blend (from clouds to clouds, from rocks to rocks, etc.) Be sure to use a soft-edged brush that is relatively large. Then release the modifier key, and with the Healing Brush paint over the seam. Click and draw gentle strokes; when you release, the image will blend to hide the seam. For more on the Healing Brush, see Chapter 11, "Repairing Images."

13. You may need to use the Blur tool (R) a little to clean up the seams as well. The Blur tool allows you to selectively defocus an area.

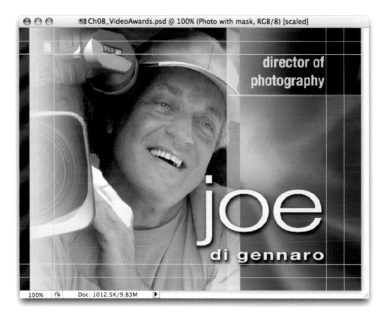

Another Look

At the start of this chapter, I mentioned how layers are often used by other applications. I've included a complex layered image for you to explore called Ch08_Video-Awards.psd. This is a graphic that has been prepared for video and it uses nonsquare pixels, which were added in Photoshop CS. This graphic (and its 12 layers) is ready to import into Adobe After Effects or Apple Motion where it can be animated for television. Feel free to explore this graphic on your own to see another approach to designing with layers.

LAYER COMPS

Photoshop CS introduced Layer Comps. These allow you to memorize combinations of layer visibility, opacity, and position. This can be useful for storing multiple designs inside one document. When experimenting with layouts, you'll often have several options in one document. You might set the headline in three different typefaces and try the main photo in two different positions. Using Layer Comps allows you to set up different options within one document (instead of having to save and keep track of several).

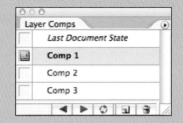

1. Open the file Ch08_LayerComps.psd to learn more.

2. Make sure the Layer Comps window is visible. If not choose Windows > Layer Comps.

3. Click the forward triangle to Apply Next Selected Layer Comp. Click through and examine the different layer comps.

4. For Layer Comp 1, move the words around onscreen to a new position.

5. Click the Update Layer Comp Button at the bottom of the Layer Comps window (it looks like two arrows in a circle),

6. Switch to Layer Comp 2. On the layer called This is, click the visibility icon next to the Layer Style Outer Glow. A black glow should be added.

7. Click the Create New Layer Comp button (it looks like a pad of paper) on the bottom edge of the Layer Comps Window. Name it Comp 2 Alternate.

8. Let's Save a copy of each Layer Comp to send to a client. Choose File > Scripts > Layer Comps to PDF. Photoshop creates a new PDF with all four Layer Comps in one document. This is a convenient way to email the project to a client for review.

Layer Comps are a bit confusing at first, but as you master what layers can do, you'll turn to Layer Comps for flexibility. Be sure to check out the Adobe Help Center for more on Layer Comps.

Using Blending Modes

9

Blending modes are both a mystery and a source of great design power. Each blending mode controls how the pixels in one layer are affected by those in another layer or by a tool from the Toolbox. Most users give up on them because the technical definitions of blending modes get very tricky. The secret is to not worry too much about the technical issues and to learn how to experiment. While we'll explore both the technology and the creativity behind blending modes, there are only a few basics that you must know to make blending modes part of your design toolbox.

About Blending Modes

There are 23 different blending options available from the Layers palette and a few additional ones that work with specific tools. How do they work? The simple answer is "It depends." Your response is likely "Depends on what?" Simply put, the effect achieved by blending two layers varies with the contents of those two layers. A blending mode compares the content of two layers and enacts changes based on the contents of both layers. You'll find blending modes in many of the tools and they can be combined with every filter.

Normal
Dissolve

Darken
✓ Multiply
Color Burn
Linear Burn

Lighten
Screen
Color Dodge
Linear Dodge

Overlay
Soft Light
Hard Light
Vivid Light
Linear Light
Pin Light
Hard Mix

Difference
Exclusion

Hue
Saturation
Color
Luminosity

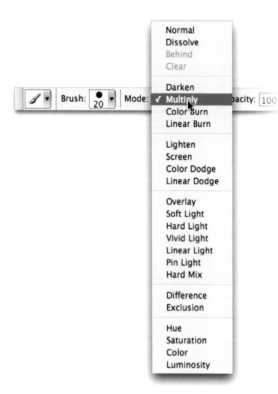

The blending mode specified in the Options bar controls how pixels are affected by a painting or editing tool. Additionally, you can set the blending mode of a layer to control how it interacts with those below it. A clear understanding of the following terms will better help you understand blending modes:

- **Base Color:** The original color in the image
- **Blend Color:** The color being applied with the painting or editing tool (or the color in the top layer)
- **Result Color:** The color resulting from the blend

List of Blending Modes

Here are the different blending modes available through the Layers palette. I have attempted to give you a clear and simple definition as well as a sample of how these images blend.

Original

 Blended Image

 Dissolve
This creates a random replacement of the pixels with the base or blend color.

 Darken
Pixels lighter than blend are replaced; darker ones are not.

 Multiply
This is similar to drawing strokes on the image with magic markers.

 Color Burn
This evaluates each channel; darkens base by increasing contrast.

 Linear Burn
This evaluates each channel; darkens base by decreasing brightness.

 Lighten
This evaluates each channel; it then uses base or blend color (whichever is lighter).

 Screen
This results in a lighter color. It is useful for "knocking" black out of a layer.

 Color Dodge
This evaluates color information and brightens base by decreasing contrast.

 Linear Dodge
This evaluates color information and brightens base by increasing brightness.

 Overlay
This overlays existing pixels while preserving highlights and shadows of base.

 Soft Light
The effect is similar to shining a diffused spotlight on the image.

 Hard Light
The effect is similar to shining a harsh spotlight on the image.

 Vivid Light
This burns or dodges by increasing or decreasing the contrast.

 Linear Light
This burns or dodges by decreasing or increasing the brightness.

 Pin Light
This is useful for adding special effects to an image.

 Hard Mix
This enhances the contrast of the underlying layers.

 Difference
This evaluates each channel and subtracts depending on greater brightness.

 Exclusion
This is similar to the Difference mode but lower in contrast.

 Hue
This mode uses luminance and saturation of the base and the hue of the blend.

 Saturation
This creates color with luminance and hue of base and saturation of blend.

 Color
This mode preserves gray levels. It's very useful for coloring and tinting.

 Luminosity
This is the inverse effect from the Color mode.

Open the file Blended_Overlay.psd from the Chapter 9 folder on the DVD-ROM to experiment with blending modes.

Blending Modes in Practice

So far we've looked at blending modes in a strictly technical sense. While it's useful to have a clear understanding of the technology, let's not lose sight of the design possibilities. Blending modes are a great way to mix layers together. For a designer, this can be a useful way to create backgrounds for speaker support (like PowerPoint presentations) or DVD menus. Let's dissect one of those backgrounds:

1. Open the file Speaker Support.psd from the Chapter 9 folder on the DVD-ROM. This seven-layer document uses blending modes to create a complex background.

2. Turn off the visibility icons for all but the bottommost two layers.

3. Select the layer Train. It is currently set to the Overlay blending mode. Changing its blending mode will create a different look.

4. A useful shortcut to cycle blending modes is Shift++(plus). This will step you forward in your blending mode list. Pressing Shift+- (minus) will step backward through the blending mode list. If you have a tool selected that has its own mode settings (such as the Brush or Gradient tools), the shortcut impacts the tool. To quickly change the mode on a layer, select the Move tool (V) or Marquee tools (M) first. Experiment with different blending modes and opacity settings to try out different looks.

5. Repeat the blending mode experimentation for the Light, Highlights, and Soft Focus layers. Try out different modes and opacity settings.

6. Select the layer Blue. It is set to the Color blending mode, which applies its color to all layers below it. This is a very useful way to tint multiple layers for a consistent look.

Feel free to continue to experiment with different combinations of blending modes and opacity settings. This sample image is just a quick glimpse into the power and flexibility of blending modes.

NOTE

Blending Mode Practice

For more practice with blending, open the files Blend Modes 1.psd and Blend Modes 2.psd in the Chapter 9 folder and experiment with different modes and opacity settings.

DESIGN "RULES" FOR BLENDING MODES

RULE #1—DON'T TRY TO MEMORIZE HOW EACH BLENDING MODE WORKS: The good news is that they are grouped by similar traits. As you make your way through the list, you will notice a gradual progression through styles. The first group darkens your underlying image, whereas the second lightens it. The third set adds contrast, whereas the last two generate dramatic results by comparing or mapping values. Depending on your sources, some blending modes will generate little or no results. Sound confusing? Keep reading.

RULE #2—EXPERIMENT: The best way to use blending modes is to just try them out. Clicking through a long drop-down menu is boring. A much better alternative is to select the Move tool and then use the Shift++ keyboard shortcut.

RULE #3—EXPLOIT THEM: Need a quick visual pop? Try blending a blurred image on top of itself. Need to tint something? Place a solid or gradient on top and change to Hue or Color mode. You'll find blending modes available to every filter (choose Fade Filter from the Edit menu) and all of your Brush tools.

23 **VIDEO TRAINING**
Blending Modes

Blending Modes in Action

Now that you've got a little practice with blending modes, it's time to explore their creative and production side in greater depth. Blending modes are part of a professional's workflow. The next four sections showcase a few different ways to better integrate blending modes for professional results.

Instant Spice

One way to improve a washed out or flat image is through blending modes. By blending a blurred copy of an image on top of itself, you can quickly create visual pop. Let's give it a try:

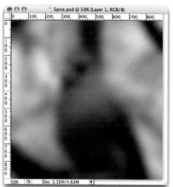

1. Open the file Spice.psd from the Chapter 9 folder.

2. Select the *Background* layer in the Layers palette.

3. Duplicate the *Background* layer by pressing Cmd+J (Ctrl+J).

4. Significantly blur the new layer by choosing Filter > Blur > Gaussian Blur. A value of 25 pixels should do the trick.

5. Select the Move tool by pressing V.

6. Cycle blending modes by pressing Shift++. Look for modes (such as Overlay or Soft Light) that increase Saturation and add visual "pop" to the image.

7. If needed, adjust the opacity of the layer to taste. You can quickly change opacity by typing in the first number of an opacity setting, such as 4 for 40% opacity. You can type 25 to quickly switch to 25% opacity, for example, if a more specific adjustment is required.

Here's a quick look at how different blending modes can be used to add instant spice to an image.

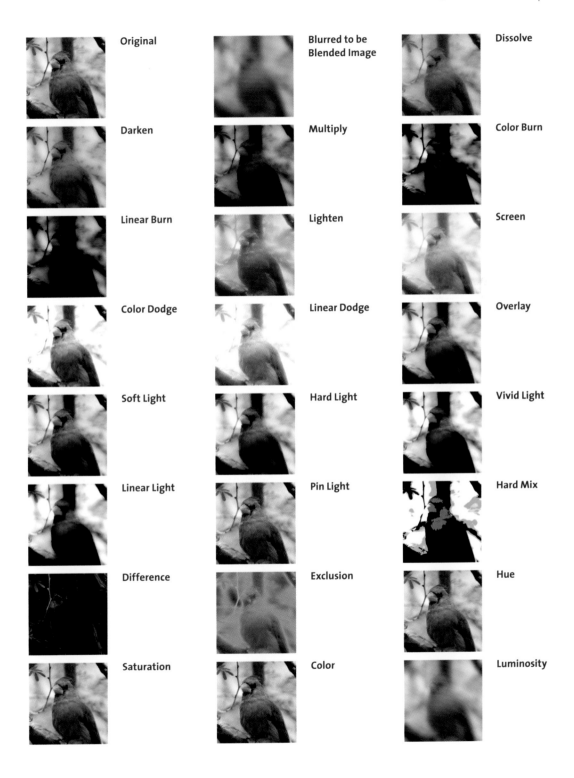

Original	Blurred to be Blended Image	Dissolve
Darken	Multiply	Color Burn
Linear Burn	Lighten	Screen
Color Dodge	Linear Dodge	Overlay
Soft Light	Hard Light	Vivid Light
Linear Light	Pin Light	Hard Mix
Difference	Exclusion	Hue
Saturation	Color	Luminosity

Fixing a Shadowed Image

If an image is completely thrown into the shadows, you can turn to blending modes to shed a little light. In fact, this is a technique that is often used by law enforcement agencies to enhance security photos or footage.

1. Open the file Meter.tif from the Chapter 9 folder.

2. Duplicate the *Background* layer by pressing Cmd+J (Ctrl+J).

3. Set the top layer to Screen mode. You can choose it from the pop-up list in the Layers palette or press the keyboard shortcut Shift+Opt+S (Shift+Alt+S). The image should appear significantly lighter.

4. You can further lighten the image by placing another duplicate copy on top. Press Cmd+J (Ctrl+J) as many times as needed. Each will lighten the image further.

Fixing a Bad Sky

You can use blending modes to enhance a flat or boring sky. In fact, through a little bit of layering, we can greatly improve the average landscape shot. Let's give it a try:

1. Open the file Desert Sky.psd from the Chapter 9 folder.

2. Create a new, empty layer. Fill it with black by choosing Edit > Fill and choose black. Name the layer Sun.

3. We are going to add a "sun" to the sky. Choose Filter > Render > Lens Flare. The Lens Flare filter normally simulates flares caused from the sun or a light source hitting the lens. Experiment with the different options and adjust the Brightness. Drag the crosshair to position the light source near the upper-left corner. Click OK.

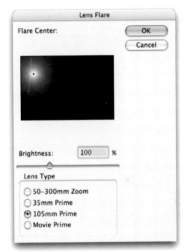

4. Change the Sun layer's blending mode to Screen. This will drop out the darkest areas and leave on the areas that are brighter than the background behind.

5. Let's further enhance the image by adding some more "rays" to the sky. Duplicate the *Background* layer and place it on the top of the layer stack. Name the copy Blur.

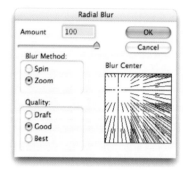

6. It's time to blur the layer using a Radial Blur. Choose Filter > Blur > Radial Blur. Set the blur method to Zoom and the amount to 100. Move the crosshair in the filter window so the Blur is directed from the upper-left corner of the image. Click OK.

7. Change the Blur layers blending mode to Overlay. Adjust the opacity to taste.

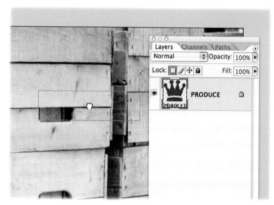

Applying a Rubber Stamp

You can also use blending modes to make one image appear as if it were applied to another. If we add the Free Transform command, we can make that stamp match the perspective of the photo. Let's give it a try:

1. Open the files Boxes.tif and Logo.psd from the Chapter 9 folder.

2. Select the Logo.psd file so it is active.

3. Activate the Layers palette. Click the thumbnail for the Logo layer and drag it into the Boxes.tif document.

4. Press Cmd+T (Ctrl+T) to invoke the Free Transform command. To harness additional transformations, right-click (Ctrl-click). Choose Distort; this will allow you to corner-pin the logo and match its angle to that of the box.

5. We now need to scale the logo smaller. Right-click (Ctrl-click) and choose Scale. Shrink the logo so it fits better on the side of the box.

6. Set the Logo layer to the Multiply blending mode and lower its opacity to 85%. This will make the Logo layer appear to be stamped on the crate.

Table 9.1 provides the keyboard shortcuts to make it easier for you to use blending modes.

Table 9.1   Blending Shortcuts

Result Windows	Windows	Mac OS
Normal	Shift+Option+N	Shift+Alt+N
Dissolve	Shift+Option+I	Shift+Alt+I
Darken	Shift+Option+K	Shift+Alt+K
Multiply	Shift+Option+M	Shift+Alt+M
Color Burn	Shift+Option+B	Shift+Alt+B
Linear Burn	Shift+Option+A	Shift+Alt+A
Lighten	Shift+Option+G	Shift+Alt+G
Screen	Shift+Option+S	Shift+Alt+S
Color Dodge	Shift+Option+D	Shift+Alt+D
Linear Dodge	Shift+Option+W	Shift+Alt+W
Overlay	Shift+Option+O	Shift+Alt+O
Soft Light	Shift+Option+F	Shift+Alt+F
Hard Light	Shift+Option+H	Shift+Alt+H
Vivid Light	Shift+Option+V	Shift + Alt+V
Linear Light	Shift+Option+J	Shift + Alt+J
Pin Light	Shift+Option+Z	Shift + Alt+Z
Hard Mix	Shift+Option+L	Shift + Alt+L
Difference	Shift+Option+E	Shift + Alt+E
Exclusion	Shift+Option+X	Shift + Alt+X
Hue	Shift+Option+U	Shift+Alt+U
Saturation	Shift+Option+T	Shift+Alt+T
Color	Shift+Option+C	Shift+Alt+C
Luminosity	Shift+Option+Y	Shift+Alt+Y

Scott Billups is a pioneer in the digital visual effects world. He has worked on major Hollywood films and television shows in various capacities—as a cinematographer, a director, and a supervisor for the special effects in the project. Despite these varied roles and need for motion, Scott relies heavily on Photoshop.

"Photoshop is probably the single most commonly used graphics application in television and motion picture production," said Billups. "There are probably as many ways to use it as there are people who use it."

Billups has created several television specials for the Discovery and History Channels. He frequently needs to take actors and insert them into historical locations. His process often involves shooting photos on location, and then inserting actors using greenscreen technology back in his California studio.

"One of my favorite budget-stretching, time-saving uses is a process I call *Super-Frames*," said Billups. "The trick is to shoot the plates cinematically. Unlike your basic holiday snapshot, a Super-Frame series needs to adhere to an established narrative structure. Since the Super-Frame is much larger than even the most advanced High Definition frame, you have plenty of room to pan and move the framing of your shot."

While he takes photos of historical locations for these shows, the photos need to be touched up. Modern buildings and power lines must be removed, often along with such items as roads and sidewalks. Billups also takes note of lighting conditions so he can match them later. Having a reference point allows for multiple shots to be color matched.

"It is very important to make a note of the lighting for each of these Super-Frames that you are creating. I've found that a simple white balloon, positioned in the area of the actors, has basically all of the information that I need to re-create a matching lighting scenario back in the studio."

Billups stressed that Photoshop is both an essential tool and a stepping-stone to other filmmaking tools.

"The Matte and Alpha Channel tools in Photoshop are used at some point on nearly every production, large or small," said Billups. "If you don't have the patience to cut a matte, you're ill suited to a career of pushing pixels."

If you are looking to get into visual effects and the motion picture industry, Billups stressed that it takes a deep sense of commitment and a respect for quality.

"It takes less effort to stay busy than it does to look busy," said Billups. "There's always a way to make something look better, so if you finish ahead of time, tweak till they pry it away from you."

For more information on Scott Billups, see his Web site at www.pixelmonger.com.

Color Correction and Enhancement 10

The primary purpose of Photoshop is to act as a digital darkroom, where images can be corrected, enhanced, and refined. How do you know an image needs touch-up? You can pretty much assume every image can look a little (or even a lot) better than how the camera captured it. Whether it's adjusting the exposure, increasing contrast, or boosting saturation, Photoshop is the place to improve an image.

Learning how to spot problems, and then matching the right correction technique, is an essential part of mastering Photoshop. There are several different tools available, some more useful than others. By analyzing the most important tools and which situations they might help you in, a more thorough understanding of color correction is possible.

Approach to Color Correction

New users often have a hard time when color correcting or enhancing images. They generally lose sight of the goal: making the image look better and believable. Many users go "too far" in their quest to fix images. If the image starts to look fake or too altered, it will be distracting. While getting it "right" will require some practice, here's some advice on getting started:

The image on the top is unretouched. The image on the bottom has been refined with three adjustment layers: one to enhance levels and two to adjust hue and saturation of the sky and vegetation.

- **Identify what's wrong:** Before you can fix a picture, be sure you have decided what's wrong. Is it too dark? Is the sky washed out? Has the picture faded over time? Make a list and prioritize the issues you find in each image. It's easier to fix one problem at a time, and if you identify those problems, you'll know when to stop twiddling with the image.

- **Work with a copy of the image:** Before you start to color correct an image, you should duplicate it. This way you can return to an original version if you make a mistake or go too far in your image touch-up. After opening your file, choose File > Save As and give the version that will be corrected a new name. Color correction is often a *destructive* process, meaning that you cannot revert to the original state at a later time. By preserving an original version, or employing adjustment layers, *nondestructive* editing is possible.

- **Edit with adjustment layers:** Adjustment layers allow you to apply most of the image correction commands as nondestructive effects. They are added as a layer above the actual image, and the adjustment layer can be blended, masked, or deleted at any time. Additionally, if you double-click the adjustment layer's thumbnail, the Image Adjustment dialog box comes back. The same modifications are available in both the Adjust menu and Adjustment Layers. You should work with an adjustment layer whenever possible as its flexibility will be important for future revisions.

- **Get a fresh opinion:** It's not a bad idea to step back and examine your work. Open up the backup copy and compare it to the image you've been working on. This comparison, literally a before-and-after, can be very useful. If you've got a fresh set of eyes nearby, ask another person for her or his opinion.

Primary Image Adjustments

While there are several image adjustments that Photoshop offers, only a few are used most often. Commands such as Levels and Curves are used by professionals to achieve outstanding results. These professional imaging techniques may take a little time to get comfortable with, but the power they offer is worth your investment.

Levels

The Levels command corrects tonal ranges and color-balance issues. With this command poor exposure can be fixed. Additionally, color correction can be performed by manually identifying a white point and black point in the image. Nearly every image can benefit from making a Levels adjustment.

VIDEO TRAINING
Color Correct—Levels

To understand Levels, it is essential to be able to read a histogram. This graph works as a visual guide for adjusting the image. If working in Photoshop CS2 (or later) you may also want to call up the Histogram palette and leave it open while color correcting. You can also choose to expand the Histogram palette by clicking the submenu and choosing All Channels View. Let's give the command a try.

1. Open the file Levels.tif from the Chapter 10 folder on the DVD-ROM.

2. Launch the Levels dialog by choosing Layer > New Adjustment Layer > Levels. While Levels is also available from the Image > Adjustments menu, the adjustment layer is more flexible. Be sure the Preview box is checked so changes update onscreen.

3. This photo was shot under low light, but we can reset the black and white points of the image to fix the exposure. Move the white Input Levels slider to the left (where the histogram starts to rise). This affects the image's white point and allows you to reassign where white should begin in the image.

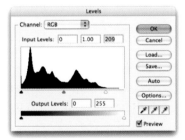

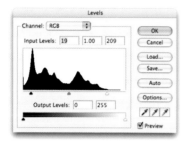

NOTE

Levels vs. Curves

A Levels adjustment does not offer as many precise adjustment points as a Curves adjustment. However, Levels adjustments can be easier to make and generally create very effective results.

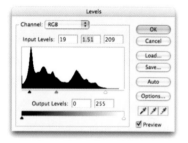

NOTE

Levels Beats Brightness/Contrast

While a Brightness/Contrast command exists, the Levels adjustment lets you perform several improvements with one command. Using a single image process cuts down on the loss of quality introduced from multiple image processing steps.

4. Move the black Input Levels slider to the right where the first amount of black starts to rise. The more you move the black slider to the right, the more contrast is introduced into the image.

5. The true power lies in the middle (gray) Input Levels slider. By moving this slider, you can modify the gamma setting. Effectively, you can use the middle Input Levels slider to change the intensity of the midtones. This adjustment can be made without making dramatic changes to the highlights and shadows. This will let you better expose an image. Move the slider to the left to add light; move the slider to the right to subtract light.

6. Click OK to apply the adjustment. If you need to re-edit the adjustment layer double-click its icon in the Layers palette.

Colorcast

In the first example, we made a Levels adjustment to all of the channels evenly. The Levels command can be further isolated to a specific channel by clicking the drop-down list in the center of the Levels dialog box. This allows you to tackle colorcast issues, such as spill from a background, a bad white balance, or a photo shot under mixed or colored lighting.

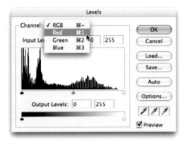

1. Open the file Levels_Color_Balance.tif from the Chapter 10 folder. Notice how the image has a greenish tint.

2. Add a Levels adjustment layer. You can click the Black and White circle at the bottom of the Layers palette and choose Levels. We will use the Levels command to fix color and exposure issues.

3. Select the Set White Point (white eyedropper) in the Levels dialog box. Click an area that should be pure white. For this image, click a bright area in the white pillar. If you click too dark an area, the whites in the image will overexpose. You can hold down the Option (Alt) key and the Cancel button changes to Reset. This will allow you to reset the Levels command. After you click, you'll see that some of the color spill has been removed.

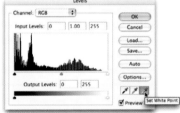

TIP

Do It Again

If you have several images from the same camera or shoot, they may need the same Levels adjustment. The Save button allows you to save a Levels adjustment (to the folder that contains the image is a good place). You can then click the Load button to apply that adjustment to another image.

4. Select the Set Black Point (black eyedropper) in the Levels dialog box. Click an area that should be pure black. Choose an area such as a jacket or a dark shadow. This will adjust the color balance and the exposure.

5. The image should now be better color balanced. Adjust the middle Input Levels slider to brighten up the image.

Manual Adjustment

The Levels command can also be used to correct skin tones and isolated areas in an image. The Set White Point and Set Black Point eyedroppers work well, but sometimes it can be difficult to find a pure white or black point in your image. Let's try fixing color and exposure the manual way.

1. Open the file Levels_Isolated.tif from the Chapter 10 folder.

2. We need to fix part of the image that has dramatically different lighting than the rest of the image. Look at the bottom-left corner; the indoor lighting is throwing off the rest of the image.

3. Use the Polygonal Lasso tool to select the door region. After making the selection, choose Select > Feather and enter a value of 5 pixels to soften the selection. Making a selection first causes the adjustment layer to attach a mask to isolate the color correction to the selected area.

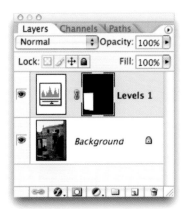

4. Add a Levels adjustment layer. We will make a Levels adjustment on each channel to fix color and exposure issues.

5. From the Channels drop-down menu in the Levels dialog, choose red or press Cmd+1 (Ctrl+1) to select the first channel. Notice how the histogram is skewed to the left. Move the white slider to the

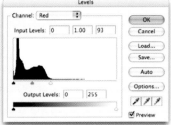

outside edge of the histogram where it begins to rise. Move the middle (gray) slider to balance the histogram data evenly on both sides.

6. Switch to the green channel by pressing Cmd+2 (Ctrl+2). Move the black and white points to the outside edges of the histogram. Adjust the middle (gray) slider to balance the histogram.

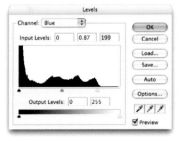

7. Make the same adjustment to the blue channel. The image should now appear color balanced. If needed, you can return to the individual channels to tweak color balance.

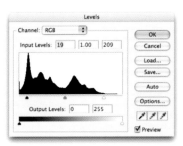

8. Switch back to the composite view by pressing Cmd+~ (Ctrl+~). You can now make a standard levels adjustment to tweak contrast and exposure. Click OK when you are satisfied.

WHAT ABOUT AUTO?

Photoshop comes with three "automatic" image adjustments:

- **AUTO LEVELS:** Attempts to fix exposure problems
- **AUTO CONTRAST:** Attempts to solve contrast issues
- **AUTO COLOR:** Adjusts contrast and color of an image by trying to automatically identify shadows, midtones, and highlights

When it comes to fixing images, Auto just won't cut it. Color and exposure are very subjective and require human intervention to make a judgment. The results these commands generate, while occasionally close, never compare to those decisions made by an experienced Photoshop user. Stay away from Auto commands; they don't improve your skills and often just leave you wanting more.

TIP

Easy Curves

When the Curves Editor is open, you can automatically add Control Points. Just Cmd-click (Ctrl-click) within the image to add a point. The Control Points will appear in the editor. These can be moved up to lighten or down to darken.

Curves

Most users will either use Curves a lot or they won't use it at all. The Curves interface is more complex than Levels, which scares many users away. While Levels gives you three control points (highlights, midtones, and shadows), the Curves dialog box allows for up to 16 control points. This can significantly open up more options when adjusting color and exposure.

Let's try the Curves command on a practice image:

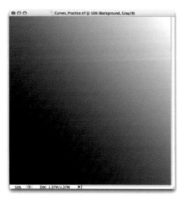

1. Open the file Curves_Practice.tif from the Chapter 10 folder.

2. Add a Curves adjustment layer by choosing Layer > New Adjustment Layer > Curves. When you open the Curves interface, there are two points (one for white and one for black).

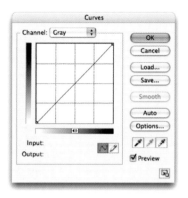

3. To make the Curves dialog box more similar to Levels, click the small white triangle on the bottom of the X axis. This will place white at the top and right in the Curves dialog box, thus using the more familiar 0–255 scale.

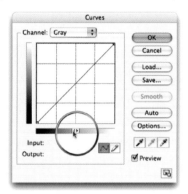

4. Add a single control point in the middle of the line (click at a Input Value of 128). Pull this new control point up to lighten the image (towards the lighter area on the Y axis). You can pull the point down to darken the image. Notice that the input and output values update as you drag.

5. The adjustment is applied gradually throughout the entire image. Multiple points can be employed for contrast adjustments based on tonal range.

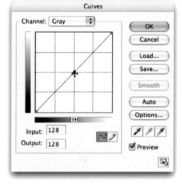

The primary advantage of Curves is that you have precise control over which points get mapped (whereas in Levels you do not). Another benefit is that Curves adjustments use a curved line (rather than Levels, which uses only three control points) to make adjustments. In this way, color correction can be applied in a more gradual manner (without the hard clipping that can be associated with Levels).

1. Open the image Curves_RGB.tif from the Chapter 10 folder.

2. Add a Curves adjustment layer. The curve has only two points on it: one representing the black point, the other, the white point.

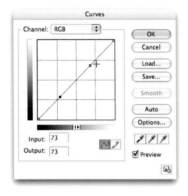

3. It's now time to add two more Control Points to refine the curve. To do this, Cmd-click (Ctrl-click) on the image itself. Add a Control Point for the highlights in the soft green background and the red of the bird's feathers.

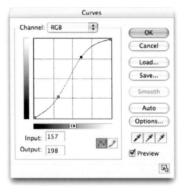

4. Experiment with adjusting the two Control Points. For best results, raise the Control Point for the soft green (this increases the brightness of the background) and lower the Control Point for the bird, which increases saturation and contrast. Continue to experiment with moving the Control Points (you can use the up and down arrow keys for precise control), then click OK when you are satisfied.

Hue/Saturation

The Hue/Saturation command lets you adjust the hue, saturation, and lightness of color components in an image. Additionally, you can simultaneously adjust all the colors in an image. This command can work in two ways:

- To adjust colors in an image that appears slightly out of phase, or skewed towards a color, such as an image that appears to have a blue overcast.

- To create stylistic changes by dramatically changing colors in an object. This could be used to try out different combinations of colors in a logo.

TIP

The Five Most Useful Image Adjustments:

- Levels
- Curves
- Hue/Saturation
- Color Balance
- Shadow/Highlights

Let's give the command a try:

1. Open the file Hue-Saturation.tif from the Chapter 10 folder. We're going to tackle a problem with the water.

2. Choose Select > Color Range and click the water to make an initial selection. Hold down the Shift key to add to the selection. Adjust the fuzziness to soften the selection. Click OK when you have a suitable selection.

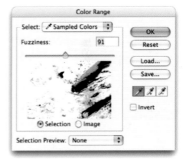

3. Choose Layer > New Adjustment Layer > Hue/Saturation to add the adjustment layer.

4. The two color bars at the bottom of the dialog box represent the colors in the color wheel. The upper bar shows the initial color; the lower bar shows the new color. Drag the Hue slider to the right until blue appears under green.

5. Additionally, you can adjust Saturation (which is the intensity of the color) and adjust Lightness (which adds white or black to the image).

6. When you're satisfied, click OK.

Recolor

A Hue/Saturation adjustment can be a very quick way to experiment with color options. You can use it to quickly change the fill colors of an object by making a global adjustment. This works well when experimenting with different color combinations. Let's try it out:

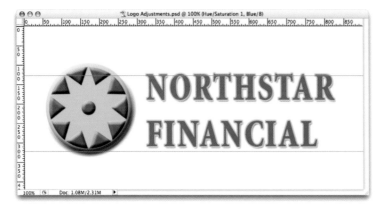

1. Open the file Logo Adjustments.psd from the Chapter 10 folder.

2. Double-click the layer thumbnail of the Hue/Saturation adjustment layer to open the Hue/Saturation dialog box.

3. Adjust the Hue slider to try out different color combinations.

Tinting a Photo

The Hue/Saturation command can also be used to tint an image. If you are working with a grayscale image, you need to convert it to an RGB image first.

PHOTO BY JAMES BALL

1. Open the file Tint.tif from the Chapter 10 folder.

2. Add a Hue/Saturation adjustment layer.

3. Click the Colorize box to tint the image.

4. Adjust the Hue slider to try out different color combinations. Adjust Saturation and Lightness to refine the tint.

5. Click OK to apply the tint.

Color Balance

The Color Balance command is a simple but useful adjustment. By using the Color Balance command, you can change the overall mixture of colors in a particular tonal range. This can be useful for generalized color correction. For example, if the shadows look too green, you can subtract green and add some red to balance the image. Color Balance allows you to constrain an adjustment to the shadows, midtones, or highlights as specified in the dialog box.

1. Open the file Color_Balance.tif from the Chapter 10 folder.

2. Add a Color Balance adjustment layer.

3. Choose to work on the Midtones in the Tone Balance section. Leave the Preserve Luminosity box checked to avoid changes in exposure.

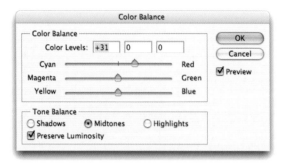

4. Add some red into the midtones by dragging the slider towards red. This places some more red into the skin tones.

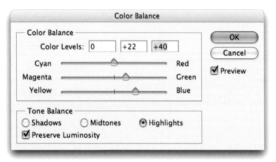

5. Switch to the Highlights in the Tone Balance section. Add some green and blue to the image to balance out the color of the tent.

6. Click OK when you're satisfied with the Color Balance adjustment.

Useful Image Adjustments

While a Levels or Curves command can usually get the color correction job done, there are often special problems that require special commands. These other commands have special purposes and should generally be reserved for the unique problems they address. Let's take a look at the specialty commands.

Match Color

The Match Color command can be used to remove colorcast from an image. It is most useful when you have a color-accurate reference photo of a subject. That can then serve as a basis for correcting other photos of the same subject. The Match Color command can be used to adjust the brightness, color saturation, and color balance in an image. The command enables fine control over luminance and color within the image. Let's give it a try:

1. Open the files Match Color 1.tif and Match Color 2.tif from the Chapter 10 folder.

2. In the document Match Color 1.tif, make a selection with the Rectangular Marquee tool in the lower-left corner (in the beach area). This will serve as a reference area for the color correction.

3. In the document Match Color 2.tif, repeat making a selection with the Rectangular Marquee tool. You should select the beach in the lower-left corner. This will serve as a target area for the color correction.

4. Choose Image > Adjustments > Match Color.

5. In the Image Statistics area, set the Source menu to Match Color 1.tif. Check both boxes Use Selection in Source to Calculate Colors and Use Selection in Target to Calculate Adjustment.

6. At the top of the dialog window, check the box Ignore Selection When Applying Adjustment. Also, make sure the Preview box is checked.

7. Adjust the Luminance slider to better match exposure. Moving the Luminance slider to the left darkens the image, to the right brightens the image.

8. Adjust the Color Intensity slider to better match color. Moving the Color Intensity slider to the left reduces the color range, to the right increases the color range and intensifies the colors.

9. Adjust the Fade slider to lessen the adjustment until it is a visually close match. Moving the slider to the right reduces the amount of adjustment. When you're satisfied click OK to apply the adjustment.

Channel Mixer

Current channels can combine to form a new channel. You can use the Channel Mixer command to solve two unique problems:

- If a digital photo had a write error to the storage card and one of the channels is damaged. You can use the two good channels to create a replacement for the third.

- If you want to manually create your own grayscale images, choose the monochromatic option. This can produce much better grayscales than by simply switching to grayscale mode or choosing Image > Adjustments > Desaturate.

Let's try out the second scenario and manually create a grayscale image:

1. Open the file Channel Mixer.tif from the Chapter 10 folder.

2. Choose Layer > New Adjustment Layer > Channel Mixer and click OK.

TIP

Special FX with Photos

To create dramatic image effects try using

- Curves (with arbitrary settings)
- Channel Mixer (load from the Presets > Channel Mixer Presets folder)
- Gradient Map

3. Check the Monochrome box and adjust the Red, Green, and Blue sliders to taste. Depending on your image, different channels should be more or less present. In general, more red looks best when skin tones are involved.

4. When you're satisfied with the new image, click OK.

5. To make the image adjustment permanent, choose Image > Mode > Grayscale. Since we've used an adjustment layer, be sure to choose merge.

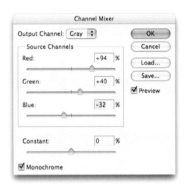

Gradient Map

The Gradient Map can be used to dramatically or subtly stylize images. The effect works best when used as an adjustment layer. The command works by mapping the colors of a gradient to the image based on the luminance values of the source image. Let's give the technique a try.

1. Open the image Gradient_Map.tif from the Chapter 10 folder.

2. Choose Layer > New Adjustment Layer > Gradient Map and click OK.

3. From the dialog window, click the drop-down menu and try a default gradient. For more on gradients, see Chapter 6, "Painting and Drawing Tools." Click OK when you're satisfied.

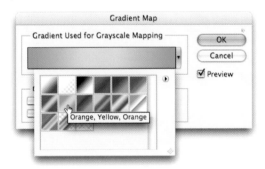

PHOTO BY JAMES BALL

4. To soften the effect, you can change the adjustment layer's blending mode. Setting it to Hue or Color creates a nice tint effect.

Photo Filter

Professional photographers often place glass filters in front of the camera lens. These can be used to "cool" or "warm" a picture, or to add special effects. Since Photoshop often tries to simulate or correct for steps not taken in the field, the addition of Photo Filters starting with Photoshop CS was a logical addition.

Adobe added to the "real time" color correction options with the addition of 20 different adjustments. These layers simulate the traditional colored glass filters. Besides the built-in presets, you can also choose custom colors from the Photo Filter interface using the standard Color Picker.

There are three main groupings for color effects:

- **Warming Filter (85 and LBA) and Cooling Filter (80 and LBB):** These adjustment layers are meant to even out photos that were not properly white-balanced. The Cooling Filter (80 or LBB) makes images bluer to simulate cooler ambient light. The Warming Filter (85 or LBA) makes images warmer to simulate hotter ambient light.

- **Warming Filter (81) and Cooling Filter (82):** These adjustment layers are similar to the previous filters but cast a more pronounced color. The Warming Filter (81) makes the photo more yellow and the Cooling Filter (82) makes the photo bluer.

- **Individual Colors:** The Photo Filter also has 14 preset colors to choose from. These can be used for two primary purposes to add a complementary color to a scene to remove colorcast or for stylistic reasons.

Let's try applying a Photo Filter adjustment layer:

1. Open the file Photo_Filter.tif from the Chapter 10 folder.

2. Choose Layer > New Adjustment Layer > Photo Filter and click OK.

3. From the Filter area, choose Cooling Filter (80) to adjust the temperature of the photo. The sky and the image should be "bluer." You can adjust the Density slider to control the intensity of the effect.

4. Click OK when you're satisfied. You can double-click the thumbnail of the adjustment layer to modify the filter.

Shadow/Highlight

Exposure problems often plague photos. Dark shadows may seem the end of a photo, but Photoshop offers a powerful command for fixing problems. The image command, Shadow/Highlight, is very flexible for solving problems. The command can help salvage images where the subject is silhouetted from strong backlight. The command can also be used to improve subjects who have been washed out by the camera's flash.

VIDEO TRAINING
Shadow Highlight Adjustment

The Shadow/Highlight command does more than lighten or darken an image. It makes adjustments by analyzing neighboring pixels. However, when first opened, the tool is too basic. It is important to check the Show More Options check box, which adds significant control. Let's give the command a try:

1. Open the file Shadow-Highlight.jpg from the Chapter 10 folder.

2. Choose Image > Adjustments > Shadow/Highlight (this command is not available as an adjustment layer). The image is brightened automatically as it boosts the shadowed areas by default.

3. Check the Show More Options check box and be sure the Preview box is checked.

4. Adjust the Shadows and Highlights of the image:

- **Amount:** Value determines how strong an adjustment is made to the image.

- **Tonal Width:** Small values affect a reduced region; larger values include the midtones. If pushed too high, halos will appear around the image.

- **Radius:** A tolerance setting that examines neighboring pixels to determine the affected area.

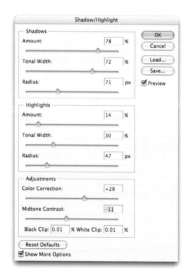

5. Modify the image adjustments to improve image quality:

- **Color Correction:** This slider modifies the saturation of the adjusted areas. Essentially, it can counterbalance washed out images.

- **Brightness:** If you're working on a grayscale image, Color Correction is replaced by a Brightness control.

- **Midtone Contrast:** This adjustment affects the contrast in the midtones of a photo. Positive values increase contrast, whereas negative values reduce contrast.

- **Black Clip and White Clip:** This adjustment modifies the black point of shadows and lowers the white point of highlights. This can lower the intensity of the effect.

6. Click Save if you'd like to store the adjustment to use on another photo. When you're satisfied, click OK to apply the adjustment.

If you'd like extra practice, you can open the image Shadow-Highlight2.tif and repeat the command.

Exposure

Starting with Photoshop CS2, support was added for 32-bit images. Generally referred to as high dynamic range (HDR), these images offer great flexibility in exposure. These images can better handle re-creating the wide range of exposures found in outdoor scenes or intense lighting conditions. The Exposure adjustment is usually used on images that exist in 32-bit space and is said to be a 32-bit floating point operation (often shortened to *float*).

Creating an HDR image is a combination of shooting techniques and a Photoshop command. It requires that the camera be secured firmly to a tripod and that you are careful when triggering or adjusting the camera to not move it. Several photos at various exposures are taken of the same scene (a minimum of three; usually five to seven is adequate). The camera should have its auto-bracket and ISO features disabled. Each shot should be about two f-stops apart. The user then harnesses the Merge to HDR command (File > Automate > Merge to HDR) to create the 32-bit image.

Since this is not a book on photography, let's jump ahead to an HDR image. The image we'll use is from the Samples folder inside your Photoshop CS2 (or newer) application folder. It is also included on the accompanying DVD-ROM in case you need it.

1. Open the file HDR.psd. You'll notice several features are grayed out. Most image adjustments do not work, nor can a 32-bit image add layers (including adjustment layers).

IMAGE COURTESY ADOBE SYSTEMS

2. Choose Image > Adjustments > Exposure. This command makes tonal adjustments by performing calculations in a linear color space (gamma 1.0) rather than the current color space. This offers extreme flexibility for future changes.

3. There are three properties that can be modified:

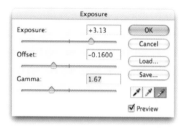

   - **Exposure:** This modifies the highlight end of the tonal range with little effect on the extreme shadows.

   - **Offset:** This darkens the shadows and midtones with little effect on highlights.

   - **Gamma:** This adjusts the gamma of the photo.

4. Additionally, there are three eyedroppers that adjust the image's luminance values.

   - **The Set Black Point eyedropper:** This sets the Offset, which shifts the selected pixel to zero.

   - **The Set White Point eyedropper:** This sets the Exposure, which shifts the selected pixel to white (1.0 for HDR images).

   - **The Midtone eyedropper:** This sets the Exposure, which shifts the selected pixel to the middle gray.

5. Make a dramatic adjustment and click OK. Let the image blow out, as this will show you the flexibility of HDR images.

6. Apply a second Exposure adjustment and bring the image back into a more accurate exposure. You'll notice the blown out areas are restored (this is impossible with 8- or 16-bit images as overexposed data is discarded).

Invert

The Invert image adjustment creates an image that is a direct inverse or negative. This can be useful in a variety of situations, including inversing a layer mask, making a positive from a scanned negative, or switching a black background to white. When an image is inverted, the brightness of each pixel is assigned the inverse value from the 256 color-values scale. This means that a 0 value would map to 255, whereas a 35 value would map to 215.

1. Open the file Invert.tif from the Chapter 10 folder. This is a negative image from a scanned film negative.

2. Choose Image > Adjustments > Invert. The negative image is now a positive image and can be further refined or color-corrected.

Equalize

The Equalize command can be used to repair a washed out photo. The command attempts to redistribute pixels so that they are equally balanced across the entire range of brightness values. The command works best when you sample a small area that will drive the overall adjustment. The Equalize command takes the lightest area and remaps it to pure white and the darkest area to pure black. Let's give it a try:

1. Open the file Equalize. tif from the Chapter 10 folder.

2. Choose Image > Adjustments > Equalize to repair the image.

3. If the image appears overexposed, you can choose Edit > Fade to reduce the intensity of the Equalize command.

Threshold

The Threshold command is used to force an image to be either black or white. When invoked, the command presents a slider that allows you to adjust the dividing point. All pixels on one side of the new midpoint are black, on the other side are forced to white. This adjustment can be used to clean up a Layer Mask or an alpha channel. Let's try it out:

1. Open the file Threshold.tif from the Chapter 10 folder.

2. Select the Channels palette.

3. Activate the alpha channel named Alpha 1.

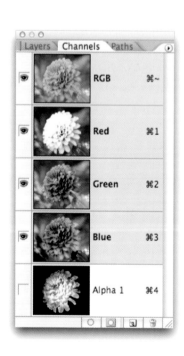

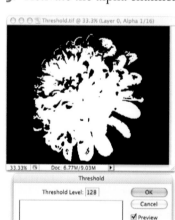

4. Choose Image > Adjustments Threshold.

5. Adjust the Threshold slider to fill the white areas in. The resulting alpha channel needs a little softening.

6. Run a three-pixel Gaussian Blur on the alpha channel to soften its mask. This will make a better edge when the alpha channel is used for keying (or compositing) in a multimedia program, or if you convert the channel to a Layer Mask.

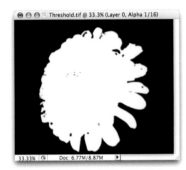

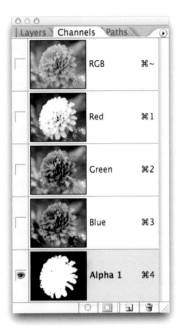

Not-So-Useful Image Adjustments

Several image adjustments can be run on your image that can cause more problems than they solve. Others (like Variations) are far less efficient than more professional alternatives. You are welcome to explore these commands, but professional users infrequently use them.

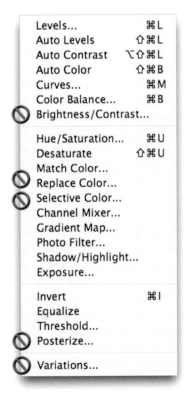

NOTE

Problem Adjustments

These adjustments may introduce new problems in your image:

- Brightness/Contrast
- Replace Color
- Selective Color
- Posterize

Brightness/Contrast

The Brightness/Contrast command is an inferior substitute to Levels and Curves. The Brightness/Contrast command affects the overall lightness or darkness. The problem with the adjustment is that it goes too far. It is impossible to adjust the Shadows without over-affecting the Highlights. The usual problems with an image are in the midtones, which are better handled by a Levels or Curves adjustment. A Brightness/Contrast adjustment will often leave your image washed out. Nothing good comes from this command, so it's best to avoid it.

The image on the left has overblown areas. When the Brightness is adjusted so the highlights are properly exposed, the shadows and midtones are too dark.

Replace Color

The Replace Color command creates a mask that is used to select specific colors in an image. Once a selection is made, the colors can be manipulated via an adjustment to the hue, saturation, and lightness of the selected areas. While this command works reasonably well, you'll see better results when you use the Select > Color Range command, and then add a Hue/Saturation adjustment layer.

While the Replace Color command works relatively well, it's hard to make changes or refine the selection. It's better to use the Color Range command and a Hue/Saturation adjustment layer.

Selective Color

The Selective Color command is similar to the Color Balance command. However, it is not as easy to use, nor does it produce professional results that a Levels or Curves adjustment would. A better option is to use the Color Range command and add a Levels or Curves adjustment layer.

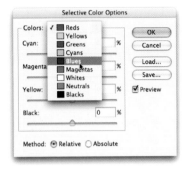

Posterize

The Posterize command reduces the number of colors used in the image. This leads to a reduced color palette and creates banding in the image. While it can be used as a special effect, lowering image quality is not desirable. Be sure to use this as an adjustment layer if you just want to experiment.

PHOTO BY JAMES BALL

Variations

The Variations command allows you to adjust the color balance, contrast, and saturation of a photo. This is done by selecting from a variety of thumbnails of alternatives. This command only works if the image is basically close to "right" and you want to experiment with subtle variations. It only works on 8-bit images, and it is a destructive adjustment that can't be modified. This command feels like a visit to the optometrist, and just takes way too long to generate average results. There's really no need to waste your time with it.

PHOTO BY JAMES BAL

When evidence is less than perfect, law enforcement agencies often turn to digital imaging tools to enhance the image. You may be thinking it must look a lot like *CSI*—but more often it's tools like Photoshop that help get the job done.

"Photoshop is used as an analysis tool for extracting information in images, which includes eliminating a distracting background from a fingerprint or piece of handwriting, enhancing a license plate from a security video camera, or measuring the height of a robbery suspect," said Reis. "Photoshop is also used to prepare comparison charts to show similarities or differences between two or more individuals, fingerprints, and samples of writing."

Photoshop's powerful correction tools can help expose vital evidence. Several features, such as Smart Sharpen, the Shadow/Highlight command, and lens correction, can bring an image into clarity. Additionally, image analysis tools like the Measure tool, Eyedropper tool, and Info palette can provide important details about an image.

"I'm simply amazed at the information that an image can contain. I first look at the image and don't expect much to be there, but then use the Channel Mixer or run a filter or two and see something that couldn't originally be seen," said Reis. "I'm amazed at how bad the security systems are; the digital systems have added severe compression to the mix, providing worse images instead of better ones. This is one area where technology caused the industry to move backward rather than forward."

Fortunately, digital tools can help counteract digital problems. "In law enforcement, in general, [digital tools] have reduced costs and improved turn-around time for photos, fingerprint images," said Reis. "They have also added capabilities in the ability to share images electronically."

The field of forensic photography and image analysis varies greatly from city to city. As such, the skills needed also vary.

"Large agencies like LAPD or NYPD will have forensic photographers who only do field photography [and] digital photo lab work," said Reis. "Other agencies will hire civilian employees to do crime scene investigation with photography as part of their duty. Some agencies have a person assigned just to do forensic video analysis. And some agencies use police officers in many of these positions. A degree in forensic science, criminal justice, or a physical science would be a good background, plus developing an eye for detail."

For those students interested in finding out more about law enforcement, Reis strongly recommends joining a Police Explorer post (a program for high school and college students). A student could also do volunteer work or seek a job as a cadet at a police agency.

To learn more about George Reis, visit www.imagingforensics.com.

Repairing and Improving Photos

11

Damage, like fashion, is often very subjective. If you show the same set of photos to five people and ask them to comment on mistakes or damage, you'll likely get five very different answers. This is because people find different things distracting: A crooked photo may bother some, whereas others may dislike a jagged edge. There are several aspects of an image that can be "wrong" but it is also impossible to have a "perfect" photo.

Because damage is so subjective, I recommend asking the clients or end customers (if possible) what needs repair. Ask them questions like "Would you like anything different?" or "Can anything be better?" You'll often be surprised

The photo on the right has had several small blemishes repaired, as well as proper contrast restored.

by their answers. Sometimes a fix will be as simple as a crop or a color correction, but more often it will involve removing (or adding) something to the picture. The world has embraced special effects and digital enhancement. You may be surprised at how much Photoshop can do.

In this chapter we'll tackle issues like physical damage such as rips, wrinkles, pushpin holes, scratches, and pen marks. We'll focus on techniques that can be performed in less than 10 minutes. With practice you can fix 90% of the problems in 10 minutes; the other 10% you either learn to live with or spend more time on.

Image Selection

While most problems can be repaired, not every problem is worth trying to fix. Most photographers shoot many exposures of a subject, so they are willing to discard several that they are unhappy with. It is best to repair images that are close to their desired state; otherwise, you may spend too much time on a project (which could send it over budget, in the professional world).

Working with Modern Images

The most common problems in modern photos are color or exposure issues (both of which we addressed in detail in Chapter 10, "Color Correction and Enhancement"). However, modern photos can still suffer physical damage. If the print is wrinkled or creased, it's always best to use the original source (either a print or the negative). If the print is dusty or smudged, gently wipe it with a soft cloth, and then try to scan or rescan it. If rescanning or reprinting is not an option (or there are issues with a digital photo), you can attempt to fix several problems within Photoshop.

This picture was straightened, color corrected, and had missing areas filled in through cloning and healing.

Working with Historical Images

Historical photos often have more problems than modern photos. There is a much greater likelihood of physical damage. You may have to repair creases, tears, water damage, or adhesive stains (from scrapbooks). It's likely that the photos will have faded and need a boost in contrast or toning. It is generally easier to remove color from a historical source while repairing it. The color can then be added back in during the final stages as an overlay or sepia tone.

The Retoucher's Toolbox

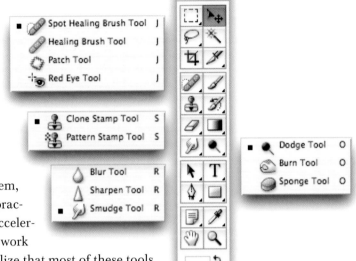

The process of repairing damage to a photo is often referred to as *retouching*. As there are several different problems that can manifest in a photo, Photoshop offers several tools to respond with. Knowing which tool to use is often a problem, but with a little bit of study and practice, the process can be greatly accelerated. Let's explore how the tools work

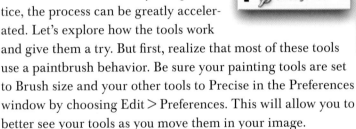

and give them a try. But first, realize that most of these tools use a paintbrush behavior. Be sure your painting tools are set to Brush size and your other tools to Precise in the Preferences window by choosing Edit > Preferences. This will allow you to better see your tools as you move them in your image.

Clone Stamp Tool

The Clone Stamp tool works by replacing bad pixels with good pixels. It's a popular tool that is relatively easy to use and achieves accurate results. The Clone Stamp tool allows you to set a sample point (where the good pixels are taken from), then paint into bad areas. This technique is very powerful, as the Photoshop paint engine allows for the softening of the stamp's edge.

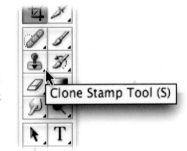

1. Activate the Clone Stamp tool by pressing S. Roll over the tools icon and be sure you have not accidentally activated the Pattern Stamp tool.

2. Select a soft-edged brush from the Options bar or Brush palette. If needed, modify an existing brush.

3. Open the file Clone.tif from the Chapter 11 folder on the DVD-ROM. You'll notice some graffiti in the upper-right corner of the sign.

For Better Results When Cloning

- Try cloning at a lower opacity and build up strokes
- Try sampling from several different places to fill in an area
- Experiment with blending modes

26 **VIDEO TRAINING**
Clone an Object

4. You need to specify the alignment for the clone:

- **Check Aligned:** The sample point and painting point move parallel as you move. If the user clones and moves the cursor to the right, the sample point moves as well. This ultimately creates more variety in the cloning, which is desirable. However, it can lead to the unwanted material instead being repeated into the stroke.

- **Uncheck Aligned:** If Aligned is not selected, the initial sample point is used (even after you stop and resume cloning). This option makes sure that you are always sampling from the same pixels when starting a new stroke.

5. If you're working with a layered image, you can clone from all visible layers by specifying Sample All Layers. If this option is deselected, only the active layer is used.

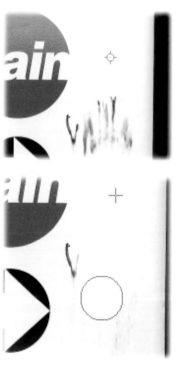

6. Option-click (Alt-click) within the current document (or even another open document set to the same color mode). This defines the source point for sampled pixel data. Click a clear white area in the sign near the pixels that will be replaced.

7. Click and paint as if you were using the Brush tool. The sampled pixels are taken from the Sample Point and cover the bad pixels. Continue cloning until all of the damage is painted over.

Pattern Stamp Tool

You'll find the Pattern Stamp tool tucked into the same position as the Clone Stamp tool. In fact, many users pick the Pattern Stamp tool by mistake, and quickly learn to avoid it, as its default settings are pretty bad. You see, the Pattern Stamp tool uses seamless patterns to fill in an area. The patterns can be Photoshop presets or custom ones you create based on a photo. The Pattern Stamp tool functions more like a brush, as you do not need to set a source point. Additionally, you may want to click the Aligned button so new strokes remain seamless with existing strokes.

Using built-in patterns

When you select the Pattern Stamp tool, you'll see a list of patterns in the Options bar. Clicking the drop-down menu will bring up a list of presets. In the Pattern Picker window you can choose a variety of seamless patterns. Additionally, you can click the submenu to load more.

Making a pattern with the Pattern Maker filter

Creating a seamless pattern from a photo is easy if you harness the power of the Pattern Maker filter. This special filter can be used to create a photorealistic pattern based on your image. It works best if there's a repeating pattern in the image and not too much detail. Images such as gravel, grass, or carpet, for example, are easy to use to create seamless patterns. Let's give it a try:

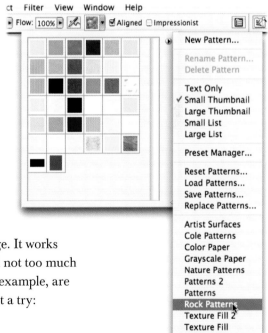

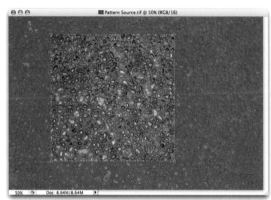

1. Open the file Pattern Source.tif from the Chapter 11 folder. This image is too large as the seamless pattern needn't be bigger than 600 × 600 pixels for most purposes. If you make the pattern too big, it will just clog up RAM.

2. Select the Crop tool (C) and type in 600 px by 600 px.

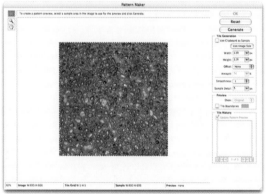

3. Convert the image to 8-bit mode by choosing Image > Mode > 8 Bits/Channel.

4. Choose Select > All or press Cmd+A (Ctrl+A).

5. Choose Filter > Pattern Maker to invoke the Pattern Maker dialog box.

6. Click the Use Image Size button to generate a pattern that matches the size of the layer.

7. The Smoothness setting adjusts the sharp edges in the pattern. By increasing the smoothness, you can reduce edges. The Sample Detail determines how much of the original detail comes through in the pattern. Higher values more closely match the original (but will take longer to generate). Set Smoothness to 3 and Sample Detail to 15 pixels.

8. Click Generate to create the pattern. You can press Esc to cancel the generation of the pattern. If you desire, you can click Generate Again to try other options.

9. When you're satisfied, click the small disk icon in the lower-right corner. This allows you to name and save the pattern as a preset. Name the pattern and click OK.

10. Try the pattern out. Create a new document sized 2000 × 2000 pixels. Select the Pattern Stamp tool and choose your new pattern from the Pattern Picker window. Click and paint to see the new pattern in action.

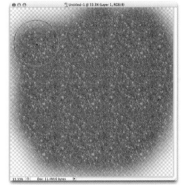

If you'd like to try out another example, tackle the image Seamless Bonus.tif from the Chapter 11 folder. Create a seamless pattern based on the trees, then pattern stamp out the reflector board.

Healing Brush Tool

The Healing Brush tool (J) is an innovative and powerful tool that can be used to repair blemishes in a photo. The Healing Brush tool operates much like the Clone Stamp tool. However, instead of just moving pixels from one area to another, the Healing Brush tool clones pixels while also matching the texture, lighting, and shading of the original pixels.

Since the Healing Brush samples surrounding areas, you may want to make an initial selection around the damaged area and feather it. This will give you better results on an area with strong contrast. The selection should be slightly bigger than the area that needs to be healed. It should follow the boundary of high-contrast pixels. For example, if you're healing a blemish on a subject's face, make an initial selection of the skin area to avoid mixing in the adjacent background or clothing. The selection will prevent color bleed-in from outside areas when painting with the Healing Brush tool.

1. Open the file Healing Brush.tif from the Chapter 11 folder.

2. Activate the Healing Brush tool by pressing J. (Be sure to closely examine the icon and not select the Spot Healing Brush tool.)

3. Select a soft brush from the Options bar or the Brush palette.

4. Set the blending mode to Replace. This option preserves noise and texture at the stroke's edges.

5. Specify a source for repairing pixels in the Options bar. The standard option is to use Sampled. This takes pixels from the area surrounding the sample point. As the brush moves, the sample point also moves to ensure variety in the sampled source.

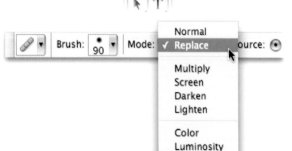

6. Specify the alignment option. If Aligned is selected, the sample point and painting point move parallel as you move the stroke. If Aligned is deselected, the initial sample point is Always. The Always option ensures that you are always sampling from the same area.

7. If you want to heal to an empty layer, check the box to Sample All Layers. This allows you to sample one layer, then apply the healing to a new empty layer above. This will provide greater flexibility in your workflow. If the Sample All Layers box is deselected, only the active layer is used.

8. Add a new, empty layer above the *Background* layer.

9. Near the bottom of the bell, Option-click (Alt-click) on the striped area.

10. Click and start to paint as if you were using a brush. Because the sampled pixels are drawn from before you click, it may be necessary to release and start over occasionally to avoid cloning the problem area.

11. After several strokes, release the mouse to merge the sampled pixels. Before the pixels blend, you will have a visible stroke. Afterward, the stroke should gently blend.

12. Continue to heal the remaining crack in the bell.

Spot Healing Brush Tool

The Spot Healing Brush tool was added to Photoshop CS2 as a way to harness powerful blending technology with less work (although the Healing Brush is pretty labor-free to begin with).

It can quickly remove blemishes and imperfections in photos without requiring a sample point to be set. The Spot Healing Brush tool automatically samples pixels from the area around the retouched area. Let's give the tool a try:

1. Open the file Spot Healing.tif from the Chapter 11 folder.

2. Activate the Spot Healing Brush tool from the Toolbox.

3. Choose a soft-edged brush from the Options bar. Make the brush only slightly larger than the problem areas. In the case of this image, we'll fix several small scratches in the tent. It's best to cover the area in need of repair with one click.

4. Set the blending mode in the Options bar to Replace. This will preserve noise, film grain, and texture at the edges of the stroke.

5. Choose a Type of repair in the Options bar:

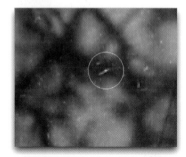

- **Proximity Match:** Pixels from the edge of the selection are used as a patch for the selected area. This should be the first attempt at repair; if it doesn't look good, switch to the Create Texture option.

- **Create Texture:** Pixels in the selection are used to create a texture to fix the damaged area. If the texture doesn't work, try dragging through the area one more time.

6. Click once on an area you want to fix. You can also click and drag over a larger area.

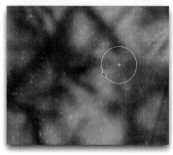

Upon close examination, you should notice that we have healed damage and flakes in the photo.

Patch Tool

The Patch tool uses the same technology as the Healing Brush tool, but it is better suited to fix larger problems or empty areas. Start using the Patch tool by selecting the area for repair, then dragging to specify the sampled area. For best results, select a small area.

The Patch tool can be used two different ways:

- **Source:** Make a selection in the area that needs repair, then drag to an area of good pixels.

- **Destination:** Make a selection in an area of good pixels. Then drag that selection on top of the bad pixels.

Let's give it a try:

1. Open the file Patch.tif from the Chapter 11 folder.

2. Activate the Patch tool by pressing J. (It's in the same well as the Healing Brush tool.)

3. Set the Patch tool to Source.

4. Make a selection around the out-of-focus cars near the right edge.

5. Drag into the tree area to sample pixels.

6. Release and let the Patch tool blend.

TIP

Making Selections

While you can make a selection with the Patch tool, you can always make a selection using any other selection tool (such as Marquees or Lassos), then activate the Patch tool. The Patch tool behaves just like the Lasso tool (as far as selections go), but it may not offer the level of control you need.

Red Eye Tool

Red eye is caused when the camera flash is reflected in a subject's retinas. This happens frequently in photos taken in a dark room, as the subject's irises are open wide. There are two solutions to fixing red eye in the field:

- Use the camera's red eye reduction feature. This will strobe the flash and adjust the eyes of your subject.

- Use a separate flash unit that can be held to the side.

While getting it right in the field is important, you can fix it in Photoshop as well. Photoshop CS2 offers a powerful Red Eye tool that can fix flash problems. It effectively removes red eye from flash photos of people and white or green reflections in the eyes of animals.

1. Open the file Red Eye.tif from the Chapter 11 folder.

2. Zoom into the red eye area. An easy way is to take the Zoom tool and drag around the problem area.

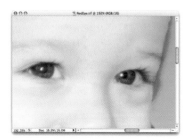

3. Select the Red Eye tool from the Toolbox or press J repeatedly to cycle through the tools.

4. Click in the red eye area to remove it. If you're unsatisfied with the results choose undo and modify the following two options.

5. Adjust the Pupil Size to a higher number if you need to convert a larger area. Adjust the Darken Pupil setting to adjust how dark the pupil will be after the conversion.

Blur and Sharpen Tools

Oftentimes a photo will need a focus adjustment. While global changes are often implemented through blur or sharpen filters, it's frequently necessary to lightly touch up an area by hand. To do this, you can use the Blur tool (to defocus) or the Sharpen tool (to add focus or detail). Both tools are driven by brush-like settings, which allow you to change size, hardness, strength, and blending mode. Remember, if the Caps Lock key is down, brush previews are disabled.

1. Open the file Blur-Sharpen.tif from the Chapter 11 folder.

2. Select the Blur tool (it looks like a water droplet) by pressing R.

3. Specify a brush size of approximately 120 pixels and a strength of 50%. The strength settings modify how quickly the tool modifies the image. Sometimes several built-up strokes are better for a gentle look.

4. Paint over an area of the photo to soften the image. The graininess in the wall is a good place for touchup.

5. Choose a blending mode of the tool. The Darken and Lighten modes are particularly useful for isolating the blurring effect to dark or light areas respectively. Try the Lighten mode and blur the cactuses.

The image on the right has had the grain softened using the Blur tool.

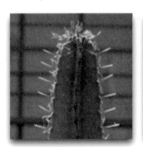 

Using the Lighten mode with the Blur tool softened the cactus and brought out the highlights.

6. Switch to the Sharpen tool and try enhancing parts of the image.

7. Be careful not to oversharpen, as it will quickly introduce visible noise and distortion.

Smudge Tool

The Smudge tool simulates dragging a finger through wet paint. The pixels are liquid and can be pushed around the screen. With the default settings, the tool uses color from where you first click and pushes it in the direction you move the mouse. This tool is useful for cleaning up dust specks or flakes in a photo. Set the tool's blending mode to Lighten or Darken (depending on the area to be affected), and you have digital makeup to touch up the problem.

1. Open the file Smudge.tif from the Chapter 11 folder.

2. Select the Smudge tool (it looks like a finger painting icon) by pressing R to cycle tools.

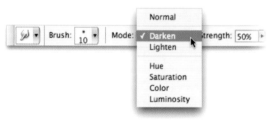

3. Zoom into the damaged area with the large tear.

4. Experiment with the Darken and Lighten modes. These are particularly useful for isolating the smudge by pushing only dark or light pixels.

5. Smudge the damaged pixels. Experiment by switching blending modes; you can always undo the smudge then change the tool's mode and resmudge.

Using the Lighten mode instead of the Smudge tool lets you push lighter pixels over darker ones.

Dodge and Burn Tools

The Dodge and Burn tools are known as toning tools. They allow you finer control over lightening or darkening your image. These tools simulate traditional techniques used by photographers. In a darkroom, the photographer would regulate the amount of light on a particular area of a print. These tools are particularly helpful when touching up faded photos, especially when repairing water damage. Let's try both tools out:

1. Open the file Dodge_Burn.tif from the Chapter 11 folder.

2. Closely examine the four faces. You should notice that the two on the right look washed out and the two on the left are a bit dark.

3. Select the Dodge tool from the Toolbox. Adjust the brush to be soft and large (approximately 80 pixels). Set the tool to adjust the Midtones.

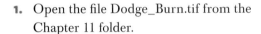

4. Paint over the shadowed faces on the left half of the picture to bring the darkest areas out a bit.

5. Select the Burn tool from the Toolbox. Adjust the brush to be soft and large (approximately 80 pixels). Set the tool to adjust the Highlights and an Exposure setting of 20%.

6. Paint over the washed-out faces on the left half of the picture to restore the contrast a bit.

7. Continue to touch up areas in the photos as needed. Lower exposure settings are generally more desirable.

Sponge Tool

The Sponge tool is very elegant and efficient. This toning tool can be used to make subtle adjustments in color saturation or grayscale contrast. This tool can be used during conversion processes to prepare images for commercial printing or television. The Sponge tool allows you to gently desaturate (or saturate) areas by brushing over them.

1. Open the file Sponge.tif from the Chapter 11 folder.

2. When converting RGB images into CMYK, there is often a shift in colors. This is because RGB has a wider color gamut than CMYK, and it can display more colors. Photoshop allows you to highlight the areas that are "out of gamut" or will shift when you convert modes. Choose View > Gamut Warning. The gray areas represent out-of-gamut areas.

3. Select the Sponge tool by pressing O to cycle tools or choose it from the Toolbox.

4. Adjust the brush to a large size and set it to have soft edges.

5. Set the tool to Desaturate and adjust the flow to a lower value. It is generally better to use a slower flow with several applications.

6. Paint over the gray gamut warning areas with the Sponge tool until they disappear.

7. If needed, you can switch the Sponge tool to Saturate to boost areas. If you see a gray gamut warning, you've gone too far.

8. When you're done, you can convert the image to CMYK using Image > Mode > CMYK. We'll cover CMYK conversion again in Chapter 17, "Outputting Specialized File Types."

Restoration in Action

Learning how to fix damaged areas in photos is not a step-by-step process. Rather it is learning how to identify problems and make strategic decisions on which techniques to employ to fix the image. Practice is the best path to becoming a skillful retoucher. However, you can expect good results if you know which tools to use. I have personally seen students become proficient using Photoshop's rich suite of tools in just a few weeks.

Alignment

Most pictures are not taken using a tripod with a bubble level. The result is that pictures can be slightly uneven. This problem can be subtle or pronounced, but it's a very easy fix.

1. Open the file Align.tif from the Chapter 11 folder.

2. Choose the Measure tool (it looks like a ruler) from the Toolbox by pressing I. Find a surface you think should be horizontal (or vertical). The stairs are a good reference point, as is the top of the door.

3. Click and drag along a line to measure the angle.

4. Choose Image > Rotate Canvas > Arbitrary. Photoshop automatically inserts the correct value from the Measure tool.

5. Crop the image to avoid the empty spaces or patch the gaps and make any additional repairs.

Apparently, I was not very "level" when I took this photo. I was 12 at the time, which may explain it. Fortunately, Photoshop offers an easy fix.

Aspect Ratio

Often, your photos will be the wrong aspect ratio for your needs. Perhaps your picture is in the portrait aspect ratio, but the layout needs a landscape-shaped photo. Remember the Crop tool, which makes this an easy fix.

1. Open the file Aspect Ratio.tif from the Chapter 11 folder.

2. Take the image full screen by pressing the F key.

3. Activate the Crop tool (C).

4. Specify a target size (such as 6 inches × 4 inches at a resolution of 200 pixels per inch) in the Options bar.

5. Make the crop; initially you will be constrained to the image's original area. After releasing, you can then grab the individual anchor points and crop beyond the image's border. This will require you to clone material in, but it allows you to include more of the original picture. Press F to cycle back to a standard view.

6. If you have empty areas, you can clone the missing pixels using the Clone Stamp or Patch tool.

Soft Focus

Cameras are much more likely to generate a soft focus under low light. Photoshop offers several sharpening filters to fix the problem. Two stand out above the rest, however: Smart Sharpen and Unsharp Mask. Both do a good job of clarifying soft focus; however, the newer Smart Sharpen is better for most problems.

Smart Sharpen

The Smart Sharpen filter was introduced with Photoshop CS2. It has the most options of any sharpening filter built into Photoshop. It allows you to choose the sharpening algorithm as well as control the amount of sharpening in shadow and highlight areas.

1. Open the file Sharpen.tif and zoom the document window to 100%. This will give you the most accurate view of the sharpening.

2. Choose Filter > Sharpen > Smart Sharpen and click the Advanced radio button.

3. Adjust the controls in the Sharpen tab:

- **Amount:** This slider sets the amount of sharpening. A higher value will increase contrast between edge pixels, which gives the appearance of more sharpness.

- **Radius:** This determines the number of pixels surrounding the edge pixels that will be affected by the sharpening. A greater radius value means that edge effects will be more obvious, as will the sharpening.

- **Remove:** This allows you to set the sharpening algorithm to be used:

  - **Gaussian Blur:** This method is used by the Unsharp Mask filter. It works well on images that appear slightly out of focus.

  - **Lens Blur:** This method detects edges and detail in an image. It provides finer sharpening of detail and can reduce halos caused by sharpening.

  - **Motion Blur:** This attempts to reduce the effects of blur caused by camera or subject movement. You will need to set the Angle control if you choose Motion Blur.

- **Angle:** Set this to match the direction of motion. It's only available when using the Motion Blur option of the Remove control.

- **More Accurate:** This allows Photoshop to spend more time processing the file. It generates more accurate results for the removal of blurring.

4. You can refine the sharpening by clicking the Advanced radio button. This will allow you to adjust the sharpening of dark and light areas by using the Shadow and Highlight tabs. These controls should be used if you start to see halos in light or dark areas.

- **Fade Amount:** This setting adjusts the amount of sharpening in the highlights or shadows regions.

- **Tonal Width:** This setting controls the range of tones in the shadows or highlights that are modified. Smaller values restrict the adjustments to smaller regions.

- **Radius:** This controls the size of the area around each pixel that determines if a pixel is considered a shadow or a highlight. Moving the slider to the left specifies a smaller region; moving the slider to the right defines a larger region.

5. When you're satisfied, click OK to apply the filter. Close the image, but don't save your changes.

Unsharp Mask

If you're working in Photoshop CS or earlier, you will likely choose the Unsharp Mask filter as it is the best option for those who don't have Smart Sharpen. The Unsharp Mask filter is used to compensate for blurring that is introduced during scanning, resizing, developing, or even photography stages.

An easy way to remember the Unsharp Mask filter is to think of it as masking (hiding) the unsharp (blurry) areas of the image. It works by detecting pixels that differ from their surrounding neighbors (specified by the threshold slider) and then increases their contrast a specified amount. You can limit the effect by adjusting the radius of comparison. The filter works best in the Lab image mode when run on the Lightness channel.

1. Open the file Sharpen.tif and zoom the document window to 100%. This will give you the most accurate view of the sharpening.

2. Choose Filter > Sharpen > Unsharp Mask. Be sure the Preview option is selected so you can see your changes. It is better to run the filter on the entire image instead of a specific area.

3. You can click the thumbnail in the Filter dialog to revert to the prefiltered state. Alternatively, you can uncheck the Preview box to compare the effect. Be sure to set your Preview window to a 100% or 50% magnification to get the most accurate preview of the filter.

4. Adjust the Amount to specify a value for how much to increase the contrast of the pixels.

5. Adjust the radius slider slightly to refine the filter.

6. Adjust the Threshold slider to taste. Threshold determines how different the sharpened pixels must be from the surrounding area before they are treated as edge pixels. A value of 2–20 is often useful for preserving flesh tones and eliminating additional noise. The default value of 0 sharpens all pixels in the image.

Faded Historical Photos

A common problem with old black-and-white or sepia-toned photos is that they fade over time. While you can use a Levels or Curves adjustment, these both often introduce color artifacts into the image. A few extra steps are needed to get the best results.

1. Open the file Fading Historical.tif from the Chapter 11 folder.

2. With the Eyedropper tool, sample the color tint if you want to retain it in the finished piece.

3. Leave the photo in RGB mode, but strip away the color. Choose Image > Adjust > Desaturate or press Shift+Cmd+U (Shift+Ctrl+U).

4. Perform a Levels adjustment and restore the white and black points. Drag the Black Input slider and White Input slider toward the center.

5. Add a Color fill layer by choosing Layer > New Fill Layer > Solid Color. Click OK. The Foreground color you previously sampled will load automatically.

6. Place the Color fill layer into the Color blending mode. Adjust the Opacity slider to taste.

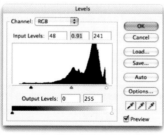

Blown-Out Skies

A professional photographer can spend a good part of a day waiting for the perfect sky and weather conditions. You, however, may not be as lucky. Skies will often be washed out and appear missing due to overexposure. My solution is to take pictures of the sky when it looks its best, then use a few techniques to combine two or more images into a new composite.

1. Open the file Fix Sky.tif from the Chapter 11 folder.

2. Use the Color Range command (Select > Color Range) to choose the sky region.

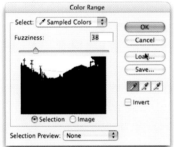

3. Subtract any stray selections in the lower half of the photo by using the Lasso tool and holding down the Option (Alt) key. Alternatively, you could switch to Quick Mask mode for more detailed touchup of the selection.

4. Double-click the *Background* layer to float it.

5. Invert the selection by choosing Select > Inverse or by pressing Shift+Cmd+I (Shift+Ctrl+I).

6. Click the Add Layer Mask button to mask the sky area.

7. Open a new sky image. You'll find a diverse collection of my favorites in the Chapter 11 folder in a subfolder called Skies. Match one that has the right color and time of day for this photo. Feel free to use the others for future projects.

TIP

Shooting Skies

I have found the desert or the ocean to be the best place to shoot the sky. This is often because the amount of environmental and light pollution is greatly reduced. Don't worry if this isn't an option for you... just keep your eyes out for a great day with beautiful skies and remember to shoot some still plates for your collection.

8. Place the sky photo on a new layer and move it behind your masked image. There will likely be fringe on the edges that will need touching up.

9. Select the Layer Mask thumbnail and run a slight Gaussian Blur (a low value such as 3 pixels).

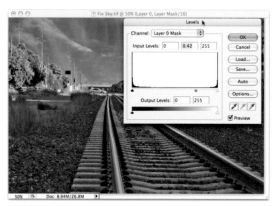

10. Run a Levels adjustment and move the middle (gray) slider to contract the mask.

11. Touch up any problem areas on the Layer Mask. Use the Smudge tool set to Darken mode to touch up the area around the trees on the right of the frame. You can also touch up the Layer Mask by using a paint-brush and black set to 20% opacity. Brush over areas that need to be blended.

12. To make the colors match better, you can place a second copy of the sky on top. Be sure just the blue sky is covering the photo. Set the blending mode to Overlay or Soft Light and lower the Opacity of the layer.

The completed image is on the disc if you'd like to examine it more closely.

Remove Grain/Noise

Oftentimes, distracting noise or grain will appear in your image. This is often caused by shooting photos with a high ISO setting on a digital camera, but it can also be caused by underexposure or long shutter speed. A lower-quality consumer camera is also more likely to exhibit noise problems. Additionally, film grain can be picked up by a scanner and cause problems as well.

The most common type of noise is luminance (grayscale) noise where the noise does not have a visible color. This noise is usually more pro-nounced in one channel of the image, usually the blue channel. By adjusting for noise on a per-channel basis, higher-image quality can be maintained. Let's give it a try:

1. Open the file Remove Grain.tif from the Chapter 11 folder.

2. Activate the Channels palette and view each channel separately. Click the chan-nel's name to isolate it. Do this for each channel.

3. You should notice a large amount of noise in the blue channel.

4. Activate all three channels by clicking the RGB composite channel.

5. Choose Filter > Reduce Noise.

6. Check the Advanced radio button to enable per-channel corrections. This allows for additional correction to be added at the channel level.

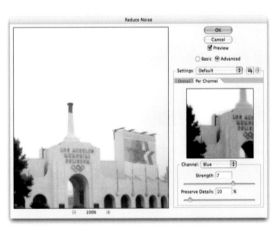

7. Switch to the blue channel within the filter dialog box and adjust Strength and Pre-serve Details to taste.

Add Grain

Sometimes you may want (or need) to add some noise back into a picture. This could be for stylistic purposes, or to keep a processed image matching the grain of others from the same camera or film stock. The key here is to put the noise on its own layer so it is easier to manage and adjust.

1. Open the file Add Grain.tif from the Chapter 11 folder.

2. Add a new (empty) layer.

3. Choose Edit > Fill and select 50% gray.

4. Generate grain by choosing Filter > Artistic > Film Grain. Adjust the three sliders to taste, then click OK.

5. Change the layer's blending mode to Overlay mode.

6. If needed you can either duplicate the grainy layer to increase the noise or adjust Opacity to taste.

Adding Lens Blur

Selectively blurring an image can help your viewer find a focal point. Starting with Photoshop CS, you now get a realistic lens blur that also allows depth-of-field blurring. This allows some objects to be in focus, while others fall out of focus. You can be very specific in regard to the blurring if you make an accurate alpha channel to serve as a depth matte. The depth matte defines how far away things are from the camera. Black areas in the alpha channel are treated as being the foreground, whereas white areas are seen as being in the distance.

1. Open the file Lens Blur.tif from the Chapter 11 folder.

2. An alpha channel has already been added to the image. It was created using the Gradient tool. Multiple gradients were combined by setting the tool to the Lighten blending mode.

3. Make sure the RGB composite channel is selected.

4. Choose Filter > Blur > Lens Blur to run the Lens Blur filter.

5. Choose the alpha channel from the Source menu. You can click the Invert box if you need to reverse the blur. For faster previews, choose Faster. When you're ready to see the final appearance, select More Accurate.

6. Adjust the Iris shape in order to curve or rotate the iris. Photoshop mimics how a traditional lens operates. Even if you are not an experienced photographer, you can twiddle and adjust to taste.

7. Move the Blur Focal Distance slider until the desired pixels are in focus. Additionally, you can click inside the preview image to set the Blur Focus Distance.

8. You can add Specular Highlights by adjusting the Threshold slider. You must set the cutoff point for where highlights occur. Then increase the highlights with the Brightness slider.

9. Finally, it's a good idea to add a little noise/grain back into the image. Normally the blur obscures this, but putting it back in makes the photo seem more natural as opposed to processed.

Using Vanishing Point

28 **VIDEO TRAINING**
Using Vanishing Point

Starting with Photoshop CS2, Adobe released a special plug-in that allows for perspective cloning. Essentially, a user can identify perspective planes (such as sides of a building) and then apply edits such as painting, cloning, copying or pasting, and transforming. All of the edits to the image honor the perspective of the plane you are working on; essentially, you are retouching the image dimensionally. This produces significantly more realistic results—but it does take some time to set up.

PHOTO BY SCOTT SNIDER

1. Open the file Vanishing Point.tif from the Chapter 11 folder.

2. Invoke the Vanishing Point dialog box by choosing Filter > Vanishing Point. This will bring up a custom interface for defining the perspective planes, as well as tools for editing the image. Your work will appear in the image.

3. We must first specify planes to define perspective in the image. In the case of this photo, we want to replace the banner. It's already been blurred, but it is still distracting to the end photo. We need to remove it as it is specific to one event and we want a generic shot of the convention center.

4. Choose the Create Plane tool and define the four corner nodes of the plane surface. You can use rectangular objects (like the windows) when creating the plane.

5. After creating the four corner nodes, Photoshop allows you to move, scale, or reshape the plane. An accurate plane means accurate vanishing point effects, so take your time. If there's a problem with a corner node's placement, the bounding box and grid turn red or yellow. You then must move a corner node until the bounding box and grid turn blue. This means that the plane is valid.

6. Grab the top edge of the plane and extend it higher for the windows in the top rows.

7. Zoom in so you can make a more accurate selection.

8. Select a window that is free from obstruc-
tion using the Marquee tool (from inside the Vanishing Point dialog box). Make a selection and you'll see it automatically matches the perspective of the grid.

9. Experiment by setting the Heal option to Luminance. This will preserve lightness values when blending. If you're unsatisfied, choose undo by pressing Cmd+Z (Ctrl+Z) and switch to Off.

10. To clone the selection, Option-drag (Alt-drag) the selec-
tion to tear off a copy. As you move the selection along the plane, it matches perspective. You can also hold down the Shift key to constrain the movement perpendicular or parallel to the plane.

11. You can press Cmd+T (Ctrl+T) to invoke a Free Transform-
like control over the cloned object.

12. Continue to experiment as you see fit. For example, you can create a plane on the cab door, then use the Vanishing Point Stamp tool (set to Luminance) to clone out the sign on the cab door. This tool functions just like the regular Clone tool except it also adjusts for perspective and luminance (which will create a much better clone).

13. When you're satisfied with the perspective cloning, click OK.

Table 11.1 shows the keyboard shortcuts to make Vanishing Point easier to use.

Table 11.1   Vanishing Point Shortcut Keys

Result	Mac OS	Windows
Zoom tool	Z	Z
Zoom 2x (temporary)	X	X
Hand tool	H	H
Switch to Hand tool (temporary)	Spacebar	Spacebar
Zoom in	Command++ (plus),	Control++ (plus)
Zoom out	Command+- (minus)	Control+- (minus)
Increase brush size (Brush, Clone tools)	]	]
Decrease brush size (Brush, Clone tools)	[	[
Increase brush hardness (Brush, Clone tools)	Shift+]	Shift+]
Decrease brush hardness (Brush, Clone tools)	Shift+[	Shift+[
Undo last action	Command+Z	Control+Z
Deselect all	Command+D	Control+D
Hide selection and planes	Command+H	Control+H
Repeat last duplicate and move	Command+Shift+T	Control+Shift+T
Fill a selection with image under the pointer	Option-drag	Alt-drag
Create a duplicate of a floating selection	Command-Opt-drag	Control-Alt-drag
Render plane grids	Option-click OK	Alt-click OK
Exit plane creation	Command+. (period)	Control+. (period)

Using the Type Tool

12

As more people start and finish their designs right inside of Photoshop, the need for better type tools has grown. While Photoshop initially had *very* primitive type tools, it has now grown significantly and become the design standard for typographic control in all Adobe applications. You'll find that working with type is fairly easy, once you understand a few key areas of the interface.

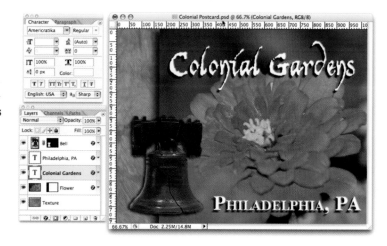

Role of Type

While many people rely on pictures to tell a story, there's just no getting around the use of type. Sure, a picture of a bus on a street sign would clue most into realizing they were at a bus stop, but you couldn't stop there. Without a few letters and numbers used properly, you'd have little confidence in the route or timing of the service. It is proper use of type that we must rely on to communicate vital information to our audiences. If we can combine this functional purpose with a better sense of style and control, then we can move our designs into a more "professional-looking" space.

©ISTOCKPHOTO/VLADIMIR TITARENKO

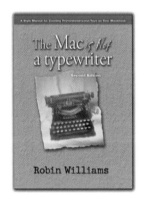

Choosing Fonts

Font choice is a very tough decision for a lot of new designers. You are likely overwhelmed with a landslide of options. To simplify the process, approach it with a triage mentality:

- **Readability:** Is the font clear to read at the size I am using it? Are all of the characters readable in the line? If I look at it quickly, then close my eyes, what do I remember about the text block?

- **Style:** Does the font convey the right emotion for my design? The text on an action movie poster is very different from that advertising the latest romantic comedy. Type is a like wardrobe; picking the right font is essential to the success of the design.

- **Flexibility:** Does the font mix well with others? Does it come in various weights (such as bold, italic, and book), which make it easier to convey significance when using that font?

While these are my three simple rules, there are other constraints at play… It's a good idea to formally study typography if you want to work in this field professionally. At the bare minimum, you can at least read a few books. I strongly recommend *The Mac Is Not a Typewriter* (Peachpit Press, 2003) by Robin Williams and *Stop Stealing Sheep & Find Out How Type Works* (Adobe Press, 2002) by Erik Spiekermann and E.M. Ginger. But since we are here together, let's get the essentials down, together.

Serif vs. Sans Serif

While there are many characteristics to a font, the presence or lack of serifs is one of the easiest to identify. Serifs are the hooks that distinguish the details of letter shape. Sans serif fonts tend to be more uniform in shape. Choosing which type of font to use will depend greatly on your needs.

SERIF
VS.
SANS SERIF

Table 12.1 shows the pros and cons of serif versus sans serif fonts.

Table 12.1   Comparison of Serif vs. Sans Serif Fonts

	PROS	CONS
SERIF	• Increased readability • More traditional • More options available due to longer history	• Thin lines can cause problems for low-resolution printing or applications like video and Internet
SANS SERIF	• More modern • Can compress more information into a smaller space • Optimal for screen usage	• Letter shapes not often as unique • Can be harder to read if too stylized

X-height, Ascenders, and Descenders

You'll quickly notice that point size for fonts is a very relative measurement. The apparent size of your text will depend on which font you choose and what resolution your document is set to. Most designers will look at the height of a lowercase *x* when deciding which font to use. This is because a lowercase x is a very clean letter with a distinct top and bottom. By comparing the x characters, you can quickly compare and contrast fonts. This measurement is combined with ascenders (strokes that go above the top of the *x*) and descenders (strokes that go below the bottom of the *x,* or the baseline). These three aspects will provide a visual clue to the font's purposes. Heavily stylized fonts (such as those used for titles or logos) will often have greater variety than those intended for a newspaper layout, where the text must take up little space, yet remain easy to read.

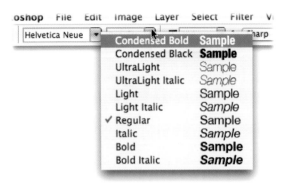

Font Weight/Font Families

If a font comes in several weights (such as bold, condensed, book, italic), it offers increased flexibility. These different versions of a font are called a font family. When choosing a font to use in a design, pros often look to font families. Some of the best designs use a single font family, but mix weights. This allows a consistent look, but with the added benefit of consistent style throughout. You'll find font families listed next to the font name in both the Options bar and the Character palette.

Using Vector Type

Now that you have a clear understanding of the basics, you can start to use text in Photoshop. Your goal should be to keep your fonts as vector type as much as possible. Type will be created as a vector if you use the Horizontal or Vertical Type tools. Vector type uses curved lines, not pixels, that can be scaled and transformed infinitely without quality loss. This will allow you to make last-minute changes like scaling the headline bigger on your print advertisement when the client requests it. This will allow greater flexibility for changes throughout the design process.

Type Tool

There are two kinds of type tools inside of Photoshop that use vectors: the Horizontal Type tool and (the much less used) Vertical Type tool. These are your tools of choice for laying out type. Let's try adding some text:

1. Create a new document by pressing Cmd+N (Ctrl+N). From the Preset list choose 800 × 600 and click OK.

TIP

Type Tool Presets

If you have a specific kind of text combo that you use a lot (say Bawdy Bold at 45 points with a tracking value of 50), you can save it. Just enter all of your text settings, as you need. Then go to the upper-left corner of the Options bar and click the drop-down menu. Here you can add new Tool Presets (just click the pad of paper icon).

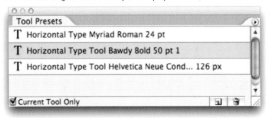

2. Press T (for *Type*) to select the Horizontal Type Tool or click the Text icon (a black letter *T*). You can then press Shift+T to cycle through your four Type tools as needed. As an alternative, you can click and hold down the mouse on the T in the Toolbox to see a flyout list of tools.

3. Notice that several options related to type are now available in the Options bar. We'll discuss these options in the following sections.

4. Click inside your document; a new type layer is added. Type a few words to make sure your Type tool works. Good? OK, let's learn what all those newly available options mean. Delete your text layer by dragging it to the trash icon on the Layers palette so we can continue.

NOTE

Spell-Checker?

Ewe betcha.... Starting with version 7, Photoshop includes a Check Spelling command (it's in the Edit Menu).

Type Mask Tool

Why does the Type Mask tool exist? To be honest, I haven't needed it in years. But in case you're the curious type (no pun intended)… here's the point (OK, pun intended that time). The Horizontal Type Mask tool or Vertical Type Mask tool is used to create a selection in the shape of the type. These selections can be used for copying, moving, stroking, or filtering (just like any other selection) on the active layer. Let's create an active selection using the Type Mask tool:

1. Create a new document using the 800 × 600 document preset.

2. Press D to load your default colors.

3. Make a new layer by pressing Shift+Cmd+N (Shift+Ctrl+N), then choose Filter > Render > Clouds.

4. Press T to select the Horizontal Type Mask tool. Click and hold down the mouse on the T in the Toolbox to choose another tool from the flyout list of tools.

5. Adjust any of the options you want in the Options bar or Character palette.

6. Click and start typing. A red (rubylith) mask will appear over the active layer. When you are finished, click the Commit button (the checkmark) in the Options bar.

7. A selection border in the shape of your text now appears in the image on the selected (active) layer. If you'd like to apply the mask, click the Add layer mask icon at the bottom of the Layers palette.

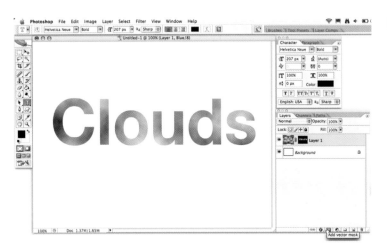

8. The completed image should contain text with a cloud texture inside of it.

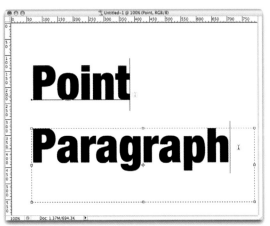

Point Text vs. Paragraph Text

When adding text to a document, you have two options that determine how that text behaves. Point Text adds text beginning at the point where you click and continuing from there. Paragraph Text constrains the text to a box, and will wrap when it hits the edge. To create a paragraph text block, click and drag using the Type tool to define the paragraph area first. Which option you choose will depend on your design needs.

Table 12.2 shows the pros and cons of using Point Text and Paragraph Text.

Table 12. 2   Point Text vs. Paragraph Text

	PROS	CONS
POINT TEXT	• Instant results • Good for small amounts of text • More flexible when using Warped Text (see "Warped Text" later in the chapter)	• Can lead to manual reformatting including inserting manual hard returns
PARAGRAPH TEXT	• Adds column-like behavior to page layout • Allows for use of hyphenation and Adobe Every-line Composer for smoother layout (more on this option in the Paragraph palette section of this chapter)	• If text is too large at the start, you may not see the text entry • Can require designer to resize text block to accommodate copy or font changes

TIP

Select Text Without a Highlight

When you double-click a text layer to select it, Photoshop responds by inversing the text with a black highlight. This can be distracting. Once you have an active selection, press Cmd+H (Ctrl+H) to hide the highlight.

Character Palette

The bulk of your control over type comes from the Character palette. This palette gives you access to control over the characters in your text block including basics such as font, size, and weight, as well as important advanced controls like kerning and baseline shift. If you don't see the Character palette icon in the Options bar, choose Window > Character. There's a lot of controls here... all of them essential, so let's take a look at each one.

Font Family

Setting the font family simply means picking the font you want to use. Nothing too complex, but navigating hundreds of fonts in your Font Family menu can be time-consuming. Here are a few tips to get things done faster:

- You can click in the Font Family field and just start typing the font name to jump through the list.

- If a text layer is active, or even just selected, you can click in the Font Family field. Use the up or down arrows to cycle through loaded fonts.

- Starting with Photoshop CS2, you can see the fonts in their actual face. Just click the Font Family field and you can see a font preview.

Font Style

Certain fonts will have multiple styles or weights; just look at the Font Style menu, which is to the right of the Font Family menu. Click the triangle to access the drop-down menu. This is where you can access variations like bold, italic, and condensed (as long as the font was designed that way.) This is a *much* better option than using the Type Enhancements buttons at the bottom of the Character palette. The Type Enhancement buttons simply thicken the character (for faux bold) or skew it (for faux italic). It is always better to use the true bold or italic versions created by the font's designer.

Font Size

Traditionally, type is measured in points. The PostScript standard (which was developed for use by commercial and laser printers) uses 72 points per inch. However, this doesn't hold up very well, as different fonts will have different x-heights.

Instead of worrying about point size, just use it as a "relative" measurement. Increase the point size to make text appear larger, decrease it to reduce the size of the text. If you need to be more precise, such as designing text for the Web, you can measure in pixels.

To switch text to pixels:

1. Press Cmd+K (Ctrl+K) to launch the Preferences window.

2. Choose the Units & Rulers tab.

3. From the Units area, switch Type to be measured in Pixels if you want.

Leading

Pronounced "*led*-ing" as in the metal, not "*lead*-ing" as in sheep. Leading is the space between lines of type. The name comes from when strips of lead were used on a printing press to space out lines of text. Adjust your leading value to improve readability of your text. Leading works best when you are using Paragraph Text. By default, the leading should be set to Auto, however, adjust as needed to fit text into your design. Just be careful to avoid setting leading too tight, otherwise your ascenders and descenders will collide with negative impact on readability.

NOTE

Finding Fonts

Here are a few of my favorite Web sites offering free and affordable fonts:

- Chank:
  www.chank.com

- Fonthead:
  www.fonthead.com

- DincType:
  www.GirlsWhoWearGlasses.com

- Fontalicious:
  www.mouserfonts.com/
  Showcase/font001.htm

- Acid Fonts:
  www.AcidFonts.com

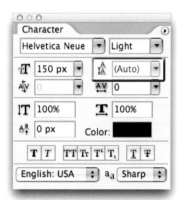

Welcome
improper kerning

Welcome
proper kerning

Kerning

The space between individual letter pairs is called kerning. "So what," you say, "why bother?" Design pros *always* check their kerning. Adjusting the space between letters produces a better optical flow. Think of each word as existing in a stream; you are trying to balance out the spacing so the water flows evenly between each pair.

Taking the extra effort will produce text that is easier to read. This is especially true the bigger your text block gets. Inexpensive fonts and freeware fonts usually have the most kerning problems because it takes a lot of effort for a fontmaker to set proper kerning for every possible letter combination. Cheap or free fonts are just that… cheap or free. While you can adjust kerning using the Character palette, here's a more "organic" method:

29 VIDEO TRAINING
Kerning

1. Click between two letters.

2. Hold down the Option (Alt) key and use the Left Arrow to tighten up the spacing between a character pair, or use the Right Arrow to loosen spacing.

3. Release the Option (Alt) key and then use the arrow keys to move to the next pair.

4. Hold down the Option (Alt) key and repeat kerning to taste.

NOTE

Good Kerning

For a more artistic example of good kerning, open the project file Surf Card.psd to examine its construction.

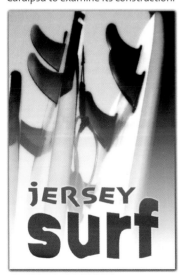

Tracking

While kerning adjusts the space between pairs of letters, tracking affects all letters in the text block or the selection. Tracking can be adjusted to fit text into a smaller space, for example if you must fit a certain number of characters on a line without reducing point

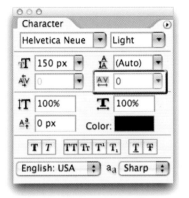

size. Conversely, you might choose a loose track to improve readability (especially if using all caps). Tracking, like kerning, is subjective and can be learned best by studying professional examples and looking for inspiration and guidance.

Vertical Scale

Need to make the text a little taller? Perhaps you want to make the text look a little skinnier or you are trying to create a stretched feeling. Well, you can adjust from 0–1000% if you are so inclined. Normally, this causes unintentional fluctuations in font appearance. If you are working on a shared computer, be sure to check this option before designing to avoid unintentional scaling.

Horizontal Scale

Horizontal scale can be used to compress (or expand) the width of text. By scaling down, you can pack more text on a line. Increasing Horizontal Scale can make the text appear "fatter." Normally, this scaling is less desirable, and you should try to find a font that better matches your design goals. Be sure to check if scaling is applied before designing with the Type tool.

Baseline Shift

Earlier we discussed baseline when we looked at x-height. This is the virtual line that the characters sit on. If you need to create a stairstep approach, adjust the baseline settings. Additionally, you can use this command to reposition elements such as quote marks or apostrophes for design purposes.

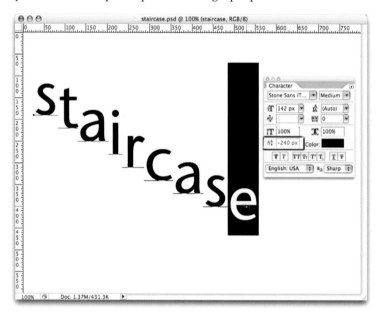

Text Color

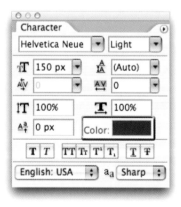

By default, text in Photoshop is black. While black is a very functional color (a third of my wardrobe is black or a shade of black) it won't always work for your designs. Click the Color Swatch to load the Color Picker window. Click a radio button for the color

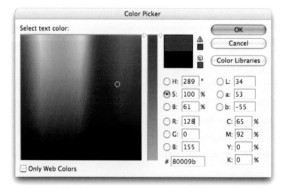

model you want to work with, and then adjust the Color slider to taste. Click in the Color Field to choose the color you want. If you need to use a Pantone color (or at least a close equivalent), click the Color Libraries button.

Type Enhancement Buttons

Herein lies a collection of treasures as well as several booby traps. Some of these buttons are truly useful, but others are just plain bad.

- **Faux Bold:** Faux is French for *fake*. Do not use a faux bold if a true bold is available within the font style you are using. All this button does is make the text thicker and harder to read.

- **Faux Italic:** Same deal here… skewing the text to the right does not make it italic. Always choose an italic version of the font you are using from the Font Style field.

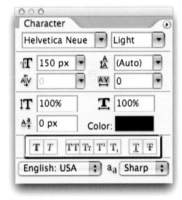

italic

faux italic

Notice the dramatic differences between choosing italic from the Font Style menu as opposed to the Type Enhancement button.

- **All Caps:** If you want the text in all uppercase, just click this button instead of retyping.

- **Small Caps:** This effect is nice on titles and in certain layouts. It replaces all lowercase text with a smaller version of the capital letter.

- **Subscript:** Used for scientific notation and other specialty purposes where a character is reduced in size and lowered below the baseline.

- **Superscript:** Used for specialty purposes such as showing mathematical power. This reduces the character and moves it above the baseline.

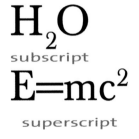

H_2O
subscript

$E=mc^2$
superscript

- **Underline:** Puts a line below the text. You may choose to manually add a line on another layer for better control.

- **Strikethrough:** Places a line through the characters.

Language Selection Menu

Computers should help make the design process easier… in this vein, recent versions of Photoshop ship with a built-in spell-checker. While not every country is represented, you do have obscure options like Nynorsk Norwegian and Turkish to get you through.

1. Select the language you are using in the Character palette.

2. Choose Edit > Check Spelling to invoke the spell-checker for all visible layers. The language chosen in this setting will also affect the hyphenation of words.

Anti-alias Menu

When designing text at low resolutions, adjusting your anti-alias settings can improve readability. Anti-aliasing blends the edge pixels of text. This option is most needed when working with complex character shapes. You have five methods to choose from:

- **None:** No anti-aliasing
- **Sharp:** Makes text appear its sharpest
- **Crisp:** Makes text appear somewhat sharp
- **Strong:** Makes text appear heavier
- **Smooth:** Makes text appear smoother

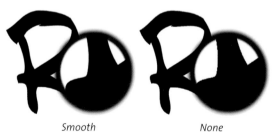

Smooth   None

Paragraph Palette

To finish out your control over text, you'll need to visit the Paragraph palette. While there are not as many choices, you will still need these controls. If it wasn't clear from its name, the Paragraph palette works best with Paragraph Text.

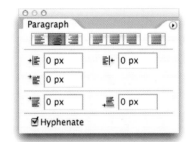

NOTE

Paragraph Art

For a more creative example of using the Paragraph palette, open the project file Concert Sign.psd to examine its construction.

Use of the Paragraph palette allowed the text on this poster to be precisely aligned.

Alignment/Justification Buttons

These buttons will attempt to align text left, right, or centered. They also add support for justification, which causes the text to be aligned to both margins through the adjustment of spaces between words.

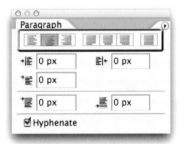

Indent Fields

These three fields allow for the indentation of the left or right margins, as well as the first line of text. If you are going to have multiple lines of text, be sure to use the first line indentation to improve readability.

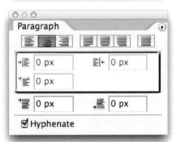

Spacing Fields

To further improve readability when multiple paragraphs are involved, use the Spacing option. You can specify how much space to add before or after a paragraph (either really works). This is a much better option than adding extra hard returns at the end of a paragraph.

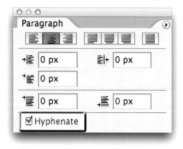

Number of Fonts

There are no hard and fast rules about how many fonts to use on a page... but here are a few "basics."

- Using a font family (with mixed weights/styles) is best.
- Using two fonts is good.
- Using three fonts is OK.
- Using four fonts (are you sure)?
- Using five fonts or more (you're in trouble)!

Enable Hyphenation

At the bottom of the Paragraph palette is a Hyphenate checkbox. If enabled, this will allow lines to break mid-word. Photoshop will use the selected dictionary from the Language Selection Menu in the Paragraph palette. While this better fills out a text block, it is not always the best for large type. It is more acceptable for a multicolumn layout or body copy. Be sure to try out the Adobe Every-line and Single-line Composer options, which can be accessed from the Paragraph palette submenu.

- **Adobe Single-line Composer:** This option determines line breaks on a line-by-line basis. While it is the default option, it can often lead to strange hyphenation or line breaks.

- **Adobe Every-line Composer:** This option examines the entire block of text and makes line breaks based on all lines of text. This can often create a better visual flow. This option is generally preferable to the Single-line Composer.

Modifying Text

If you need to tweak your text a little more, you're in luck. Photoshop has even more options for typographic effects. These five options can take your typographic treatments even further.

Free Transform

Because our text is vector-based, it can be sized and modified using the Free Transform command with no loss of quality. The text will "redraw" itself after the command is applied. The Free Transform command lets you rotate, scale, skew, distort, and add perspective in one continuous operation. This will ensure the highest quality of your text. Let's experiment with this command:

1. Select your text layer and press Cmd+T (Ctrl+T) or choose Edit > Free Transform.

2. Do one or more of the following options:

- To scale by dragging, drag a handle.

- Press Shift while dragging a corner handle to scale proportionately.

- Press Option (Alt) while dragging a corner handle to scale from the center.

- To rotate by dragging, move the pointer outside the bounding border. Notice that the pointer changes to a curved, two-sided arrow. Click and drag.

- To distort freely, press Cmd (Ctrl) while dragging a handle.

- To skew press Cmd+Shift (Ctrl+Shift) while dragging a handle.

- To apply perspective change, press Cmd+Option+Shift (Ctrl+Alt+Shift) while dragging a handle. You may also need to combine this with scale to achieve a believable perspective change.

- If you forget any of the above, right-click/ Ctrl-click a corner of the transform box to display a pop-up list of options.

3. Click the Commit button (checkmark in the Options bar).

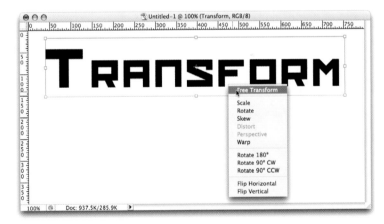

Text on a Path

Placing text along a vector path used to be a job for Illustrator. This would allow you to make text follow a curved line or other geometric shape. Starting in Photoshop CS, this ability moved into Photoshop.

1. Add a path to your document using the Pen tool or Shape tool.

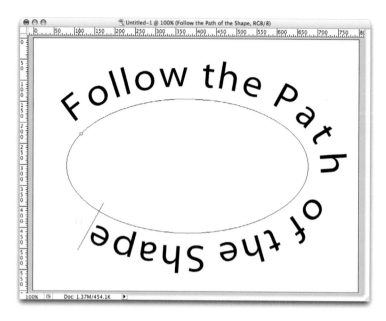

2. With your Horizontal Type tool selected, move over the path until your cursor changes to a new icon (an I-bar with a curved path).

3. Click and start typing.

4. Use the Direct Selection tool to move the margin of the text for repositioning. You can also pull up or down to move the text to the inside or outside of the path.

5. Adjust the baseline and tracking as needed for improved readability.

Warped Text

With names like Flag, Fish, and Wave, the Warp Text dialog box doesn't scream *useful*. However, a lot of powerful (and useful) distortions are available. These vector distortions allow you to reshape text, which is particularly helpful for advertising-style type effects:

1. Select an existing text block.

2. Click the Create Warped Text button in the Options bar.

3. Choose a Style for the Warp and specify Horizontal or Vertical.

VIDEO TRAINING
Warped Text

4. Additionally, experiment with the Bend, Horizontal Distortion, and Vertical Distortion properties.

5. Click OK when you're satisfied.

6. To modify the effect in the future, double-click the T icon in the Layers palette.

Using Layer Styles

Text often needs a little style, and Layer Styles allows you to add a stroke, shadow, bevel, or even texture to your text. At the bottom of the Layers palette you'll see a small *f* inside a circle. This is the easiest way to access Layer Styles. But be sure to show good taste and not go wild with effects. Let's work with some prebuilt Styles to see the possibilities available to you:

1. Select or create a text layer.

2. Choose Window > Styles to open the Styles palette.

3. From the palette's submenu (the triangle in the right corner) choose Text Effects.

4. Click a style's thumbnail to apply the effect; just click another to apply an additional effect.

Some of these effects are attractive and useful; many are gaudy (but that is my personal taste). The best approach is to create your own styles. Be sure to see Chapter 13, "Layer Styles," for more information.

Filters on Text

If you want to run a filter on text, Photoshop will rasterize the text. This process converts the text from being vector-based (and scaleable) into pixel data (which cannot be enlarged without visible softening of the edges due to blowing up pixels). When you have a text layer selected and you want to apply a filter, Photoshop will warn you that it is going to rasterize the type and leave

it uneditable. Click OK if you are sure. I recommend making a duplicate text layer as a backup (with the visibility icon turned off) before filtering text, or try to create the effect using Layer Styles and Warped Text instead. Open the file Light.psd to see an effect that combines the Radial Blur–Zoom filter with Layer Styles.

TIP

System Performance

Having too many fonts active can impact performance of your system by hogging RAM and slowing system boot and application launch times. Instead, use a font manager like FontBook or Suitcase to better manage your font collection.

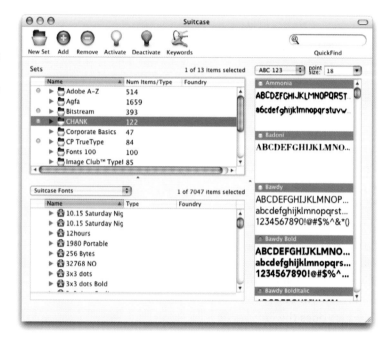

Layer Styles

13

Photoshop comes with several built-in effects: shadows, glows, bevels, textures, and strokes. These effects allow for quick changes to a layer's appearance. Layer Styles are "live" effects, which is to say as the content of a layer updates, so does the effect. For example, if you have a bevel and shadow applied to a type layer, changing the type will cause the effect to be applied to the new characters.

The effects that are applied to a layer become the layer's custom style. You can tell that an effect has been applied if an *f* icon appears to the right of the layer's name in the Layers palette. A Layer Style can be expanded by clicking the triangle icon next to the *f* icon to reveal the layer effects in the palette. This makes it easier to edit the effects to modify the style. Let's start exploring the powerful options of Layer Styles.

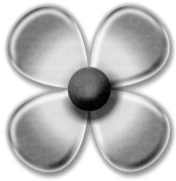

This flower was created from two basic shapes. The beveling, textures, and colorization were all done with Layer Styles. You can open the file Flower_Style.psd from the Chapter 13 folder on the DVD-ROM to explore the effects.

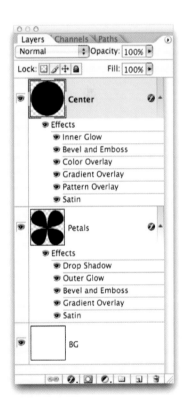

Adding a Layer Style

Photoshop offers 10 effects to choose from. Each offers several options for customization and can be used to create unique and dynamic Layer Styles. Each effect has its own interface, with many shared commonalities; however, each deserves close exploration.

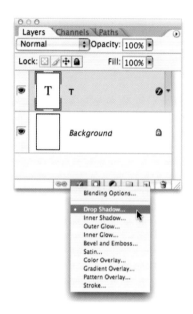

1. Create a new document and choose the 2 × 3 preset.

2. Select the Type tool and add the letter T. Use a thick sans serif font and set the point size large enough to fill the canvas. If you are not yet familiar with the Type tool, you can open Layer_Style_Start.psd from the Chapter 13 folder.

3. At the bottom of the Layers palette, click the circular *f*, and choose the first effect, Drop Shadow.

4. The Layer Style dialog box opens, and you have control over the effect.

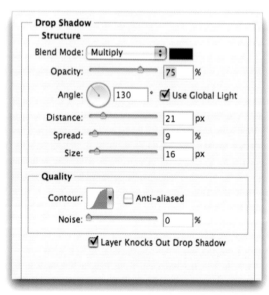

Drop Shadow

The Drop Shadow effect is straightforward, useful, and serves as an introduction to the Layer Styles. Several of the Drop Shadows interface elements appear in other effects. Let's examine its window closely.

- **Blend Mode:** You can specify the blending mode for the shadow. This allows the shadow to more realistically blend with lower layers. The Multiply blending mode is the most common for shadows. This mode causes the darkness of the shadow to mix with background colors, which more closely simulates a natural shadow.

- **Color:** By default, the shadow is set to black. But shadows often pick up the color of the light source or background. To change the color of the shadow, click the color rectangle to load the Adobe Color Picker.

- **Opacity:** Adjust the opacity to taste. Opacity is the opposite of transparency: the higher the number, the less you can see through the layer.

- **Angle:** This sets the direction of the shadow.

- **Use Global Light:** The Global Light option allows you to use a consistent light source for all layer effects. It's a good idea to leave the Global Light box checked so that your designs have realistic (and consistent) lighting.

- **Distance:** The Distance option affects how far the shadow is cast. You can also click in the window and manually drag the shadow into position.

- **Spread:** This affects how much the shadow disperses.

- **Size:** This modifies the softness of the shadow.

- **Contour:** Most users skip the Contour settings. This is a terrible mistake. The contour is essentially a curve; it is representative of how Photoshop fades transparency. There are several presets to try, and we'll explore this setting more later on.

- **Anti-aliased:** The Anti-aliased box gives you a smoother onscreen appearance. This is important if you are creating titles for screen usage (such as Internet or video).

- **Noise:** This option places noise in the shadow, which adds random dispersion to your style.

- **Layer Knocks Out Drop Shadow:** This option is checked by default (and should probably stay that way). It ensures that the shadow does not bleed through partially transparent text.

Uncheck the Drop Shadow box to remove the shadow, and then click the Inner Shadow box.

VIDEO TRAINING
Type Effects

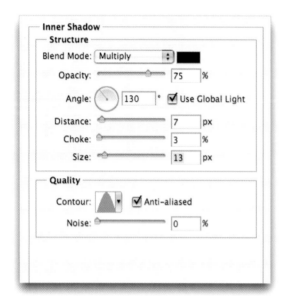

Inner Shadow

The Inner Shadow effect casts a shadow in front of the layer. This effect can be used to create a "punched-out" or recessed look. It looks best when the shadow is set to a soft setting. Inner shadows look good when used in combination with other Layer Styles, but are distracting when overused. The controls of this effect are nearly identical to the Drop Shadow; the only new setting is Choke.

The Choke slider shrinks the boundaries of the Inner Shadow prior to blurring.

Uncheck the Inner Shadow box to remove the shadow, and then click the Outer Glow and Inner Glow boxes.

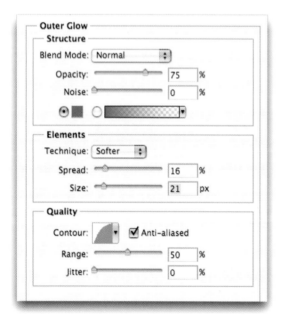

Outer Glow and Inner Glow

The Outer Glow and Inner Glow effects create a glow on the outside and inside edges. Both effects allow you to set the color, amount, and shape of the glow. If you choose a darker glow, you might need to change its blending mode to see it.

The key difference is that the Inner Glow lets you set where the glow emanates from, the edges of the layer or the center of the layer. Inner glows signify light coming from behind the layer. It is unlikely that you would need to apply a Drop Shadow and a glow simultaneously. Tweak the contour and quality for a variety of shapes to your glows.

- **Technique:** You can choose to use Softer (which does not preserve as many details). Choose Precise if the source has hard edges (like text or a logo).

- **Source:** An Inner Glow can emanate from the edges or the center of a layer.

- **Range:** This helps target which portion of the glow is targeted by the contour.

- **Jitter:** This will vary the application of the glow's gradient. It affects color and opacity.

Uncheck the Outer Glow and Inner Glow boxes to remove the glows, and then click the Bevel and Emboss box.

Bevel and Emboss

The Bevel and Emboss effect is very versatile, but you'll need to be careful not to overdo it. You can use bevels in combination with other effects to create realistic depth. This effect has five different kinds of edges:

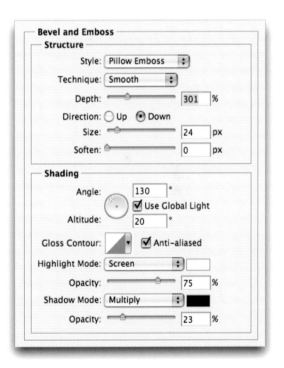

- **Outer Bevel** effect adds a three-dimensional beveled edge around the outside of a layer. This bevel is created by adding a clear edge.

- **Inner Bevel** effect generates a similar effect inside the edge. Instead of a clear edge, it uses the layer's own pixels.

- **Emboss** effect combines inner and outer bevels into one effect.

- **Pillow Emboss** combines the inner and outer bevel effects, but it reverses the outer bevel. This causes the image to appear stamped into the layer.

- **Stroke Emboss** must be used with the Stroke Layer Style. These two effects combine to create a colored, beveled edge along the outside of the layer.

TIP

Bevel Overuse

Don't over-bevel. A subtle bevel helps a text or logo element lift off the page or screen and adds subtle depth. Overuse, however, looks amateurish.

The Bevel and Emboss effect allows significant control over the edges. You can change the lighting source and direction of the bevel, as well as the bevel's thickness, softness, and depth.

- **Depth:** This is how thick the bevel is.

- **Direction:** The bevel can go up or down to change the look of the bevel.

- **Altitude:** You can set the altitude of the light source between 0° and 90°. The higher the number, the more the bevel appears to go straight back.

- **Gloss Contour:** This command creates a glossy, metallic appearance. The Gloss Contour is applied after shading the bevel or emboss.

THE FLEXIBLE POWER OF CONTOUR SETTINGS

The least understood option of Layer Styles is the Contour setting. Most users leave Contour set to the default linear slope setting. The easiest way to grasp the Contour setting is to think of it as a cross-section of the bevel (it represents the shape of the bevel from a parallel point of view).

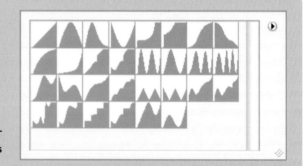

The basic linear contour reflects light with predictable results. However, irregularly shaped contours can generate metallic highlights or add rings to the bevel. The Contour setting is extremely powerful and unlocks many looks. Be sure to choose the Anti-aliased option for smoother results.

YOU HAVE A FEW OPTIONS AVAILABLE TO MODIFY A CONTOUR:

- Click the drop-down menu and select a preset.

- If you don't like the 12 included contours, you can load additional contours. Loading contours is similar to loading styles: just click the submenu triangle.

- You can make your own contours by defining the shape of the curve. Click the curve and add points. If the Preview box is checked, the curve will update in near-real time. This is the best way to learn how the Contour controls work. You'll find Contour controls on glows, shadows, and bevels.

You'll find an extra set of contours called UAP contours.shc in the Chapter 13 folder.

- **Highlight Mode and Opacity:** This specifies the blending mode and opacity of the highlight.

- **Shadow Mode and Opacity:** This specifies the blending mode and opacity of the shadow.

- **Contour:** The flexibility of the Contour controls is the bevel effect's best option. There are two Contour settings: the first affects the bevel's lighting, the specialized Contour pane alters the shape of the edge.

- **Texture:** This option allows you to add texture to the bevel. You'll find several textures available in the Pattern Picker and additional ones can be added by loading them from the picker's submenu.

Uncheck the Bevel and Emboss boxes to remove the bevel, and then click the Satin box.

Satin

The Satin effect can be used to add irregular ripples or waves in your Layer Style. It can be used to create liquid effects and subtle highlights. This effect requires experimentation as its controls are very sensitive. To create different looks, experiment with different colors, contour settings, and blending modes. The Satin effect works very well in combination with other effects.

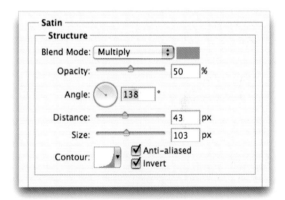

Uncheck the Satin box to remove the satin, and then click the Color Overlay box.

Adding Soft Highlights

Satin is an underused effect that can add soft highlights to a layer.

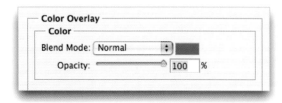

Color Overlay

The Color Overlay style replaces the contents of your layer with new fill color. This can be a great timesaver and allows for fast design of text effects or Web buttons. Additionally, blending modes can be used to create tinting effects.

Uncheck the Color Overlay box to remove the color, and then click the Gradient Overlay box.

Gradient Overlay

The Gradient Overlay allows you to overlay a gradient on top of the layer. You can harness the full power of the Gradient Editor. For more on gradients, see Chapter 6, "Painting and Drawing Tools."

Uncheck the Gradient Overlay box to remove the gradient, and then click the Pattern Overlay box.

> **TIP**
>
> **Change the Color of Several Layers at Once**
>
> 1. Apply a Color Overlay Layer Style.
> 2. Copy the Layer Style by Ctrl-clicking (right-clicking) the small *f* icon and choose Copy Layer Style.
> 3. Select multiple layers that you want to change.
> 4. Ctrl-click (right-click) and choose Paste Layer Style.

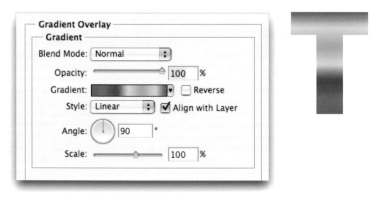

Pattern Overlay

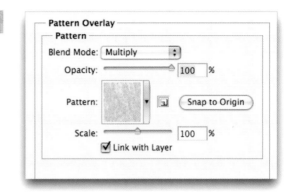

A Pattern Overlay uses photo-realistic patterns or seamless tiles. To create more believable effects, combine patterns with blending modes. Photoshop ships with several seamless patterns and you can make more using the Patternmaker filter (see Chapter 11, "Repairing and Improving Photos").

Uncheck the Pattern Overlay box to remove the pattern, and then click the Stroke box.

VIDEO TRAINING
Photo Effects

CREATING DUOTONES WITH LAYER STYLES

The Color, Gradient, and Pattern overlays are very useful when working with photos. If you're working with groups of historical sources or grayscale photos, you can use Layer Styles to create consistent tinting effects. Often, it is easier to strip all of the color data out of a historical photo before restoring it. You can then add the duotone or sepia tone effect back in as the last step.

1. Open the file Photo Styles Practice.tif from the Chapter 13 folder.

2. Load the Layer Styles set, UAP Photo-Styles.asl from the Chapter 13 folder as well.

3. Double-click the Background layer to float it. Name the layer photo.

4. Click the different styles to try them out.

5. Open the effect window and examine how blending modes and textures can be harnessed for powerful effects.

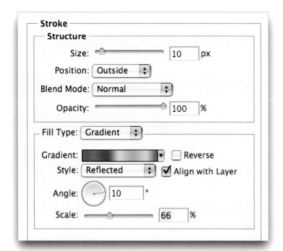

Stroke

The Stroke effect places a colored border around the edge of a layer. This is a much better replacement for the Stroke command found under the Edit menu. You can choose from inner, outer, or center strokes, as well as advanced controls such blending modes, textures, and gradients. If you'd like to emboss the stroke, combine it with the Stroke Emboss effect.

TIP

Is There a Soft-Edged Stroke?

Sure—it's called Outer Glow. Adjust the size and spread for a better appearance.

LAYER STYLE SHORTCUTS

Adobe created a few useful shortcuts that will increase the efficiency of Layer Styles:

- **Double-click a layer in the Layers palette (except on the name), and the Layer Style dialog box opens.**

- **To edit a specific effect, double-click its name in the Layers palette.**

- **Turn an effect's visibility off by clicking the eye icon next to it.**

- **Copy and paste Layer Styles by Ctrl-clicking or right-clicking the effect icon in the Layers palette and choosing Copy Layer Style. You can then Paste Layer Styles to other layers by Ctrl-clicking or right-clicking and choosing Paste Layer Style.**

- **You can move a Layer Style from one layer to another by dragging it.**

- **You can Option-drag (Alt-drag) a Layer Style from one layer to another to copy it.**

Working with Layer Styles

Harnessing Layer Styles is an important part of a professional user's workflow. The efficiency and flexibility offered by styles are huge timesavers. They can also add consistency to a designer's techniques. Be sure to fully explore all the ways Styles can be useful to you.

Using Prebuilt Layer Styles

Adobe Photoshop includes some very good layer style presets to work with. These are an excellent way to learn what is possible with Layer Styles. By seeing the possibilities, you can learn how to combine effects to create your own custom looks.

1. Open the file Style Practice.psd from the Chapter 13 folder.

2. Activate the Styles palette by choosing Window > Styles. Each swatch represents a Layer Style. To apply a style, highlight any layer (other than the Background layer or a locked layer) and click a swatch.

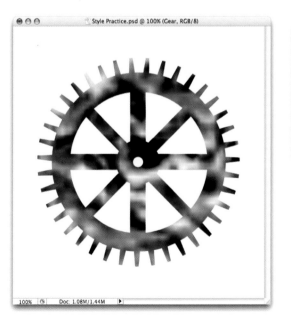

You'll find these and 22 other styles in the UAP Styles set on the DVD.

TIP

Scaling Styles

When changing the Image Size (Image > Image Size), specify that you'd like styles to scale proportionately.

3. If you need more looks, click the Styles palette submenu. You'll find several options built into Photoshop. When you select a new set of styles from the Preset list, you are presented a choice:

- **Append:** Adds new styles to the bottom of the current list

- **Cancel:** Does not load anything new

- **OK:** Replaces the current list with new presets

4. You can also load styles that don't appear in the preset list. Choose Load Styles from the Styles palette submenu. You'll find a collection of styles called UAP Styles.asl in the chapter's folder. If you'd like these new styles to appear in your preset list, locate the Presets folder inside your Photoshop application folder. Any Layer Style library copied into the Styles folder will appear as a preset the next time you launch the program.

LOOKING FOR MORE STYLES?

One of the best places to find more Layer Styles (as well as other resources) is Adobe Studio's Exchange (www.adobexchange.com). This is a popular free site (don't be thrown off when it asks you to register). You'll find a plethora of free content available for all Adobe products.

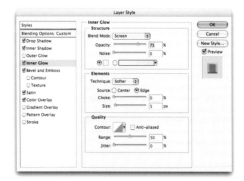

Creating Your Own Layer Styles

It's a pretty straightforward process to create your own Layer Styles. You simply add one effect at a time and experiment with different combinations. Options like Contour and blending modes go a long way toward creating appealing Styles. Styles are quick to learn and easy to master; just continue to experiment with many options.

Saving Layer Styles

Once you've created an original style (or even modified an existing one), you may want to save it. There are two ways to save a style:

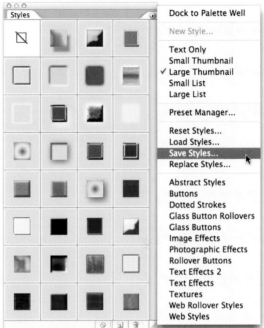

- **Embed:** Photoshop embeds the Layer Style information into the layered files. Be sure to save the document in a layered format (such as Photoshop Document, Layered TIFF, or Photoshop PDF). Three months from now, when your project comes back to life, you can open your source files and start making changes. Remember, Layer Styles will automatically update as you make edits to the layer.

- **Save as a Library:** After creating a Layer Style, you can add it to the open style library by clicking an empty space in the Styles window. A new thumbnail swatch is created, and you are prompted to name the swatch. It is then available to you until you load another style library.

If you want to save styles permanently, you must save a Styles library (or set) from the loaded swatches. It's a good idea to create a personal set in which to store your styles. There is no "new set" option. Simply create new styles and then delete any styles you don't want by dragging them into the trash can at the bottom of the palette or Option-clicking (Alt-clicking) an unwanted style. When you're ready to save, choose Save Styles from the Styles palette submenu.

You should store styles in *<Photoshop Application folder>* > Presets > Styles. Styles placed in this default location will appear in your pop-up menu when you restart Photoshop.

Maximizing Filters

14

Filters are among Photoshop's most popular features. These specialized add-ons can be used to boost productivity or add special effects. Photoshop ships with over 100 built-in plug-ins, and there is a rich array of others available from third-party developers. Filters are so popular that you'll find more tutorials online than you could ever make it through in a lifetime. There are also several books for sale that are overflowing with filter combinations (or recipes).

Photoshop almost did not ship with filters, as many at Adobe thought they were too "gimmicky." However, John Knoll, cocreator of Photoshop, managed to "sneak" them in. Those early execs were partially right, though: When used improperly (or too often) filters can definitely be gimmicky. Think of filters like spices: When used properly they can add to a meal but if overused they can ruin it—and no one can live on spices alone.

Both built-in and third-party filters were run on this image. You would not normally run as many filters on a single image, but you can see just how diverse filters can be.

THIRD-PARTY FILTERS

When you're looking for filters, a great starting place comes to mind: *Photoshop User* magazine frequently reviews plug-ins. Members of the National Association of Photoshop Professionals (NAPP) often get discounts as well. Go to its site (www. photoshopuser.com) and click the Magazine link to find out more.

Filters Defined

The proper use of filters can significantly extend Photoshop's capabilities. Filters can allow you to achieve what otherwise

Plug-Ins
30 items

would be time-consuming results more quickly; they can even unlock options that could not be done with built-in tools. By definition, a filter must reside in Photoshop's Plug-Ins folder. Other features, such as Actions and Layer Styles, should not be confused with filters.

Filter Interfaces

A few filters have no user interface (for example, Average, Despeckle, Facet). If a filter does not have ellipsis (…) after its name, it means there is no user interface. These filters are fairly limited and will likely fall off your favorites list.

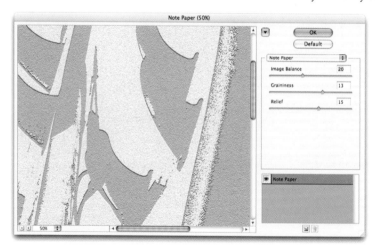

Most filters, however, will have some form of a user interface. Some filters have their own window; others use the Filter Gallery. No matter which interface you use, consider checking the Preview box option. This allows you to see the filter's results to your canvas before applying it. Here are a few more tips about using a filter's interface:

- Click in the Preview window and drag your view. This allows you to change the preview area.

- Use the + or - button under the Preview window to zoom in or out. Additionally, you can zoom in to the Preview window using Cmd+= (Ctrl+=) and zoom out with Cmd+- (Ctrl+-).

- Once you're in a dialog box, fully explore it. Try adjusting all of the variable sliders one at a time. If there's a Load button, try loading presets that shipped with the product.

Using the Filter Gallery

As of Photoshop CS, Adobe changed how several filters work. Forty-seven of the built-in filters now use the Filter Gallery interface. This larger window allows for the application of multiple filters in one pass, as well as to preview the effects before applying them.

Many users wonder why only some filters are in the gallery. Adobe placed most of the filters that were meant for artistic or experimental purposes (such as the Sketch filters) into the gallery. Effects that are more surgical (such as the Smart Sharpen filter) have their own windows. The primary benefit of the Filter Gallery is that you can see the results of combination effects. Let's explore the Filter Gallery interface:

1. Open the file golden_gate_night.psd from the Chapter 14 folder on the DVD-ROM.

2. Launch the Filter Gallery by choosing Filter > Filter Gallery.

3. You are initially presented with a large thumbnail of the effects organized by filter submenu. You can click the Show/Hide button near the upper-right corner to make more room for the image preview.

PHOTO BY DIGITAL ANARCHY (WWW.DIGITALANARCHY.COM)

4. Click the New Effect Layer button to add an effect. The added effect will be Accented Edges because it falls first in the list alphabetically. Experiment with the sliders or choose a different effect from the Effects list.

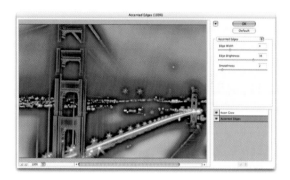

5. You can add additional effects by clicking the New Effect Layer button again. You can also delete or rearrange the stacking order of the effects. Changing the stacking order often results in new looks.

6. In order to temporarily disable an effect layer, just click its visibility icon.

7. When you're satisfied, click OK to apply the effect.

Getting Better Results

Many people simply "slap" filters on their images and expect great results. This bandage approach does not usually create award-winning results. With a little bit of care, you can achieve significantly better looks.

NOTE

Color-Correct Before Filtering

An image should be color-corrected properly before filtering. Remember: GIGO (garbage in = garbage out).

Better Define the Target Area

We spent a lot of time on accurate selections in Chapter 5, "Selection Tools and Techniques" (if you skipped it, reviewing it now will help you get the most out of this chapter). For the best results, you'll want to accurately select the area to be filtered. Depending on what you want to achieve, filters may be run on the entire image, a small portion, or even a single channel. Also, it's not a bad idea to test a filter first by running it on a small area.

Smooth the Edges

A hard-edged selection creates a visible border of where the filter processed. It is absolutely essential to soften your selections. There are two techniques that both work well (and can be combined).

- Choose Select > Modify > Smooth to round out hard corners in your selection.

- Choose Select > Feather to create a gradual edge. This is similar to the difference between a line drawn by a ballpoint pen and one by a felt-tip pen.

Check the Color Mode and Bit Depth

You'll want to make sure that you are working in RGB mode if at all possible (Image > Mode > RGB). This will ensure that you have the most filters available. Very few filters work in CMYK mode.

Depending on Color Mode or Bit Depth, a filter may be grayed out (and unavailable).

It's also important to keep an eye on bit depth. While a 16-bit image can be processed more without showing banding or posterization, you may need to work in 8-bit mode. That's because several filters don't work in 16-bit space. In fact, as of Photoshop CS2, only 36 of the built-in Photoshop filters worked in 16-bit mode. If you can work in 16-bit mode, then do so—but be prepared to lose some functionality.

Fade and Blend

The Fade command is a little-known secret in Photoshop. It allows you to further modify filters by harnessing the power of blending modes. This command allows you access to all of the 22 blend modes besides Normal. That makes your filter collection 22 times larger.

TIP

Using the Fade Command

If you forget to invoke the Fade command, step backwards through your History palette until the filter is removed. Then run the last filter again (with the same settings) by pressing Cmd+F (Ctrl+F). You can then invoke the Fade command.

VIDEO TRAINING
Fade a Filter
33

The Fade command must be chosen immediately after the filter is run (even before you deselect the active selection). Let's try it out:

1. Open the file Pumpkins.tif from the Chapter 14 folder.

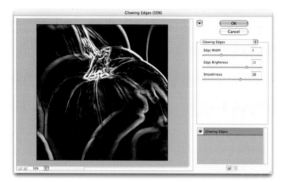

2. Choose Filter > Stylize > Glowing Edges.

3. Adjust the sliders to taste until you have an image that looks much like a black velvet painting.

4. Click OK

5. Invoke the Fade command by choosing Edit > Fade <*name of filter*>. The shortcut is Cmd+Shift+F (Ctrl+Shift+F). To remember this shortcut, think of it as you want to command (or control) the shifting (fading) of the filter.

6. Try different blending modes and opacity settings to modify the look of the filter.

The Standard Filter Guide

Want to know more about filters? Then keep reading. The rest of the chapter walks you through what each filter is for and gives recommendations on different uses. We'll look at the filters in the order they are presented in the menu. This is for ease of reference when you want to come back and look things up.

Next to each description you'll see the filter in action, processing an image. I've rendered two different outcomes with each filter. The left image is a more "traditional" use of the filter. The right image uses more extreme settings or blending modes to achieve a different look. You'll find the source images in the Chapter 14 folder. Feel free to open the image and try the filters out.

KEYBOARD SHORTCUTS

Repeat previous filter
Cmd+F (Ctrl+F)

Reopen previous filter with same settings Cmd+Opt+F (Ctrl+Alt+F)

Fade previous filter
Cmd+Shift+F (Ctrl+Shift+F)

Artistic Filters

The Artistic Filters are direct descendants of the Gallery Effects filter package. These effects were originally sold as a stand-alone product, but were bundled with Photoshop when Adobe bought Aldus (original creator of the page layout program PageMaker). These filters are "old" and their looks are often overused.

Colored Pencil

The Colored Pencil filter produces a very predictable result. The key to achieving variety depends on the color loaded as your background color, as this becomes the "paper" that shows through. Shorter stroke width combined with a higher pressure setting generally produces the best results. Using white as the background produces a natural look. To further enhance the filter, choose Fade immediately after running it and set the filter to Hard Light mode.

Cutout

The Cutout effect produces a very pleasing look where the image is simplified to the point that it looks like pieces of colored paper that have been roughly cut out and glued together to form an image. A higher setting of edge simplicity produces a better look.

Dry Brush

The Dry Brush produces a very traditional paint effect, somewhere between oil and watercolor. The strokes are very defined, and it is possible to introduce a visible texture.

Film Grain

At low values, Film Grain can be used to introduce a fairly realistic grain. This can be employed when mixing computer-generated graphics with material shot on film. At high values, the effect produces a gritty posterization effect. This can be useful for stylizing items for an aggressive, youthful look.

Fresco

Fresco is a traditional art technique in which earth colors are dissolved in water, then pressed into fresh plaster. What you get with this filter is a darker image with small swirls. The look can be useful for simple photos, but gets too "mushy" on photos of people or small objects.

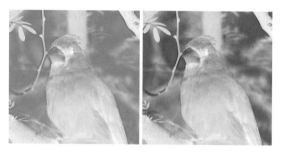

Neon Glow

The Neon Glow filter uses three colors to produce its results: the foreground, background, and one additional color specified within the filter's dialog box. This effect can be used to add a variety of glows to an image, as well as colorizing and softening.

Paint Daubs

Paint Daubs is the most versatile of Photoshop's Artistic Filters. It comes with six paint styles and 50 brush sizes, which give you a lot of variety. Brush types include simple, light rough, dark rough, wide sharp, wide blurry, and sparkle. If you need a painterly look, choose Paint Daubs.

Palette Knife

A palette knife is a thin, flexible blade used by artists to mix paints. This filter reduces detail in an image, giving the effect of a thinly painted canvas. This gives the appearance of the canvas's texture showing through.

Plastic Wrap

The Plastic Wrap filter is better suited for producing text effects, although most of its results can be generated by Layer Styles. When using it on an image, it simulates the effect of coating the object in shiny plastic. To gain finer control, fade this filter, and then adjust blending and opacity controls.

Poster Edges

The Poster Edges filter posterizes an image (removes the number of color steps or gradients). It also finds the edges of the image and draws black lines throughout the image. This filter produces a lot of detail in the resulting image.

Rough Pastels

Rough Pastels is a pleasant effect that simulates the image being drawn with strokes of colored pastel chalk on a textured background. The chalk appears thick in light areas, and the texture shows through more in darker areas. This filter is very flexible as it lets you load your own textures.

Smudge Stick

The Smudge Stick filter softens an image using short diagonal strokes. These strokes smudge or smear the dark areas of an image. The light areas lose some detail and become brighter.

Sponge

The Sponge filter simulates the traditional art technique of painting with a sponge. Images are highly textured with areas of contrasting color. The resulting images will be clearer if you fade the filter.

Underpainting

The Underpainting filter is very similar to Rough Pastels. Its texture controls are where its true power lies. The filter gives the appearance of a softly painted image over a textured background.

Watercolor

The Watercolor filter paints the image in a watercolor style. Details are simplified because of the larger brush size. Saturated areas will become darker as well.

Blur Filters

You'll often need to soften an image, and Photoshop offers plenty of choices. Some are more useful than others, so be sure to understand your options. Beyond obvious uses, Motion Blur and Radial Blur can be used as design effects, especially when faded or blended. If applying a Blur filter to a layer with transparency, make sure the Preserve Transparency option in the Layers palette is turned off; otherwise, the image will defocus but have crisp edges.

Average

The Average filter is a newer filter and was a welcome addition to Photoshop CS. This filter analyzes the color of selected pixels in a selection to determine an average value, then fills with that color. While that may sound pretty tame, it's a great way to kill off noise in a sky or grain in your shadows. This filter works well with the Select Color Range command.

The pixel values of the image were averaged to a single value.

Blur and Blur More

If ever two filters could be replaced (or simply forgotten), these are they. Blur slightly (practically unnoticeably) softens an image. Blur More will do the same about three times more. Both require repeated applications and are inferior to the Gaussian Blur filter.

Box Blur

The Box Blur filter softens an image based on the average color value of neighboring pixels. You can use this filter to create special effects. Try adjusting the size of the area used to calculate the average value for a given pixel. By using a larger radius, you'll achieve greater blurring.

Gaussian Blur

Gaussian Blur is the blur filter you will use most often. The term *Gaussian* is frequently used to signify normal distribution. This filter is appropriately named as it generates a bell-shaped curve when Photoshop applies a weighted average to the pixels. This filter is very fast and has great controls. It is typically used to defocus an area or an entire image. It can be run on drop shadows or glows to add natural softness. Blurring an image, then fading it opens up a whole new world of stylized color correction.

Lens Blur

The Lens Blur filter adds a very needed depth-of-field blur to Photoshop. Before running this filter, create an alpha channel to serve as the depth map. Be sure to check out Chapter 11, "Repairing and Improving Photos," for more information.

Motion Blur

The Motion Blur filter produces a very photo-realistic simulation of a delayed exposure. This can be used to simulate motion or to add streaks of light from an image. This filter blurs an equal amount in two directions, which can be set from an angle dial. The intensity settings range from 1 to 999 pixels. This filter also produces very nice results when it is faded.

Radial Blur

The Radial Blur filter is plagued by a poor interface, but can be used to produce nice effects. It is designed to simulate the blur of a zooming or rotating camera. Spin blurs along concentric circles; Zoom blurs along radial lines. Both allow a variable between 1 and 100. Move the center point in the filter dialog box to aim the blur's center.

Shape Blur

The new Shape Blur filter was added to Photoshop CS2 and allows you to use a specified kernel to create the blur. Choose the kernel from a list of custom shape presets, then adjust the radius slider to change its size. Additionally, you can experiment by loading different shape libraries by clicking the triangular submenu.

Smart Blur

The Smart Blur filter can be thought of as a "selective" blur. The filter allows you to set a tolerance setting (threshold) for finding dissimilar pixels and specify a radius so it knows how far to search. These pixels can then be blurred a specified amount and quality setting. The filter can blur the entire image (normal mode) or focus on the edges (Edge Only and Overlay). These last two modes often produce unexpected results.

Surface Blur

The new Surface Blur filter allows you to blur an image while preserving edges. It can be useful for removing noise or graininess. Adjust the Radius option to specify the size of the area sampled for the blur. The Threshold option controls how much the tonal values of neighboring pixels must differ from the center pixel value. Pixels with sufficiently different tonal value (less than the Threshold value) are not blurred.

Brush Stroke Filters

The Brush Stroke filters should have been named Artistic Filters Part II. They are also leftovers from the Gallery Effects package and are meant to give a painterly or fine arts look. These filters use brush-and-ink stroke effects to produce a variety of looks. They can also be used to add grain and texture to an image.

Accented Edges

Use the Accented Edges filter to accentuate the edges of an image. This filter generates a traced edges look. When the edge brightness is set to a low value, the accents resemble black ink. When set to a high value, the accents look like white chalk. This look is very pleasing and has a nice softening effect.

Angled Strokes

The Angled Strokes filter "repaints" an image using diagonal strokes. You can choose the balance between right and left strokes. The lighter areas of the image are painted in strokes going down to the right, whereas the darker areas are painted going down to the left.

Crosshatch

The Crosshatch technique shades an image with two or more sets of parallel lines. This filter preserves the original details of an image, but adds texture and roughens the edges. The technique resembles the use of a pencil hatching.

Dark Strokes

The Dark Strokes filter is a bit unusual in that it appears to "burn" the image. The dark areas of an image are moved closer to black with short, tight strokes. The lighter areas of the image are brushed with long, white strokes. This filter can be used as a "grunge" filter, especially when combined with blend modes and fading.

Ink Outlines

The Ink Outlines filter redraws an image with fine narrow lines. These lines go over the original details, simulating a pen-and-ink style.

Spatter

The Spatter filter produces rough edges while simulating the effect of a spatter airbrush. When using this effect, be sure to simplify it.

Sprayed Strokes

The Sprayed Strokes filter is very similar to Spatter. It produces rough strokes of the dominant colors in the image.

Sumi-e

The Sumi-e filter tries to simulate a popular Japanese painting style. The image "looks" like it was painted with a wet brush full of black ink on rice paper. The result is a soft blurry image with rich blacks. This filter closely resembles Dark Strokes.

Distort Filters

The Distort filters allow you to bend, push, squish, and completely reshape your image. These tools can simulate 3D space and can be quite useful when building backgrounds. Many of these filters are memory intensive, so if your computer is slow, be patient.

Diffuse Glow

The Diffuse Glow filter acts very much like a diffusion filter applied to a camera lens. It is possible to get a very subtle or dramatic effect. The glow color is driven by your loaded background color; a white, or off-white looks best. If you get strange results, choose a different color. The image will be rendered with film grain and white noise, with the glow fading from the center of the selection.

Displace

In the two examples of the Displace filter, I've used a grayscale file (the left image) to displace (distort) the source photo. Can this filter do a lot? Yes. But it requires you to build your own displacement maps (grayscale files) for it to work.

1. Create or locate a grayscale file to act as a displacement map. Black areas will move pixels to the right, down, or both. White pixels will move the image left, up, or both. And 50% Gray will have no effect. You must save the map as a flattened Photoshop format file.

2. Choose Filter > Distort > Displace.

3. Enter the scale for the magnitude of the displacement. You are able to specify the horizontal and vertical displacement separately.

4. If the map is a different size than your image, specify if the edges should wrap or repeat to fill in empty pixels.

5. Click OK.

6. Navigate to and select the displacement map. There is one provided in the Chapter 14 folder called map.psd. The distortion is applied to the image rather quickly.

So, was it was worth it? Maybe not, as the filter lacks a Preview box and takes a lot of steps. Some users swear by the Displace filter (others just swear at it).

Glass

The Glass filter is a versatile filter that allows you to distort an image so it appears as if it is being viewed through different types of glass. There are some presets to choose from, or you can create your own glass surface as a Photoshop file and apply it. With controls for scaling, distortion, and smoothness settings, quite a bit is possible. This filter can also be used for creating pleasant ripple or haze effects. To create your own map, follow the instructions for the Displace filter.

Lens Correction

The Lens Correction filter is designed to fix common lens flaws such as barrel and pincushion distortion. It can also remove vignetting and chromatic aberration.

- **Barrel distortion** is a defect that causes straight lines to bow out toward the edges.

- **Pincushion distortion** is the opposite, where straight lines bend inward.

- **Vignetting** is a defect where edges of an image are darker than the center.

- **Chromatic aberration** appears as color fringe along the edges of your subject as the camera is attempting to focus on different colors of light in different planes.

You can store settings that match your lens. Additionally, the filter can be used to fix perspective problems caused by vertical or horizontal camera tilt.

Ocean Ripple

The Ocean Ripple filter should have been called Glass Lite. It does a very similar effect, adding randomly spaced ripples to the image's surface. The intent of the effect is to make the image appear as if it were underwater. The effect is not very convincing, but can be useful as another glass filter.

Pinch

Think of the Pinch filter more as a "pucker & bloat" filter. It is possible to take a selection and squeeze it in with a positive value (up to 100%). The opposite effect of pushing the image out can be achieved with a negative value (up to -100%). Applying this filter to only a portion of the image adds a nice "pop-up" effect.

Polar Coordinates

Let me suggest you give up on understanding the Polar Coordinates filter. This filter is designed to change an image or selection from its rectangular to polar coordinates, and vice versa, according to a selected option. Technically, it is designed to counteract shooting with curved lenses or mirrors; however, some cool effects can be generated.

 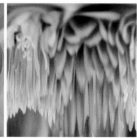

When combined with other filters, the Polar Coordinates filter provides a nice way to "scramble" an image. This can be quite useful in creating backgrounds or patterns. This way the source image is unrecognizable, but the colors come through nicely.

Ripple

The Ripple filter adds a pattern similar to ripples on the surface of water. You have three sizes of ripples to choose from, as well as control of quantity of ripples. For greater control, use the Wave filter instead.

Shear

The Shear filter uses a curve to distort the image. To form a curve, simply drag the line in the filter control box. You can add additional points by clicking on the line and pulling. Click Default to reset the curve to a straight line. You can also specify whether edge pixels wrap or repeat.

Spherize

The Spherize effect is very similar to the Pinch filter. It simulates a 3D effect by wrapping a selection around a spherical shape. It can distort an image by making it appear to wrap around the outside or inside of a sphere.

Twirl

The Twirl effect rotates a selection more sharply in the center than at the edges. If you fade this filter immediately after running it, you can get a nice effect. The only control of this filter is specifying an angle that produces the twirl pattern. To produce a more realistic effect, run this filter several times with a lower twirl amount.

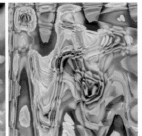

Wave

The Wave filter is very powerful. You have tremendous control over the shape of waves, quantity, amplitude, and wavelength. The Randomize option is also helpful. This filter produces very realistic wave distortions.

Even better, though, this filter is very useful in generating background patterns. Just push the number of generators way up, and play with the other settings.

ZigZag

The ZigZag filter produces a different kind of ripple, one that radiates from a center point, much like a drop hitting a flat surface of water. You have three types of ridges to choose from, as well as a quantity slider. This effect also produces a nice effect on text.

Noise Filters

The Noise filters are used to remove or add noise. This can be helpful when blending a selection into the surrounding area. Noise filters can create textures or grain. They can also remove problems that cause moiré effect.

Add Noise

The Add Noise filter introduces random noise to the image. It can be grayscale (monochromatic) or multicolored. The Add Noise filter is also useful for reducing banding in gradients. If you have done a lot of retouching, add noise to match previous grain. You have two distribution methods for adding noise. Uniform distributes noise using random numbers for a subtle effect; Gaussian distributes noise for a speckled effect.

Despeckle

The Despeckle filter combines edge detection with blurring. It is useful for finding speckles in an image, and softening them. This produces the effect of removing or limiting noise in an image. There are no sliders to adjust, just keep repeating the filter [Cmd+F (Ctrl+F)] until the desired result is achieved.

Dust & Scratches

The Dust & Scratches filter provides a more powerful way to remove noise from an image. Dissimilar pixels are modified to achieve a balance between sharpening and hiding defects. You'll want to try different settings on your image, as a wide variety of results are possible. It may be helpful to run the filter on only part of your image at a time.

To use the filter, follow these steps:

1. Make a selection or use the entire image.

2. Choose Filter > Noise > Dust & Scratches.

3. It is a good idea to keep the preview zoomed in to 100% and pan to see the scratches.

4. Set the Threshold slider to 0. This turns off the value, so that all pixels can be examined. Threshold is used to determine how different pixels must be before they are removed.

5. Move the Radius slider left or right, or choose a value from 1 to 16 pixels. The radius determines how far to search for differences among pixels. Overuse of Radius blurs the image; you'll need to balance how much noise is removed, versus when softening occurs.

6. Gradually increase the Threshold to the highest value that still produces the desired effect.

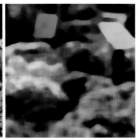

Median

The Median filter is most useful as a way to eliminate moiré patterns. If your scanner does not have a descreen option, run this filter on your scans. This filter is very sensitive, so only use a low value for image correction. High values can be used to get an interesting softening effect. The filter examines the radius of a pixel selection for pixels of similar brightness. Any nonmatching pixels are discarded and replaced with the median brightness value of the searched pixels.

Reduce Noise

The Reduce Noise filter is a new filter to Photoshop CS2. It can be used to reduce noise, as well as smooth out JPEG artifacts. To use the filter

1. Choose Filter > Noise > Reduce Noise.

2. Zoom in on the preview image to get a better view of noise. Try to view the image at 100%.

3. Adjust the following options:

- **Strength:** This controls the amount of luminance noise reduction applied to the image's channels.

- **Preserve Details:** This preserves edges and image details such as hair. Using a value of 100 preserves the most image detail, but reduces luminance noise the least. You'll need to play with the balance of Strength and Preserve Details to fine-tune noise reduction.

- **Reduce Color Noise:** This removes random color. Use a higher value to reduce more color noise.

- **Sharpen Details:** This sharpens the image. Removing noise will reduce image sharpness.

- **Remove JPEG Artifacts:** This is used to remove blocky image artifacts and halos caused by JPEG compression.

4. If noise is more present in one or two color channels, click the Advanced button. Now you can choose individual color channels from the Channel menu. Then use the Strength and Preserve Details controls to reduce noise in the problem channels.

Pixelate Filters

The Pixelate filters can be used to produce a variety of pixel types. They work by clumping similar color values in cells together into new cells. You can use these to process an image into a different look, often slightly stylized. These filters also work well at high pixel sizes for creating background layers.

Color Halftone

The Color Halftone filter simulates the effect of getting too close to the Sunday comics. An enlarged halftone screen is very visible on each channel. The image is divided into rectangles, and each rectangle then becomes a circle (sized proportionally to the brightness of the rectangle).

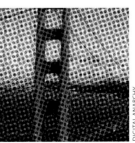

Crystallize

Pixels are clumped into polygons with a solid color. The Crystallize filter can generate a stained glass look at a small cell size, or simplify a complex image into a bed of color for use in composite building.

Facet

The Facet filter produces a very subtle change to pixels. Don't be confused when you run it; no dialog box appears. It may take several repetitions to notice the effect, so keep pressing Cmd+F (Ctrl+F). Similarly colored pixels are clumped together into blocks of like-colored pixels. This provides for a nice painterly effect.

Fragment

Four copies of the image are created, averaged, and then offset from each other. The Fragment filter produces a blur effect that may make you feel dizzy.

Mezzotint

Mezzotints are a traditional Italian process of engraving copper or steel plates by scraping and burnishing. This produces areas of extreme light and darks. These plates were often used to make prints that would contain random pattern of black-and-white areas or of fully saturated colors. Stick with the longer dot patterns from the Type menu in the dialog box; you may also need to soften the resulting image. This is a nice effect for stylizing images.

Mosaic

The Mosaic filter clumps pixels into larger pixels (square blocks) to form images. These new pixels are the averaging of the original colors in the selection. Think of this as your classic video game filter.

Pointillize

The Pointillize filter simulates a pointillist painting. The image is broken up into randomly placed dots. The background color loaded acts as the "paper" color. If you set the cell size extremely large, you can generate acceptable texture plates.

Render Filters

The Render filters are a mixed bag. Some, like Clouds and Lighting Effects, produce beautiful photo-realistic results. Others, like 3D Transform, are clunky and slow. Spend a little extra time on these, as they can be quite handy.

3D Transform

The 3D Transform filter maps your image to crudely created cubes, spheres, and cylinders. These shapes can then be rotated or distorted. This filter is slow and appears to be an idea that didn't make the complete leap from the old application, Adobe Dimensions. Starting with Photoshop CS, you must manually install 3D Transform. You'll find it on your Adobe Photoshop CD in the Goodies Folder.

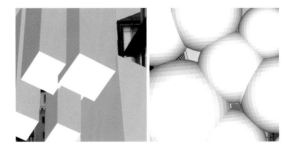

Clouds

The Clouds filter is incredibly useful. It generates a soft cloud pattern from random values between the foreground and the background colors. Every time you run this filter, you get new results, so if you don't like the clouds generated, just press Cmd+F (Ctrl+F) to run the filter again. To create starker cloud patterns, hold down the Option key (Alt key) when you run the filter.

For retouching work, it can create nice clouds that you add into blown-out skies. Simply load your foreground and background as off-white for the clouds and a blue for the sky. This filter is also the starting point for many background textures.

Difference Clouds

The Difference Clouds filter is very similar to the Clouds filter, but it blends the new cloud data with the existing data using a difference-blending mode. Running the filter for the first time will invert portions of the image. Applying the filter several times creates a marble-like effect. This filter uses the foreground and background colors.

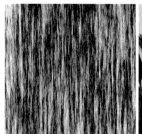

Fibers

Photoshop CS adds a new texture generator called Fibers to simulate natural fibers. Your foreground and background swatch affect the fibers, but you can always change the color afterward with an image adjustment. You can experiment by clicking the Randomize button.

Lens Flare

The Lens Flare filter creates what many see as mistakes. A lens flare is the refraction caused by shining a bright light into the camera lens. You can specify where the flare occurs by clicking the image thumbnail or by moving the cross-hair. Many designers use this as an element or for down-and-dirty lighting effects. Photoshop CS adds a new flare type: Move Prime.

Lighting Effects

Lighting Effects is a diverse filter that lets you simulate 3D lights being added to your shot. You have a lot of choices with this filter, so start with the presets. You can pick from 17 light styles, three light types, and four sets of light properties. All of these can be tweaked and repositioned.

Texture Fill

The Texture Fill filter is fairly obsolete. It lacks controls over the size of the texture as well as blending options. A much better option is to create a pattern fill layer and modify its more flexible options to taste.

Sharpen Filters

The Sharpen filters are direct opposites of the Blur filters. These filters attempt to focus soft images by increasing the contrast of adjacent pixels. You can have moderate success with sharpening, but be careful not to oversharpen or you will get distortion such as grain and pixelization.

ABBA SHAPIRO

Sharpen and Sharpen More

The Sharpen and Sharpen More filters offer an all-or-nothing approach and are not very useful. While they add focus to a selection, they have no controls. The Sharpen More filter applies a stronger effect than the Sharpen filter. Skip these and just use the Unsharp Mask or, better yet, Smart Sharpen.

Sharpen Edges and Unsharp Mask

Sharpen Edges and Unsharp Mask filters help find areas where significant color changes occur and sharpen them. While it has no controls, the Sharpen Edges filter does a good job. It only affects edges, thus preserving overall image smoothness.

The Unsharp Mask filter is an even better way to go. This filter lets you adjust the contrast of edges by producing a lighter and darker line on each side of the edge. This helps add emphasis to edges and produces a very satisfactory result. You'll find detailed instructions on the Unsharp Mask filter in Chapter 11.

Smart Sharpen

The Smart Sharpen filter is new to Photoshop CS2. It has superior sharpening controls not available with the Unsharp Mask filter. It allows you to set the sharpening algorithm and control the amount of sharpening that occurs in the shadow and highlight areas. The Smart Sharpen filter is covered in depth in Chapter 11.

Sketch Filters

The filters in the Sketch category add texture to images. They are useful for creating a hand-drawn look. Most of these filters rely on the foreground and background colors you have chosen. Experiment with different colors for very different looks.

Bas Relief

The Bas Relief filter does a great job of transforming the image to appear carved into stone. You also can control the direction of light and its softness value. Dark areas of the image use the foreground color; light colors use the background color.

Chalk & Charcoal

The Chalk & Charcoal filter creates the look of an artist using chalk and charcoal to form an image. The midtones are turned to gray, the highlights are turned to chalk (in the foreground color), the dark areas charcoal (in the background color).

Charcoal

The Charcoal filter redraws an image, creating a smudged, posterized effect. Charcoal is the foreground color; the paper is the background color. This can create a nice, simplified look that works well in video.

Chrome

The Chrome filter attempts to look like polished chrome. Adobe recommends using a Levels adjustment after running this filter to get a better look. There are much better third-party effects for chrome, and you can experiment with Layer Styles to achieve metal as well.

Conté Crayon

Conté crayons are usually very dark or pure white. The Conté Crayon filter uses the foreground for dark areas and the background for light ones. To replicate the traditional look, use a dark red, brown, or black for the foreground color. This filter can also be used as an optional way to achieve a historical-looking sepia tone.

Graphic Pen

The Graphic Pen filter uses fine strokes to replicate the original image. The foreground color acts as ink; the background color acts as the paper.

Halftone Pattern

The Halftone Pattern filter is useful for stylizing an image. You can choose between dots, circles, and lines. This can be used to create a scan line look or a unique twist on pixelization. The foreground and background colors are very important. Be sure to use the Fade command on this filter.

Note Paper

The Note Paper filter creates a look of the image being constructed of handmade paper. Its results are marginal, but worth the occasional try.

Photocopy

Photocopy does what its name implies: It makes the image look like you made a photocopy on a 1970s copy machine. Large areas of darkness will copy only around their edges. Midtones tend to drop off to pure black or white. This filter is useful for simplifying a photo for use as a design element.

Plaster

The Plaster filter simulates a molded image made of plaster. The foreground and background colors are used to colorize the image. Dark areas are raised; light areas are recessed.

Reticulation

Reticulation is a developing technique where the controlled shrinking and distorting of film emulsion generates an image that appears clustered in the shadows and grained in the highlights. This is a nice alternative to a duotone effect.

Stamp

The Stamp filter creates a woodcut or rubber-stamp look. It's a good way to simplify images for use in multilayered compositions. The foreground and background colors are important.

Torn Edges

The Torn Edges filter works well on high-contrast images and text. It makes the image appear to be constructed of torn paper. The foreground and background colors then tint the image.

Water Paper

The Water Paper painterly effect looks like paint blotches on fibrous, damp paper. The colors of the source appear to flow and blend. This filter softens the original image.

Stylize Filters

The Stylize filters work by displacing pixels and adding contrast to edges. Use of the Fade command and blending modes will significantly extend the usefulness of these filters.

Diffuse

The Diffuse filter is very subtle and may take a few passes to be noticed. It attempts to diffuse an image to make the selection look less focused. Normal moves pixels randomly. Darken Only replaces light pixels with darker pixels. Lighten Only replaces dark pixels with lighter pixels. Anisotropic shuffles pixels toward the direction of least change in color.

Emboss

Emboss gives the appearance of a raised or stamped image. You can specify the angle, height, and amount of color. To better preserve color, fade the filter immediately after running it. You can try Bevel & Emboss Layer Style for greater flexibility.

Extrude

The Extrude filter creates a 3D texture. You can choose from Blocks or Pyramids, as well as specify the size and depth. This is a nice look for background images; it looks particularly good on simple backgrounds or even solid colors.

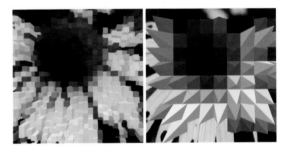

Find Edges

The Find Edges filter creates a very nice stroked edge effect. Try blending it to create a cel-shaded cartoon look.

Glowing Edges

The Glowing Edges filter is an inverse of the Find Edges filter. It also identifies edges, but produces an inverted color scheme. This filter looks best when blended via the Fade command.

Solarize

The Solarize filter blends a negative and a positive image together. Be sure to use the Fade after running the filter to open it up to more possibilities.

Tiles

The Tiles filter breaks the image up into tiles. You can specify the size, amount of movement, and what lies beneath.

Trace Contour

The Trace Contour filter locates transitions of major brightness areas and thinly outlines them. Each color channel is identified. The effect is designed to simulate contour lines on a map.

Wind

The Wind filter creates small horizontal lines to simulate a wind effect. You can choose left or right, as well as three methods: Wind, Blast, and Stagger.

Texture Filters

The Texture filters give the appearance of depth in an image. They can be used to make an image appear to be on an organic surface. When run on images, they give the appearance of the image being mapped or repainted on additional surfaces.

Craquelure

The Craquelure filter simulates paint on a plaster surface. It creates cracks that follow the image's contours.

 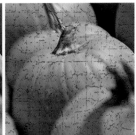

Grain

The Grain filter can create regular, soft, sprinkles, clumped, contrasty, enlarged, stippled, horizontal, vertical, or speckle grain. This filter is very useful for stylizing images and backgrounds.

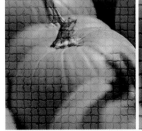 

Mosaic Tiles

Don't confuse the Mosaic Tiles filter with the more useful Mosaic filter. This filter is similar to Craquelure, but not very useful.

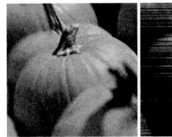 

Patchwork

The Patchwork filter can be thought of as an alternate Mosaic filter. It cuts the image into smaller squares filled with the predominant color in that area. The squares have a random depth assigned to them.

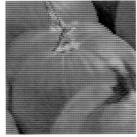 

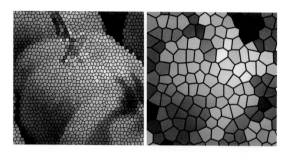

Stained Glass

The Stained Glass filter simulates stained glass windows. The image is repainted as single-colored cells, outlined in the foreground color. Try layering a filtered copy with an original version.

Texturizer

The Texturizer filter is very diverse, if you have textures. Any flattened grayscale Photoshop format file can be used as a texture. Look in your Photoshop folder or on your installation disc for extra textures.

Video Filters

The Video filters are designed for professional video work. These two are both pretty straightforward, but important to video pros. To learn more about Photoshop and Video, visit www.PhotoshopforVideo.com.

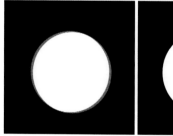
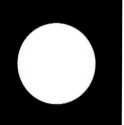

De-Interlace

Video frames in a camera are often recorded between 24 and 30 frames per second. These still images create movement when played back. For smoother motion, adjacent frames are blended together or interlaced.

If you are working with a freeze frame from a video, you may choose to remove interlacing. You can replace the discarded line via interpolation or duplication. Generally speaking, replacing odd or even fields does not matter, but interpolation generates better results than duplication.

NTSC Colors

Like CMYK color space, video graphics have a narrower gamut. The NTSC Colors filter adjusts the colors of your Photoshop graphic to match the NTSC standard (used by broadcasters in North America). Unfortunately, this filter hard clips color information that falls outside of safe color range for the NTSC model. Instead of gently fading these colors, a hard clip is quite visible. If you're using Photoshop CS2 (or later), be sure to try the Broadcast Saturation action (part of the Video set).

Other Filters

The Other filters did not fit into any of the other categories. So the descriptive term *other* was put through months of development and testing. You can use these filters to make your own filters, modify masks, or adjust colors. It's a true grab bag, but an important mix.

Custom

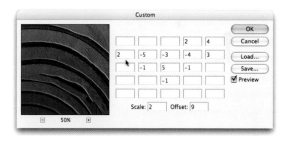

Some users like the Custom filter, but it's pretty tough to use. Essentially, you are multiplying, adding, and subtracting color information. Look up the instruction in the Help Center, and feel free to explore.

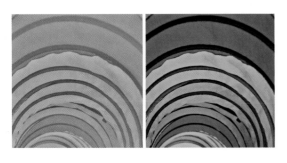

High Pass

The High Pass filter is used to keep edge details within the specified radius, while suppressing the rest of the image. The filter is an anti-Gaussian Blur filter.

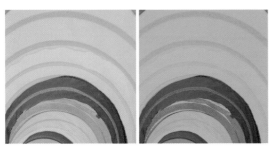

HSB/HSL

The HSB/HSL filter allows you to convert between RGB, HSB, and HSL mode. This is helpful if an image is being wrongly interpreted. If run on an image that does not need it, you will get severe color shifting.

Minimum and Maximum

The Minimum and Maximum filters are used for modifying masks or alpha channels. The Minimum filter acts as a matte choker. Black is expanded, whereas white is shrunk. The Maximum filter has the opposite effect as a matte spreader; white is expanded, whereas dark is contracted. These filters can also be run as a different pixelization effect, and produce a nice mosaic look for an image.

Offset

You can use the Offset filter to move an image a specified distance, either horizontally or vertically. The pixels can leave an empty place, wrap around to the other side, or continue the color at the edges.

Actions and Automation

15

While Photoshop is an extremely efficient program, you're truly missing out if you don't learn how to harness actions and automation. Photoshop has three categories of technology that can streamline your workflow and save you hours of work per week. These powerful commands can take the most repetitive tasks and automate them completely:

- **Actions** record a series of commands for playback on future images. They can be used to generate extremely complex results. You can also use batch processing to run an action on an entire folder of images.

- **Automate commands** perform complex production tasks (like thumbnail sheets or Internet galleries) with minimal effort.

- **Scripts** can perform tasks that are more complex than actions. Scripts were unveiled with Photoshop CS and have made a strong impact on complex workflow issues.

Actions

Photoshop's actions technology lets you record nearly every command (or better yet, a series of commands) and then play them back on another image. You can use basic actions, such as a resize or file format change, to quickly convert files at a push of a button. These simple actions can be recorded, and then mapped to empty function keys (F-keys, F1–F12) on your keyboard. By using combinations of Shift and Option (Alt) as key modifiers, a standard keyboard has 48–60 customizable keys.

TIP

Actions as F-keys

Actions can be assigned to F-keys for easy access. Just double-click to the right of an action's name and pick an F-key. You can also add modifier keys to extend the number of F-keys.

If your Actions palette looks like this, you are using Button mode. This is a useful way to access actions, but you cannot create or modify actions when using Button mode.

PHOTO BY DIGITAL ANARCHY (WWW.DIGITALANARCHY.COM)

Meet the Actions Palette

To use actions, let's take a closer look at the Actions palette. If the Actions palette is not visible, choose Window > Actions. If the palette does not look like a list, go to the palette's submenu and make sure that the Button mode is not checked.

If you look at the interface, it has fairly clear controls. There are Stop, Record, and Play buttons, and they behave as you expect. The folder icon creates a new set to store actions, and the page icon creates a new (empty) action. The trash icon can be clicked to delete the highlighted items, or you can drag actions or sets into it.

Let's practice with actions by using some of the built-in actions:

1. Open the file ocean-bay-day.psd from the Chapter 15 folder on the DVD-ROM.

2. From the Actions palette submenu, choose Image Effects. This menu item loads a set of actions that will process the image to a different look using a combination of filters and adjustments.

3. Choose the Action Sepia Toning (layer) and press Play.

4. The action should take very little time to process the image.

5. Delete all but the bottommost layer and try other actions from this set to see the diversity.

6. You can explore the steps in an action by clicking the triangles in the Actions palette to look at how elaborate some actions are. You may be thinking that these are interesting, but will get stale quickly as they create the same look each time.

This is not the case. It's very easy to modify an action. The easiest way to do this is by turning dialog boxes on. Normally, an action will play all the way through, using the original values assigned to the filters or image adjustments. However, if you click in the column next to each step, you can enable dialog boxes for a filter or adjustment (click a second time to disable). These dialog boxes let you enter variables and influence an action's outcome.

7. Let's try this out. Go back to the Sepia Toning (layer) action. Click the actions triangle so you can expand it and see all of its steps. You may find it useful to expand individual steps to better see what command they perform.

8. The final step, Make, creates a new adjustment layer for the tinting. Click next to its name to enable the dialog box.

9. By modifying these actions, several different outcomes are possible. Expand the triangle next to the action's name to see the list of steps. It is possible to turn on only some of the dialog boxes by clicking next to a specific step.

10. Run the action again. This time a dialog box opens for the final step and you can customize the tint effect. Click OK to create the adjustment layer. You can now modify the tint effect, and then click OK to finish the action.

We have only scratched the surface of what's possible. Actions open up all sorts of options, both for creative and technical outcomes.

Working with Third-Party Actions

There are an innumerable amount of actions available on the Internet. The previously mentioned Adobe Studio Exchange Web site (www.adobexchange.com) is an excellent starting point. Most actions are available for free; some of the most creative and useful are sold affordably by both small and large developers. Let's try out some third-party actions and learn how to load and use them.

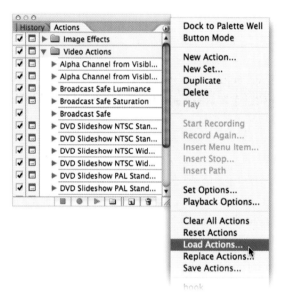

1. Open the file ocean-bay-day.psd from the Chapter 15 folder. If it is still open from before, choose File > Revert.

2. In the Actions palette, click the submenu to choose Load Actions.

3. Also inside the Chapter 15 folder you'll find a folder called Panos FX. The folder contains four sets of actions from the creative mind of Panos Efstathiadis (www.PANOSFX.com). Load the action Stamp v2 by Panos.atn.

4. Select the README first! action and press Play to run the action. Follow the onscreen instructions.

5. Select the !!! STAMP !!! round stamp action and press Play.

6. Follow the detailed onscreen instructions. You can substitute the Enter button for clicking the Commit check mark if you want.

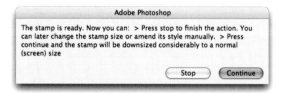

7. When the action gets to the very end, it asks you to make a choice. You can stop and preserve the high-res version or click Continue to reduce the image to a very small size for screen resolution. I recommend clicking Stop.

8. All of the important layers are in a group (also called set) already. You can drag this group into a new document or save it to use later.

There are three more sets and a total of nearly 20 actions to explore. These are some wonderful samples of how powerful and devoted the Photoshop community is.

 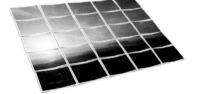 

Creating Actions

By now, actions should seem pretty appealing. You've explored using built-in actions, as well as loading (and finding) third-party actions. Now it's time to create your own.

You must first create a set to hold your personal actions. Sets hold actions, and there's no limit to how many actions can be placed into a set, or how many sets you can load. Let's give it a try:

1. Open the file downtown_close_day.psd.

2. Call up the Actions palette and click the folder-shaped button to create a new set.

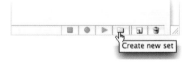

3. Name the set using your name and click OK.

4. Click the New Action icon. You can give the action a name now or rename it later. In this case, I called it Cartoon Look.

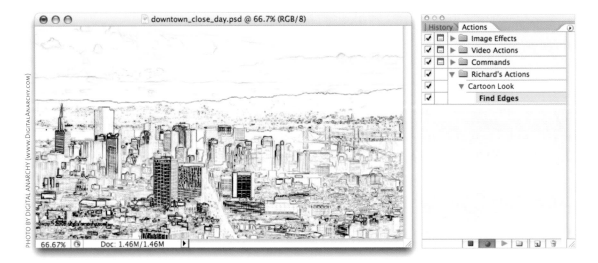

5. Run the Find Edges Filter by choosing Filter > Stylize > Find Edges. There is no dialog box for this effect.

6. To achieve the look we need to fade the filter, choose Edit > Fade Find Edges.

7. Try the Overlay blending mode and adjust the Opacity slider to taste. Depending on the source image, you may need to try different blending modes.

8. To enable flexibility, turn on the dialog box for the Fade step.

9. Click Stop

Congratulations, you've created your first action from scratch. The recipe above is one of my own, but the technique works with most filter recipes. Let's try making one more.

1. Open the file downtown_close_day.psd or, if it is still open from the last action, choose File > Revert.

2. Click the New Action icon. You can give the action a name now or rename it later. In this case, I called it Zoom Blur. The action is now recording.

3. Duplicate the background layer by pressing Cmd+J (Ctrl+J).

4. Strip the color from the duplicate layer by pressing Cmd+Shift+U (Ctrl+Shift+U).

5. Now we'll make the image zoom from a center point. Choose Filter > Blur > Radial Blur. Set the method to zoom and use an amount of 100 at Good quality. Move the center point by dragging within the dialog box, then click OK.

6. Repeat the Blur filter by pressing Cmd+F (Ctrl+F).

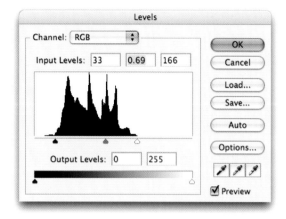

7. On the topmost layer, make a Levels adjustment by pressing Cmd+L (Ctrl+L). Bring the black and white Input sliders towards the center. Move the gray slider (the midpoint) away from black.

8. Change the blend mode of the top layer to Screen mode.

9. Press Option+[(Alt+[) to select the previous layer.

10. Press Cmd+Option+F (Ctrl+Alt+F) to run the zoom filter again with options.

11. Set the amount to 30 and click OK.

12. To achieve the look we need to fade the filter, choose Edit > Fade Radial Blur. Lower the Opacity of the effect to 30% and click OK.

13. Click Stop

Experiment and create your own looks. Virtually every menu command or button can be recorded (although items from the Toolbox do not record properly). Actions can be duplicated, modified, and deleted. Be sure to explore all of the options in the Actions palette submenu. Be sure to dissect actions made by others to get ideas of what is possible. With a little practice and imagination, you'll be amazed at what you can accomplish.

If you want to check out the actions we just created, compare them to a set I've saved in the Chapter 15 folder.

Saving Actions

Actions are stored in a temporary cache. If you delete the set or load a replacement, your new actions could be overwritten. Therefore, it's important to save your actions so they can be backed up and reloaded in the future.

1. Click an action set; you can use the one created in the previous exercise. You must click the whole set, not just an action in that set.

2. Go to the Actions palette submenu and choose Save Actions.

3. The Photoshop Actions folder (inside the Presets folder) will be chosen by default. If it isn't, manually locate it in your Presets folder.

4. If you add to the set later, just be sure to resave it to the same location with the same name.

TIP

Sharing Actions

If you create useful actions, you can post them to the Adobe Studio Exchange community to share with other users (www.adobexchange.com).

TIPS FOR CREATING BETTER ACTIONS

- Brush strokes, cloning, and most manual tools from the Toolbox do not record properly with actions. Instead, use an alternative, such as a Gradient Fill layer (Layer > New Fill Layer > Gradient) instead of the Gradient tool.

- To play a single step of an action, double-click it.

- If you make a mistake in an action, click Stop. Delete the incorrect steps by dragging them into the Actions palette trash can. Choose Edit > Step Backward as many times as needed. Then click Record and start again from the last good point.

- Button mode lets you launch actions quickly—just click an action and it runs. You can access the command from the Actions palette's submenu. You'll need to disable Button mode to access recording and editing features.

- Choose Playback Options from the Actions palette submenu. Specify that you want the actions to play back an action accelerated. Photoshop can process faster than it can redraw the screen.

- Be sure to back up your custom actions to two locations; the default location and a secondary backup location. This way, a reinstall or upgrade won't blow your custom actions away.

- To create an action that will work better on all files, set the rulers set to measure using percentage.

- Use File > Automate > Fit Image to resize an image for a specific height or width.

- Photoshop records the names of layers as you select them. This may cause playback issues, because the action will look for specific names. Use keyboard shortcuts to select layers and such so that the action won't look for a specific name for that step. For more on layer shortcuts, see Chapter 8, "Compositing with Layers."

Outcome	Mac	PC
Choose layer above	Option+]	Alt+]
Choose layer below	Option+[	Alt+[
To move the current layer		
Up the layer stack	Cmd+]	Ctrl+]
Down the layer stack	Cmd+[	Ctrl+[
To the top	Shift+Cmd+]	Shift+Ctrl+]
To the bottom	Shift+Cmd+[	Shift+Ctrl+[

Automate Commands

Photoshop offers several commands for speeding up profession-al imaging workflow. We'll explore each option available as of this writing. If you are working with an older version of Photo-shop, you might not have some of these automation tools. Each is a significant timesaver, and you should attempt to integrate them into your workflow as often as feasible.

Batch

If you liked actions, you'll love the Batch command. The Batch command allows you to apply an action to a group of images. This is a huge timesaver, especially for mundane tasks like resizing. You can also use it to batch process an entire roll of images and run the same Levels adjustment to each image. Let's give it a try.

Let's start by making the action "batchable."

1. Open a TIFF image from the Batch 1 folder.

2. Call up the Actions palette.

3. Choose File > Save As and save a copy to the desktop. This is a temporary copy to prep the action and can be thrown away when you're done.

4. Create a new action called Zoom Blur Batch and start to record.

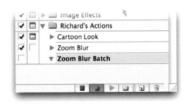

5. Click the Zoom Blur action and press Play (an action can record the running of another action).

6. When the action completes, choose File > Save As. Navigate to your desktop and save the file. Uncheck the Layers box and click Save.

7. Choose a compression option; in this case LZW is very efficient.

8. Click Stop.

9. You can discard the two temp images from your desktop now (or later).

TIP

Batch Jams

A Batch process can get stuck on file closings, especially with JPEG or TIFF compression, which asks for user interaction. You'll want to either batch-convert the files ahead of time to another format (like PSD) or record the close-and-save step as part of the action. Be sure to check the Override Action "Save As" Com-mands option. This will ensure that your files are saved in the folder specified by the Batch command.

The action is now ready to be applied to a folder of images.

1. Choose File > Automate > Batch to invoke the Batch window.

2. Specify a Set and an action from the set that you'd like to use. The action must be currently loaded if it is to appear in this list. In this case, use the Zoom Blur Batch action that we created earlier.

3. Choose the files that you want to process from the Source pop-up menu:

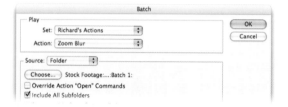

- **Folder:** This option processes all items in a specified folder. Click Choose to navigate to and select the folder. A folder can include additional subfolders as well. For our images, choose Folder. Click Choose and navigate to the folder called Batch 1 in the Chapter 15 folder.

- **Import:** This option processes images from a digital camera, scanner, or a PDF file. A useful batch and action would be to create an action that sets a documents resolution to 300 pixels per inch without resampling. You could then run this action on all items you import from a digital camera.

- **Opened Files:** This option processes all open files.

- **Bridge:** This option works on all selected items in Adobe Bridge. First, you would select several images in Bridge and choose Tools > Photoshop > Batch.

4. You now need to set processing options that guide what is and is not processed as well as how to handle errors or files:

- **Override Action "Open" Commands:** If your action contains an Open command that refers to specific file names rather than the batched files, you'll want to deselect the Override Action "Open" command.

- **Include All Subfolders:** This option applies the action to all files in the subdirectories of the specified folder.

TIP

Batch Multiple Folders

You can batch multiple folders at once. Create aliases or shortcuts within one folder that point to the desired folders. Be sure to click the Include All Subfolders option.

- **Suppress File Open Options Dialogs:** This option hides File Open Options dialog boxes. It's a good idea to use this when batching actions on camera raw image files. Photoshop will then use the latest settings. For maximum compatibility, check this option.

- **Suppress Color Profile Warnings:** This option ignores color profile warnings, which can cause an action to hang and wait for user interaction. For maximum compatibility, check this option.

5. You need to specify a destination for the processed files by choosing one from the Destination menu:

   - **None:** This option leaves the files open without saving changes.

   - **Save And Close:** This option saves the files in their current location. This is a destructive edit as it will over-write the original files.

   - **Folder:** This method saves the processed files to another location (this is the safest option). Click Choose to spec-ify the destination folder. For this Batch, navigate to the desktop and create a new folder called Batch Processed.

6. If the action you're using includes a Save As command, choose Override Action "Save As" Commands. Otherwise, the image may write to the wrong folder. For maximum compatibility, check this option.

7. If you chose Folder as the destination, you'll need to specify a file-naming convention. Several pop-up fields are avail-able for easy file naming. These fields make it very easy to rename files from a digital camera or to specify a serial number. As photos from digital cameras often end up with the same name, this is a very good idea as you can create more accurate and descriptive names for each image. In this case choose the following settings:

   - **Field 1:** Fruit Stand (manually type in)

   - **Field 2:** _ (manually type in)

   - **Field 3:** mmddyy (date) (from pop-up list)

TIP

File Naming Compatibility

For File Naming Compatibility, be sure to choose Windows and Mac OS to ensure file names are compat-ible with the OS.

TIP

Converting File Formats

The Batch command cannot con-vert file formats. This can easily be done in advance using the Image Processor script that ships with Photoshop CS2. If you're using an older version of Photoshop, you can record a Save As command followed by the Close command as part of the original action (remem-ber you can go back and duplicate the action, then modify it). Be sure to choose Override Action "Save In" Commands for the Destination when setting up the Batch process.

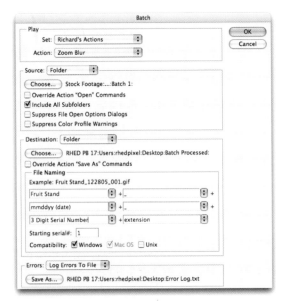

- **Field 4:** _ (manually type in)
- **Field 5:** 3 Digit Serial Number (from pop-up list)
- **Field 6:** extension (from pop-up list)

These settings will result in a name like Fruit Stand_122705_001.tif

8. You need to set an option for error processing from the Errors pop-up menu:

   - **Stop For Errors:** This option suspends the process until you confirm the error message. Only choose this option if you will be monitoring the Batch process closely.

   - **Log Errors To File:** This option records each error into a file without stopping the process. After processing, a message will appear to tell you if any errors occurred. For this Batch, choose Log Errors To File. Save a file called Error Log.txt on the desktop

9. Click OK to run the Batch. Photoshop will batch-process the images. Depending on the speed of your computer, this may take a few minutes. You can abort a Batch by pressing Esc at any time.

PDF Presentation

Several documents can be combined into a single PDF document. This can be useful to send a lot of files to a client or as a way to present your work.

VIDEO TRAINING
PDF Presentation

1. Choose File > Automate > PDF Presentation.

2. In the PDF Presentation dialog box, click the Browse button. Navigate to the folder you want to use. In this case, navigate to the folder PDF Presentation in the Chapter 15 folder and open it. Shift-click to select multiple files or Cmd-click (Ctrl-click) to select discontiguous files in a list. Additionally, you could also choose the Add Open Files option to add files already open in Photoshop.

3. Drag the files into the order you want the pages (or slides) to appear. The topmost files are presented first. Just drag them to reorder the images.

4. In the Output Options area of the PDF Presentation dialog box, you need to choose from the following options:

   - **Multi-Page Document**: This creates a PDF file with each image on a separate page.

   - **Presentation:** This creates a PDF slide show presentation.

5. If the Presentation option is chosen, you can specify the following options:

   - **Advance Every [5] Seconds:** This allows you to specify how long each image is shown. The default duration is 5 seconds. Unchecking this option causes the slides to be manually advanced. In this case choose every 5 seconds.

   - **Loop After Last Page:** This tells the presentation to automatically start over after reaching the end. This can be useful if the presentation is to be self-running at a kiosk. For this presentation, choose this option.

NOTE

Duplicate a File

If you want a file to appear more than once in the presentation, select the file and click the Duplicate button. You can then drag it to a new position in the PDF.

- **Transition:** You can specify a transition to use between slides. For this presentation, choose Wipe Down.

6. Click Save to create a PDF file. Navigate to the desktop and name the file Presentation.pdf.

7. The Save Adobe PDF dialog box opens. You can choose an Adobe PDF preset or specify detailed options for the PDF document. Use High Quality Print if printing is a concern or Smallest File Size to make the file easier to email.

8. Click Save PDF. Photoshop will create the PDF file. A dialog box appears telling you if the PDF presentation was created successfully.

Create Droplet

Saving Droplets

Save your droplets in a convenient location for drag-and-drop.

A droplet is a lot like a permanent batch. The interface is almost the same as the Batch command in that you choose an action and set naming and destination options. The key difference is that you don't set an input source. Instead, a droplet is created that allows you to drag an image (or folder of images) onto it to run.

1. Choose File > Automate > Create Droplet. The Droplet interface opens and should appear similar to the Batch window.

2. Click the Choose button in the Save Droplet In section of the dialog box and navigate to a location in which to save it. In this case, name the droplet *Aged Photo* and save it to the desktop.

3. Select the set and action that you want to use. In this example, choose the Image Effects and the Aged Photo action.

4. The Override commands in the Play area are identical to the Batch command. In this case, leave the Suppress Color Profile Warnings box checked. It's also a good idea to check Include All Subfolders Processes files in subdirectories.

5. Choose a destination for the processed images. In the Destination menu, choose Folder and create a new folder on the desktop called Droplet Results.

6. Specify the file-naming convention and select file compatibility options for the new files. Feel free to choose a naming convention that makes sense to you. Be sure to make the files Mac and PC compatible.

7. Choose to log errors to a file. Set the log to write to the desktop in a file called Error Log.

8. Click OK to create the droplet.

9. To prevent the Batch from stopping to ask about file compatibility, let's change a File Handling option. Press Cmd+K (Ctrl+K) to call up Photoshop's preferences.

10. Choose File Handling from the pop-up menu.

11. Uncheck Ask Before Saving Layered TIFF files. If you're running CS2 or later, check the box for Enable Large Document Format (.psb) and set Maximize PSD and PSB File Compatibility to Always.

12. In the Chapter 15 folder, you'll find a folder called Droplet. Drag it on top of the new droplet you created (Aged Photo) to run the action on the entire folder.

13. Sit back and wait; the batch should run without errors. Droplets can be useful as well if you want to set up a time-intensive task and walk away from your computer for a while. Just be sure to test a few images before leaving.

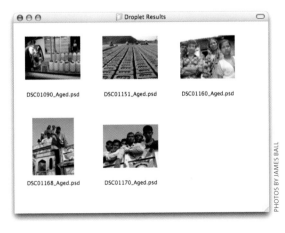

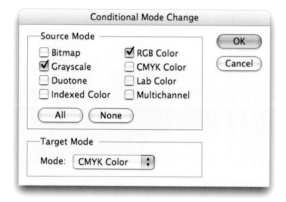

Conditional Mode Change

The Conditional Mode Change command is meant to be used within an action. It allows you to specify conditions for a mode change to occur during an action. Recording a mode change into an action can result in an error if the action is run on an image that has a different image mode. For example, if one step of an action were to convert an image from a source mode of RGB to a target mode of CMYK, applying this action to an image in Grayscale mode would result in an error. The command allows you to specify one or more source modes and a mode for the target mode.

Contact Sheet II

VIDEO TRAINING
Contact Sheet II

In traditional photography, it is a common practice to create a contact sheet from rolls of film. This allows the photographer (and clients) to select images they'd like to see printed at full size. This step is done for both convenience and cost-savings.

This best practice also works in the digital domain. Contact sheets are a convenient way to get images in front of a client without having to make expensive prints or wasting paper. Creating a contact sheet is easy; let's give it a try:

1. Choose File > Automate > Contact Sheet II.

2. In the Contact Sheet II dialog box, specify which images to use. This can be done by choosing from the Use menu in the Source Images area:

   • **Current Open Documents:** This uses all images that are currently open in Photoshop.

   • **Folder:** You must click Choose (Browse) then navigate to a folder containing images. You can also specify to Include All Subfolders to include images within any subfolders. For our example, click Choose (Browse) and navigate to Historical Contact Sheet in the Chapter 15 folder.

- **Selected Images From Bridge:** If you've selected images in Bridge choose this command, then Photoshop will use those for the contact sheet.

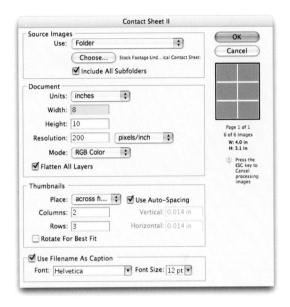

3. In the Document area, you must specify the dimensions of the paper, a resolution, and color mode for the contact sheet. For this sample, enter a page size of 8 inches × 10 inches, a resolution of 200 ppi, and an RGB color mode. These settings will work well for both email and an inkjet printer.

4. Select Flatten All Layers to put all images and text on a single layer. This will result in a smaller file. If you want the ability to edit photo captions, uncheck this box.

5. In the Thumbnails area, you can specify options for the thumbnail previews and layout.

- **Place:** You must choose to arrange thumbnails across (from left to right, then top to bottom) or down (from top to bottom, then left to right).

- **Columns/Rows:** Enter the number of columns and rows you want for each contact sheet. Photoshop automatically creates new contact sheets when the current one is full. As you modify these settings, you'll see a visual preview of the specified layout. In our sample, the folder contains six images, so choose 2 columns and 3 rows to maximize thumbnail size.

- **Use Auto-Spacing:** Select Use Auto-Spacing and Photoshop will optimize the amount of space between each thumbnail.

- **Rotate For Best Fit:** Deselect Rotate For Best Fit so the images appear properly oriented. If you check this option, some thumbnails will be larger (but rotated 90°).

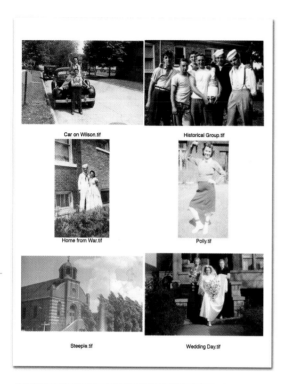

6. Check Use Filename As Caption to label each thumbnail using its source file name. This is an important option so you and the client can clearly identify each image. You can use the menu to specify a font and size for the captions.

7. Click OK to run the script.

8. When the file is done, choose Save As and save the file as a PDF file for maximum compatibility and easy email use.

Crop and Straighten Photos

When scanning images, it's often possible to fit more than one image on the scanner bed. Scanning multiple images at once can save input time when loading images into Photoshop. Fortunately, the Crop And Straighten Photos command picks up and keeps the efficiency going. Let's give it a try:

1. Open the file Crop and Straighten.tif from the Chapter 15 folder. If you would rather, just scan in a few images on your own scanner.

2. If you're working in a multilayered image, select the layer that contains the images. If you only want some of the images, draw a selection border around one or more images.

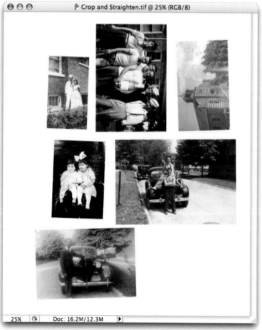

3. Choose File > Automate > Crop And Straighten Photos.

4. Each image should be cropped, straightened, and moved into its own document window.

Fit Image

The Fit Image command is another that is meant to be inserted into an action. It allows you to specify a maximum width and height (in pixels) that the image cannot exceed. This is useful when sizing images for the screen or Internet.

Picture Package

The Picture Package command allows you to fit multiple pictures onto a page. This can be helpful as it allows you to bundle multiple images into a single sheet for printing, thus saving you time and money. Let's give it a try:

1. Choose File > Automate > Picture Package.

2. In the Source Images area, choose to use a File (you can also use a folder or the open document).

3. Click Choose and navigate to the Chapter 15 folder. Inside you'll find a folder called Picture Package. Open that folder and choose the first image.

4. In the Document area choose a Page Size (8 × 10 works best for most inkjet printers). The RGB mode and 300 ppi work best for inkjet work as well. In the Layout drop-down menu, you have several choices (it will feel like grade school picture day all over again).

5. In the Picture Package dialog box, choose a layout from the Layout menu. For this example, choose the (1) 5X7 (2) 3.5X5. Photoshop rearranges and sizes the images in the Layout preview.

Crop and Straighten Best Results

For best results, you need to keep 1/8 inch between the images in your scan. If the Crop And Straighten Photos command does not succeed (which is rare), you should process the individual images using the Crop tool.

VIDEO TRAINING
36
Picture Package

6. Let's add more images into this layout. Click the bottom-right image. Navigate to the Picture Package folder and choose the second image in the list.

7. Click the bottom-left picture and pick the third image from the Picture Package folder.

8. Click OK to create the Picture Package. The package is now ready for printing. A paper cutter or Xacto knife with a straight-edge metal ruler works best to separate your pictures—just be careful when cutting.

Web Photo Gallery

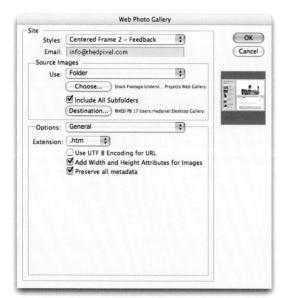

37 VIDEO TRAINING
Web Photo Gallery

Photoshop's Web Photo Gallery command is one of the most popular in Photoshop. Power users and amateurs alike have discovered the power and flexibility of creating entire galleries right within Photoshop. Without knowing any HTML or Flash, users can quickly create online galleries for their images. If they are familiar with Web programming, they can customize the templates for quicker results.

1. Choose File > Automate > Web Photo Gallery.

2. Choose a style for the gallery from the Styles pop-up menu. You can see a preview of the main page for the chosen style in the preview area. Photoshop CS2 includes 30 different templates including interactive ones for client feedback and impressive galleries powered by Flash. For our sample, choose Centered Frame 2–Feedback.

3. Enter an email address if you want the client to be able to send you feedback.

4. Choose the source files to use for the gallery from the Use menu. In our sample use a Folder and click Choose. Navigate to the folder Web Gallery in the Chapter 15 folder.

5. Click Destination and navigate to a place to create the Web site. It is best to target a folder, not a drive. Navigate to the desktop and create a folder called *Gallery*.

6. There are several options that you can customize (and they vary by the template you pick). Pick each option and modify it to taste.

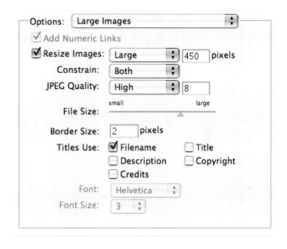

- **General:** Includes metadata with your images so shooting info is included. You can also choose to use the extension .htm or .html, depending on your server requirements.

- **Banner:** Specify information to be included in the banner area of the Web page.

- **Large Images:** Set the size for the images displayed on the detail pages. Be sure to balance size versus download time.

- **Thumbnails:** Set how large the thumbnail images are for the index pages.

- **Custom Colors:** Some templates allow you to change colors of certain elements. These colors will not affect every template.

- **Security:** Watermark images with security information. This will put some clients' minds at ease.

7. Click OK. Photoshop creates a Web page and stores all of the HTML and JPEG files in the destination folder.

8. The resulting Web site can be posted to the Internet if you have a Web site or Web hosting (many Internet Service Providers provide hosting as part of their Internet access plans). You can also zip the file and send it to a client via email (clients can then click to expand the archive and open the index.htm file). With the Feedback template, the client can approve and add comments to each image (they must click Save before switching images). They can then click Email to send the feedback to you.

Photomerge

The Photomerge command allows you to merge several (adjacent) photographs into one continuous image. This command is used to make panoramic images. We covered this command in depth back in Chapter 8. If you skipped that hands-on activity, feel free to flip back to Chapter 8. If you'd like another practice image, you'll find a folder called Photomerge in the Photoshop Application folder (Photoshop > Samples > Photomerge).

Merge to HDR

The Merge to HDR command is new to Photoshop CS2. It allows you to take multiple exposures of a subject (shot from a locked tripod or camera mount) and merge them into a new image that better displays highlights and shadows. The resulting image is also a 32-bit image that allows great flexibility for adjusting exposure. We covered HDR images in depth in Chapter 10, "Color Correction and Enhancement." Let's create an HDR image:

1. Choose File > Automate > Merge To HDR.

2. Within the Merge to HDR dialog box, click Browse to navigate to the source images. You'll find an HDR sample in the Sample Images folder (Photoshop> Samples> Merge to HDR). Click Open. In the folder, Shift-click images 1–4 to select them. Click Open.

3. A second Merge to HDR dialog box opens. You'll see thumbnails for each of the images used as well as a resulting image.

4. Leave the Bit Depth set to 32 Bit/Channel.

5. Adjust the slider below the histogram to set the white point.

6. Click OK to create a new HDR image.

Scripts

Photoshop scripting offers a more powerful automation technology than actions. Scripts allow for the execution of more elaborate tasks than what actions can do. This is because scripts recognize conditional states. Scripting was introduced in Photoshop CS, and powerful built-in scripts automate the processing of multiple layers or layer comps.

Creating original scripts requires you to use a scripting language such as AppleScript, JavaScript, or Visual Basic. Photoshop includes a script editor and debugger for JavaScript. JavaScript is the preferred language as the scripts are cross platform. Scripting is complex and is essentially computer programming. There are plenty of resources available for those who want to learn scripting, but be

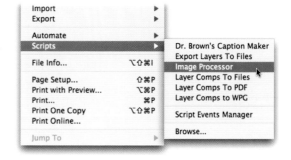

prepared to spend some time. You'll find a folder called Scripting Guide in the Photoshop application folder. In it you'll find sample scripts and a PDF with detailed information.

Fortunately, there are some wonderful examples of scripting available at the Adobe Studio Exchange Web site (www. adobexchange.com). Be sure to look for scripts by Photoshop guru Russell Brown. Load new scripts by choosing File > Script > Browse. To permanently add a script to the Script menu, copy it into the Scripts folder inside your Presets folder. For now, let's explore the built-in scripts.

Export Layers to Files

There are certain production situations where it is useful to export a layered PSD file to separate images. This might be the case if you are trying to bring a layered file into another application that does not read layered files.

VIDEO TRAINING
DVD Slide Show

Photoshop allows you to convert a layered file into a series of individual files. You can choose to create a PSD, BMP, JPEG, PDF, Targa, or TIFF for each layer. Layers are named automatically as they are created; however, you have some options you can modify for naming. Let's give it a try:

1. Open the file Script Sample.psd

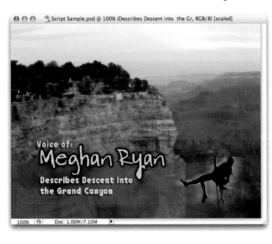

2. Choose File > Scripts > Export Layers To Files.

3. In the Export Layers To Files dialog box, choose Destination by clicking Browse. For our sample, create a folder on the desktop called Script Export.

4. Enter a name in the File Name Prefix text box. This will serve as a prefix for the exported files.

5. Choose a File Type and set options for the exported file. For our sample choose PSD.

6. Select the Visible Layers Only option if you only want to export layers that have visibility enabled.

7. Choose the Include ICC Profile option if you want the working space embedded in the exported files. This is important if you're working in a color-managed workflow.

8. Click Run.

Image Processor

The Image Processor command can be used to convert and process multiple images. It made its official debut in Photoshop CS2, but you can find it at Adobe Studio Exchange under the name Dr. Brown's Image Processor. (If you're still using Photoshop CS, you can download and use version of this useful script.)

The Image Processor differs from the Batch command in that you don't have to first create an action. The image processor can be used for any of the following tasks:

- To convert a set of files to JPEG, PSD, or TIFF format. You can also convert files simultaneously to all three formats.

- To process a set of camera raw files using the same camera raw options.

- To resize images to fit within a specified pixel dimension.

- To embed a color profile into images or convert files to sRGB and save them as JPEG images for the Web.

- To include copyright metadata into the processed images.

TIP

Apply One Setting to All

If you need to process a group of camera raw files taken under the same lighting conditions, open and adjust only the first image to your satisfaction. You can then apply the same settings to the other images by checking this option's box.

NOTE

Batch Processing

The Image Processor is another way to batch-process images (and you don't need to go through the extra steps of the Save As command). The Image Processor script can be more flexible than the Batch command.

TIP

Saving Settings

You can click Save to save the current settings in the Image Processor dialog box. These settings can be reloaded for a later job if needed.

The Image Processor works with PSD, TIFF, JPEG, or camera raw files.

1. Choose > File > Scripts > Image Processor.

2. Choose the images you want to process. You can use open images or navigate to a folder to choose images. Click Select Folder and navigate to the folder called Batch 1 in the Chapter 15 folder.

3. Select a location to save the processed files. You can choose the Script Exports folder on the desktop.

4. Select the file types and options you want to convert to:

   - **Save As JPEG:** Sets the JPEG quality between 0 and 12. You can also resize the image and convert it to the sRGB color profile.

   - **Save As PSD:** Sets the PSD options. You can also resize the image and check Maximize Compatibility.

   - **Save As TIFF:** Saves images in TIFF format with LZW compression. You can also resize the image.

   For our example, choose JPEG and choose to resize to 800 × 600 pixels with a compression of 10.

5. You can choose other processing options as well:

   - **Run Action:** If an action is loaded into Photoshop, you can run it on the image during the process.

   - **Copyright Info:** This includes any text you enter in the IPTC copyright metadata for the file. Text overwrites the copyright metadata in the original file.

   - **Include ICC Profile:** This embeds the color profile with the saved files.

   For our example, choose an Image action to run on the processed images.

6. Click Run. Photoshop processes the images to the specified folder.

Layer Comps to Files, PDF, and WPG

Three scripts work with Layer Comps. Layer Comps allow you save different arrangements of layer visibility, position, and effects. Layer Comps are covered in depth in Chapter 8.

1. Open an image that uses Layer Comps. You can use your own or the file called Script Sample.psd from the Chapter 15 folder.

2. You have to choose from three different ways to export layer comps. Choose File > Scripts and then choose one of the following scripts:

   - **Layer Comps To Files:** This exports all layer comps to individual files, one for each comp. You can choose to create BMP, JPEG, PDF, PSD, Targa, or TIFF files.

   - **Layer Comps To PDF:** This places all layer comps into a PDF file. This is a useful way to send a layer comp set to a client for review. The options are identical to the PDF slide show command.

   - **Layer Comps To WPG:** This creates a Web Photo Gallery from each layer comp. By default, the style is set to Simple for the gallery. You can change the style, but must do so manually (there's no pop-up list). Just copy the name of the Web gallery style; you can navigate inside your Photoshop application folder (Photoshop > Presets > Web Photo Gallery). Copy the exact name of a template and paste it into the style box.

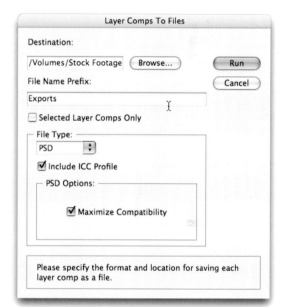

Script Events Manager

The Script Events Manager allows you to have certain events (such as the opening or saving of a file) trigger a JavaScript or a Photoshop action. Several default events are included, or you can add your own by following the guidelines in the Photoshop Scripting Guide.

Let's create a useful script that resets Photoshop's interface on launch. This can be particularly useful in a mixed user environment like a computer lab.

1. Call up the Actions palette.

2. Select the Default Actions set (if its not loaded, choose it from the Actions palette submenu).

3. Create a new action called Reset.

4. Choose Window > Workspace > Default Workspace. Photoshop resets all of the palettes and tools.

5. Select the Actions palette and click Stop.

6. Select the Default Actions set and save it back into your Presets folder (overwriting the previous version).

We can now set up an event and an action to go with that event.

1. Choose File > Scripts > Scripts Events Manager.

2. Make sure the box Enable Events to Run Scripts/Actions is checked.

3. From the Photoshop Event menu, choose an event that will trigger the script or action. For our example, choose Start Application as the event.

4. You can choose to add a script or an action. In this example, choose the newly created Reset action from the Default Actions folder.

5. Click Add. The event and its associated script or action is now listed in the dialog box.

6. When you're finished, click Done. The dialog window closes. The Reset script will run each time you launch Photoshop.

TIP

Disable or Remove Events

To disable or remove individual events, call up the Script Events Manager. Select the event in the list and click Remove. To disable all events but still keep them in the list, you can deselect Enable Events To Run Scripts/Actions.

Printing and PDF Essentials

16

At some point, you will need to send your images to an output device. Several different devices are available including paper and film printers, plates, or a digital printing press. Whether you are printing on a desktop inkjet printer or sending your images to prepress, there are some essentials you should know. Understanding the core technology will ensure your print jobs go more smoothly and that your images turn out as desired. The material in this chapter serves as a primer on printing and PDF technology, but you should realize that professional printing is a trade that takes a lot of experience and specialized knowledge.

Professional Printing Options

Depending on the type of image you have, you need to determine the right type of printer. This will be a balance of budget and availability. The simplest images, such as line art, use only one color. An illustration may use several colors, and those can be printed using CMYK inks to create the different colors or spot inks that exactly match.

The most complex images are photographs because they use varying colors and tones to simulate the image. These types of images are generally referred to as continuous-tone images.

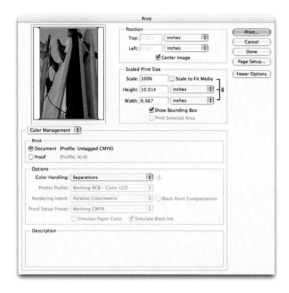

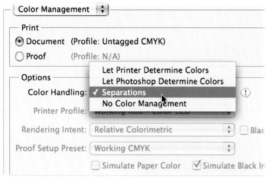

Color Separation

If your multicolored image is intended for commercial output (that is to say printing on a large press), it will need color separation. This process allows for a master plate to be created for each color. Generally, the plates created are for cyan, magenta, yellow and black—also called key—(CMYK) inks.

These plates can be created in several ways. Usually, the process is handled by a printing professional. However, let's take a quick look at how these separations can be created in Photoshop.

1. Open the file Surfboards.tif from the Chapter 16 folder on the DVD-ROM.

2. Check to make sure that your document is in CMYK Color or Multichannel mode.

3. Choose File > Print With Preview.

4. Click the More Options button (if it is already selected, you'll see the Fewer Options button).

5. Choose Color Management from the pop-up menu.

6. Choose Separations from the Color Handling pop-up menu.

7. Click Print. Your printer will print separations for each of the colors in the image.

Halftoning

To simulate continuous tones in images, commercial printers break down images into dots. For those images printed on a press, this process is referred to as halftoning. By varying the size of the dots, the halftone screen creates the optical illusion of variations in tone.

While an inkjet printer also uses dots, it's not the same. An inkjet printer's dots are very small and uniform in size.

Quality of Detail

How clear an image prints depends on its resolution and screen frequency. Professional printing devices are often capable of high resolution. As such, they require a finer screen ruling (lines per inch). For more on resolution, you can revisit Chapter 3, "Acquiring Digital Images." It's a good idea to discuss resolution requirements with your printer before starting a job.

Desktop Printing Options

The majority of Photoshop users print their images on desktop printers most of the time. These printers generally fall into three categories:

- **Inkjet:** These printers are the most popular and widespread. They offer relatively affordable printing. For best results look for inkjet printers with cartridges for each color.

- **Dye Sublimation:** These printers allow for printing of lab quality prints. The price on these printers has recently plummeted. These printers do not use dots; rather, transparent film (using CMYK dyes) is heated up and transferred to the paper. The vaporized colors absorb into the printer paper. This method is less vulnerable to fading over time.

- **Laser Printer:** Laser printers use static electricity to affix powder to the page to form the image. These printers are generally more expensive than inkjets, but can usually print faster and at a higher quality. For more information on laser printing, see an information article at http://computer.howstuffworks.com/laser-printer1.htm.

RGB vs. CMYK

While inkjet printers use CMYK inks, they prefer to ingest RGB images. If the image is in RGB mode, there is no reason to convert if you're using an inkjet printer. Desktop printers are designed to do their own CMYK conversion using internal software. Sending a CMYK image to an inkjet printer will usually result in a second (and unpredictable) color conversion. It is important to realize that the computer screen can display more colors than the printer can print. You might want to use the Gamut Warning command (View > Gamut Warning) to identify areas that need to be toned down before printing.

Printing Paper

Several specialty papers are available for desktop printers. You will not get good results trying to print on plain white copy paper. These specialty papers must be selected in the printer window. It's a good idea to identify the paper you are using so the print driver can adjust the density of the ink coverage to match the paper stock. To conserve paper, you might want to create and print a contact sheet or picture package with several smaller images first.

Printing Commands

Several commands are associated with printers. Those specific to your printer are controlled by the printer driver, which can be clearly explained by visiting the printer manufacturer's Web site. There are many different drivers available, so instead of focusing on the multitude of manufacturers and hardware options, we'll focus our efforts on what can be controlled within Photoshop.

Page Setup

The Page Setup command is the best way to identify the paper size you intend to print on.

1. Choose File > Page Setup. The exact options available depend on your printer, printer drivers, and operating system.

2. Select a printer from the Format for: pop-up menu.

3. Choose the paper size from the Paper Size: pop-up menu.

4. You can also adjust the orientation of the page as well.

5. Do not adjust the scale of the image. Instead use the Print with Preview command.

Print with Preview

The Print with Preview command offers the greatest flexibility when printing in Photoshop. The command allows you to adjust the size of the image, its position on the page, and to specify color management policies. Learning to control this window will allow you to get better results.

1. Open the file Silhouette.tif from the Chapter 16 folder.

2. Choose File > Print With Preview or press Cmd+Option+P (Ctrl+Alt+P).

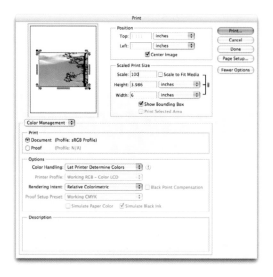

3. For the best results, make sure that More Options is selected. If you see the Fewer Options button displayed and Color Management is visible, you are working with More Options.

4. In the Print area, choose Document. The profile for the image is displayed in parentheses on the same line.

5. In the Options area, choose Let Printer Determine Colors for Color Handling. This is generally the best option as it lets the printer use its specialty software to get the most accurate color.

6. In the Options area, you need to specify the Rendering Intent. This is how the colors will be converted for the destination color space. Most non-PostScript printer drivers ignore this option and use the Perceptual rendering intent, but there are four options to choose from:

   - **Perceptual:** This method attempts to present color so it is natural to the human eye, even though the color values may change.

   - **Saturation:** This method tries to produce vivid colors in an image; however, it may sacrifice color accuracy.

   - **Relative Colorimetric:** This method compares the highlights of the source color space to the destination and shifts all colors accordingly.

   - **Absolute Colorimetric:** This method leaves colors that are in gamut untouched while clipping those colors that are out of gamut for the destination color space.

7. You will need to access additional Color Management options for the printer driver from the second print dialog box. The second box automatically appears when you click Print. Under the Mac OS you access printer options from a pop-up menu. Windows users need to click the Properties button to access printer driver options.

COLOR MANAGEMENT BY SOFTWARE

In the color management by software workflow, Photoshop does all the color conversion. This method works best when you have a custom ICC profile for each specific printer, ink, and paper combination. This method is more commonly used in professional printing environments when working with higher end devices that have been professionally calibrated.

8. Inkjet printers label color management options as either ColorSync (Mac OS) or ICM (Windows). You want to select this category, and then specify to let the printer driver handle the color management during printing.

9. Click Print.

VIDEO TRAINING
Printing Dialog Box

39

COLOR MANAGEMENT BY PRINTER

The color management by printer workflow approach lets the printer hardware handle the color conversion. Instead of performing the color management, Photoshop sends all of the necessary details to the printer. This method is the best method when printing to inkjet photo printers. This is because each combination of paper, printing resolution, and additional printing parameters requires a different profile.

Using this option is generally best, but it does require you to set printing options and turn on color management in the printer driver. If you're working with a PostScript printer, you can harness powerful options. PostScript color management allows for color separations and complex color management.

TIP

Your Image Is Larger Than the Paper's Printable Area

If you get a warning that the image is too large for the paper, clipping will occur. You can choose File > Print With Preview, and select the Scale To Fit Media box. If you are certain the image should fit, you may want to check the Page Setup window and verify orientation.

Print One Copy

If you are in a rush and don't have any special needs, you can choose the Print One Copy command. This command prints one copy of a file using the latest setting you have loaded.

Print Online

The Print Online command allows you to use a variety of online printing services. These services update automatically because they are Web-enabled.

1. Open the file Silhouette.tif from the Chapter 16 folder.

2. When you choose this command, it requires you to save the image as a JPEG first. Choose to use the maximum quality setting (12) when saving.

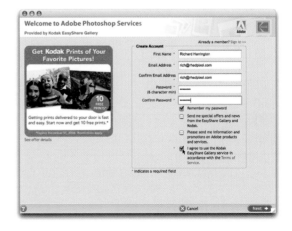

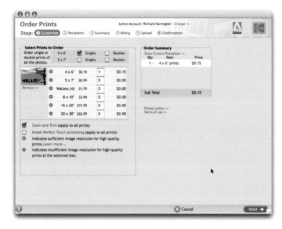

3. If you have not set up an account, you will be guided through the process.

4. You can order various-sized prints and then choose to send them directly to others.

PRINTING VECTOR DATA

If your Photoshop document contains vector data (such as shape or type), you will want to send that data to a PostScript printer. When you choose to send vector data, Photoshop prints a separate image for each vector layer. These images are composited together in the printer. The vector graphics will print at the printer's maximum resolution, which is a good option for type or vector logos.

1. Choose File > Print With Preview.

2. Make sure that More Options is selected.

3. Choose Output from the pop-up menu (it's in the same space as Color Management).

4. Choose the Include Vector Data option.

PDF Essentials

The Portable Document Format (PDF) is a file format that Adobe invented. PDF was unveiled in 1992 and was intended to be an extension of PostScript. A PDF can describe any combination of text, images, multimedia, and layout. It is independent of the device it was created on, and can be viewed on virtually every operating system.

The PDF is an open-standard, which means that the computer industry is able to create applications that can read or write PDFs without paying Adobe additional fees. This openness led to the quick adoption of PDF, and it is utilized online extensively.

The most powerful PDF authoring tool is Acrobat from Adobe. This software is bundled with Photoshop in the Adobe Creative

Suite Premium package. However, Photoshop (and most Adobe programs) have the ability to create PDFs. The PDF file format is an excellent way to send files to a service bureau or print shop as the file can be stored at print resolution with embedded vector files and high-quality output options.

Compression Options for Adobe PDF

When you choose to save artwork as a Photoshop PDF, you are presented with the Save Adobe PDF dialog box. You can choose to compress text and line art as well as downsample bitmap images. Depending on the chosen settings, you can significantly reduce the size of a PDF file with little or no loss of detail.

In the Save Adobe PDF dialog box, you can choose an Adobe PDF preset. This is a fast way to specify what is meant for commercial printing, distributed via email, and so on. You can click Save PDF to generate the file right away, or keep modifying the settings for special purposes.

ADOBE PDF STANDARDS

You can choose to create a PDF that matches the most widely used standards for print publishing. There are two different types of PDF/X formats:

PDF/X-1A (2001 AND 2003)

PDF/X-1a is an industry-recognized standard for graphic exchange. Choosing PDF/X-1a requires all fonts to be embedded and for the appropriate PDF bounding boxes to be specified. PDF/X-compliant files must contain necessary information describing the condition for which they were prepared to be printed. PDF/X-1a compliant files can be opened in Acrobat 4.0 and Acrobat Reader 4.0 and later.

PDF/X-3 (2002 AND 2003)

The main difference in this newer version of PDF is that it allows for the use of color management. Additionally, it supports device-independent color as well as CMYK and spot colors. Additionally, ICC color profiles can be used to specify color data later on in the workflow. PDF/X-3 compliant files can be opened in Acrobat 4.0 and Acrobat Reader 4.0 and later.

For more information on PDF/X, see www.adobe.com/products/creativesuite/pdfs/pdfx_white_paper.pdf

Compression

The Compression area of the Save Adobe PDF dialog box offers several options for reducing file size. You do not need to downsample, but you might want to if you want to better match the output resolution of a particular printer or to reduce file transfer times.

The chosen interpolation method determines how pixels are deleted:

- **Average Downsampling:** This method averages the pixels in a sample area and replaces the entire area with the average pixel color.

- **Subsampling:** This method chooses a pixel in the center of a sample area and replaces the entire area with that color.

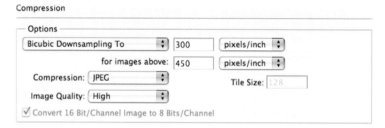

- **Bicubic Downsampling:** This method uses a weighted average to determine pixel color. It generally yields better results than Average Downsampling. This is the slowest, but most accurate, method.

- **Compression:** Three methods of compression are available to use:

  - **ZIP compression:** This works well for images with large areas of single colors or repeating patterns.

  - **JPEG compression:** This is suitable for grayscale or color images. JPEG compression eliminates data, so it usually results in much smaller file sizes than ZIP compression.

  - **JPEG2000:** This is the new international standard for image data compression. Like JPEG compression, JPEG2000 compression is suitable for grayscale or color images. It also provides additional advantages, such as progressive display.

- The Image Quality setting determines how much compression is applied. The settings will vary based on the compression method chosen, but they are clearly labeled.

- You can check the convert 16 Bit/Channel Image To 8 Bit/Channel if you're working with a 16-bit image. This can significantly reduce file size, but is not a good option if you're creating a PDF for professional printing. This option is grayed out if the image you are working with is already in 8-bit mode.

Output

The most common way to create accurate color when creating a PDF is to stick with the PDF/X standard. However, you can choose to modify settings in this area and embed color profiles. Be sure to check with your printer or service bureau regarding color profile settings.

Security

The PDF format supports several different security options. This can be useful to protect the document from unauthorized viewers or to preserve copyright by blocking copying or printing functions. Here are some of the most important security options:

- **Require a password to open the document:** The viewer must enter a password to view the PDF document.

- **Use a password to restrict printing, editing, and other tasks:** Several options can be placed on the document. You can restrict printing and block modifications to the page.

Summary

The Summary area provides a single pane view of all of the settings you have used. This is a quick way to check the options you've enabled.

When you're finished, you can click Save PDF to create the PDF file. You can also click Save Preset if you want to save the settings you've modified for future PDF creation.

Outputting Specialized File Types

17

While Photoshop is a feature-rich and truly enjoyable program, it is frequently not the end of the road for a designer or artist. Most often, professionals (and even hobbyists) will need to save their files for use in other software packages and environments. Whether it's a JPEG for a Web site, an EPS for a professional printer, or a PICT file for video editing, Photoshop can create it. In fact, Photoshop supports more than 20 file formats by default. Additional formats used by cameras or other software packages can be added via plug-ins.

On the Photoshop installation disc you'll find additional plug-ins to install. You can install additional file formats by navigating to *<PS Application folder>* > Plug-Ins > File Formats. To access special formats choose File > Save As and pick a file type from the Format list. Not all formats will work with every color space or image type, but each has a special purpose. Let's explore file types in depth.

```
  Photoshop
✓ Alias PIX
  BMP
  CompuServe GIF
  ElectricImage
  Photoshop EPS
  Genuine Fractals
  IFF Format
  JPEG
  JPEG 2000
  Large Document Format
  PCX
  Photoshop PDF
  Photoshop 2.0
  Photoshop Raw
  PICT File
  PICT Resource
  Pixar
  PixelPaint
  PNG
  Portable Bit Map
  Scitex CT
  SGI RGB
  SoftImage
  Targa
  TIFF
  Wavefront RLA
  Photoshop DCS 1.0
  Photoshop DCS 2.0
```

File Formats Explained

There are too many file formats to ignore. Unfortunately, each industry is different; 3D animators need different images than magazine designers. A brief overview of file types will be useful to identify the formats that you will need. Then just revisit this chapter when you need to brush up on a new format.

Image.psd

Photoshop (.psd)

Layers	8-bit	16-bit	32-bit
Bitmap	Grayscale	Duotone	Indexed Color
RGB	CMYK	Lab	Multichannel

*Not all color spaces work in 16- and 32-bit modes

Photoshop format is the default file format. This format supports all of Photoshop's features. It's a good idea to save your design files in this format for maximum editability. Additionally, many other software packages recognize Photoshop layers.

Alias Pix (.pix)—Optional Plug-in

Layers	**8-bit**	16-bit	32-bit
Bitmap	**Grayscale**	Duotone	Indexed Color
RGB	CMYK	Lab	Multichannel

Alias is a 3D software company best known for the Maya animation software. Some of its software tools use the file format PIX for individual images.

From the Save As dialog box, you can select from several file formats. Certain ones may be unavailable due to bit depth or image mode.

BMP (.bmp)

Layers	8-bit	16-bit	32-bit
Bitmap	**Grayscale**	Duotone	**Indexed Color**
RGB	CMYK	Lab	Multichannel

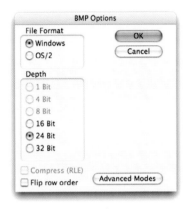

When saving a BMP file, you have several options available. These options optimize the file for use with other applications.

Microsoft Paint's BMP is a standard Windows image format on DOS and Windows computers. The BMP format supports RGB, Indexed Color, Grayscale, and Bitmap color modes. The BMP format supports several lower-quality modes and is most used by video game developers.

Cineon (.cin or .dpx)

Layers	8-bit	16-bit	32-bit
Bitmap	Grayscale	Duotone	Indexed Color
RGB	CMYK	Lab	Multichannel

Cineon is a common file format for digital film work and is used in the motion picture industry. It is a subset of the ANSI/ SMPTE DPX file format, which represents each color channel of a scanned film negative in a "10-bit log" format. Photoshop does not have a 10-bit space, so instead handles the images in 16-bit mode. The DPX file format is derived from the output file format of the Kodak Cineon film scanner. The Cineon format has been replaced by a related format called DPX.

CompuServe GIF (.gif)

Layers	8-bit	16-bit	32-bit
Bitmap	**Grayscale**	Duotone	**Indexed Color**
RGB	CMYK	Lab	Multichannel

Online service provider CompuServe originally developed the Graphics Interchange Format (GIF). This format displays

Compare a JPEG (left) and a GIF (right). Notice how the GIF uses fewer colors. This format can reduce file size, but often creates banding or color shifts.

8-bit or indexed-color graphics and images in HTML documents on the Internet. You'll hear the file called both "giff" and "jiff"; both are acceptable. GIFs use a color table (with no more than 256 colors) to represent the image. This can lead to a small file size, but also banding in the image. If you need transparency in a Web graphic, GIF is one of two choices (the other is PNG). There are also animated GIFs, which are GIF frames displayed one after the other to create animation. Unless you need transparency or animation, JPEG is a better option for Web delivery.

ElectricImage (.img)—Optional Plug-in

Layers	8-bit	16-bit	32-bit
Bitmap	Grayscale	Duotone	Indexed Color
RGB	CMYK	Lab	Multichannel

This is a very uncommon file format associated with animation software from Electric Image.

Photoshop EPS (.eps)

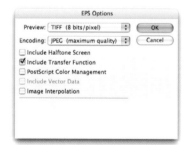

You can embed an image preview into an EPS file, which makes previewing your image easier in a page-layout program.

Layers	8-bit	16-bit	32-bit
Bitmap	Grayscale	Duotone	Indexed Color
RGB	CMYK	Lab	Multichannel

The Encapsulated PostScript (EPS) language file format can contain both vector and bitmap graphics. It is nearly universal and is supported by virtually all graphics, illustration, and page-layout programs. EPS format is used to transfer PostScript artwork between applications. When you open an EPS file that contains vector graphics, Photoshop rasterizes the image.

Filmstrip (.flm)

Layers	**8-bit**	16-bit	32-bit
Bitmap	Grayscale	Duotone	Indexed Color
RGB	CMYK	Lab	Multichannel

The Filmstrip format is used for movie files created by Adobe Premiere and Premiere Pro. Every frame of video is saved to one file, which you can open in Photoshop for Rotoscoping (painting on video or film frame-by-frame). If you change resolution, delete alpha channels, or alter the color mode, you won't be able to save it back to Filmstrip format. This format is becoming much less common as most users turn to After Effects for this sort of work.

Genuine Fractals (.stn)—Third-Party Plug-in

Layers	**8-bit**	**16-bit**	**32-bit**
Bitmap	Grayscale	Duotone	Indexed Color
RGB	**CMYK**	**Lab**	Multichannel

While the Genuine Fractals plug-in is a third-party product (and costs extra), it is so common in certain industries that it bears mention. Most versions of the plug-in write to the .stn format (often called Sting). There are two versions of Genuine Fractals: one that supports only RGB images and a Pro version that adds CMYK and Lab support. The major benefit of the format is that an image can be saved as an .stn file, then scaled up to 800% larger. While some image degradation occurs, it is much less than what Photoshop would cause by upsampling. The file format also allows for large amounts of visually lossless compression to reduce file size. This format is very common in the large format print industry (such as billboards or product displays).

FORMATS THAT SUPPORT SPOT COLOR CHANNELS

Do you need spot color channels for special printing jobs? Then you'd better stick to these file formats:

- Photoshop
- Genuine Fractals
- JPEG 2000
- Large Document Format
- Photoshop PDF
- Photoshop Raw
- TIFF
- Photoshop DCS 2.0

IFF Format (.iff)—Optional Plug-in

Layers	8-bit	16-bit	32-bit
Bitmap	**Grayscale**	Duotone	**Indexed Color**
RGB	CMYK	Lab	Multichannel

Most of you reading this book are too young to remember Commodore computers. The manufacturer produced computers between 1976 and 1994 and is often remembered for the Commodore 64, which was a very successful personal computer in the early days of computing. A follow-up computer was the Commodore Amiga. The Amiga Interchange File Format (IFF) is the standard raster file format for the Commodore Amiga. You can use this format to transfer images between the Macintosh/Windows systems and Amiga computers. You'll also occasionally see this format used in animation programs. Some paint programs on IBM computers also support this format. RGB, Indexed Color, Grayscale, and Bitmapped modes can be saved in this format. Besides supporting Amiga output, the file can also export for Maya.

JPEG (.jpg)

Layers	8-bit	16-bit	32-bit
Bitmap	**Grayscale**	Duotone	Indexed Color
RGB	**CMYK**	Lab	Multichannel

The Joint Photographic Experts Group (JPEG) format is most often used to display continuous-tone images (such as photos) on the Internet. Most digital cameras use JPEG as it provides excellent compression; the maximum setting provides comparable quality to much larger files. Occasionally the print industry (especially newspapers) will use JPEGs.

Name	Size	Kind
Boards.jpg	2 MB	Adobe Photoshop JPEG file
Boards.psd	17 MB	Adobe Photoshop file

Notice the difference in file-size savings between the two formats. The JPEG (even at maximum quality) is almost nine times smaller. File savings make JPEG a popular format for digital cameras and the newspaper industry.

The JPEG format supports RGB, CMYK, and Grayscale color modes, but does not support alpha channels. JPEG is a lossy compression, which means that some data is discarded during compression of the image. JPEGs should not be used as an archive or production file format. You should generally only save JPEG files once, as resaving continues to discard data and lower image quality.

If you are using it as a source format, be sure to set the digital camera to Maximum quality. The best way to create JPEGs for the Internet is with the Save For Web command (discussed in depth at the end of this chapter).

JPEG 2000 (.jpf)—Optional Plug-in

Layers	8-bit	16-bit	32-bit
Bitmap	**Grayscale**	Duotone	Indexed Color
RGB	**CMYK**	**Lab**	Multichannel

The JPEG 2000 format is a significant improvement upon the JPEG standard. It offers more options and greater flexibility, and is designed for use by the Web and print publishing industries (although the video and film industry is examining it as well). Not all Web browsers support the JPEG 2000 format natively and may require a plug-in.

While traditional JPEG files use lossy compression, the JPEG 2000 format supports optional lossless compression. It can also work in 16-bit mode for greater color fidelity and retain transparency, alpha channels, and spot color channels. In fact, by using an alpha channel, you can specify a region of interest. This area will have more details preserved while the rest of the image can have greater compression (which reduces file size).

The JPEG 2000 dialog box offers significantly greater control over image compression than the standard JPEG format.

Image.psb   Image.psd

The two file formats are virtually identical. Using the Large Document Format does not increase file size, it just allows a larger sized file to be saved.

Large Document Format (.psb)

Layers	8-bit	16-bit	32-bit
Bitmap	Grayscale	Duotone	Indexed Color
RGB	CMYK	Lab	Multichannel

There is normally a 2 GB file size limit in older versions of Photoshop and most other computer applications. To respond to the need for larger file sizes, Adobe launched the Large Document Format (PSB). It supports documents up to 300,000 pixels in any dimension (up to 100 inches at 300 ppi). All Photoshop features, such as layers, effects, and filters, are supported.

Additionally, 32-bits-per-channel images can be saved as PSB files. It's important to remember that files saved in the PSB format can be opened only in Photoshop CS or Photoshop CS2. Other applications and earlier versions of Photoshop cannot open documents saved in PSB format. Also, to save a document as a PSB file, the Enable Large Document Format option must be enabled in your Preferences.

OpenEXR (.exr)

Layers	8-bit	16-bit	**32-bit**
Bitmap	Grayscale	Duotone	Indexed Color
RGB	CMYK	Lab	Multichannel

OpenEXR is a specialized file format used by the visual effects industry for high dynamic range images. It was developed by Industrial Light and Magic and released under an open source license. The format supports multiple lossless or lossy compression methods. It is designed to support both 16-bit and 32-bit images (although Photoshop currently supports only 32-bit images). Its primary benefit is that it allows for over 30 stops of exposure (which gives it incredible range of light to dark). For much more information, see www.openexr.com/about.html.

PC Paintbrush (.pcx)

Layers	8-bit	16-bit	32-bit
Bitmap	Grayscale	Duotone	Indexed Color
RGB	CMYK	Lab	Multichannel

PC-compatible computers can use the PC Paintbrush format. The format is designed to match the standard VGA color palette. PCX supports RGB, Indexed Color, Grayscale, and Bitmap color modes, but does not support alpha channels. It is most often a compressed file and supports bit depths of 1, 4, 8, or 24. Because of its small color range and compressed images, this format is not very useful.

Photoshop PDF (.pdf)

Layers	8-bit	16-bit	32-bit
Bitmap	Grayscale	Duotone	Indexed Color
RGB	CMYK	Lab	Multichannel

The Portable Document Format is a cross-platform, cross-application file format. PDF files are designed to accurately display and preserve fonts, page layouts, and both vector and bitmap graphics. You can also transfer Photoshop's annotation notes (both text and audio) into a PDF.

The Photoshop PDF format is the only PDF that Photoshop can save and it's a hybrid. It supports layers and other Photoshop features, but not all PDF features. You do have several choices, though, in the Save Adobe PDF dialog box (including password and permissions). You do not need to flatten to save a PDF file. This file can then be transferred to coworkers or clients for review and comment using Adobe Acrobat or viewed using the free Adobe Reader. This is an excellent format for review purposes.

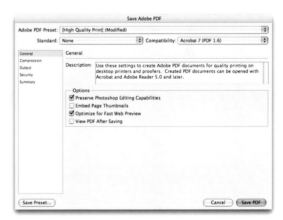

The PDF dialog box allows for several options including security. This allows you to password-protect a file from opening or being modified.

FORMATS THAT SUPPORT LAYERS

Layered files are very important for the flexibility they offer for future changes. Not all file formats store layers, so be sure to keep a copy of your layered image by saving to one of these file formats:

- Photoshop
- Large Document Format
- Photoshop PDF
- TIFF

Photoshop 2.0

Layers	8-bit	16-bit	32-bit
Bitmap	Grayscale	Duotone	Indexed Color
RGB	CMYK	Lab	Multichannel

File this format under the "just-in-case" category. If you need to send a file for use in Photoshop 2.0, choose to export to this format. It will only allow you to save a copy and all layer information will be discarded. Occasionally, some third-party software application may require a Photoshop 2.0 file; however, this file format is fairly obsolete.

Photoshop Raw (.raw)

Layers	8-bit	16-bit	32-bit
Bitmap	Grayscale	Duotone	Indexed Color
RGB	CMYK	Lab	Multichannel

The raw format is a flexible file format for transferring files between applications and computer platforms. Essentially, a text file is written containing a stream of bytes describing the color information for the image. Every pixel is described in binary format. It's important to note that a Photoshop raw image is not in the same file format as a camera raw image. Most users can completely avoid this format.

PICT File (.pct)

Layers	8-bit	16-bit	32-bit
Bitmap	Grayscale	Duotone	Indexed Color
RGB	CMYK	Lab	Multichannel

The Macintosh Picture format is widely used by video editors who initially grew up on Macintosh-based editing systems. Its popularity can be traced back to many software packages, which historically required graphics to be in the PICT format. The PICT format is very effective at compressing large areas of solid color. This compression results in a huge file savings for alpha channels, which are mostly black or white. On the Mac platform, you have choices of additional JPEG compression. Avoid these as they cause import problems on PCs, and the file-size savings are not worth the quality loss.

PICT Resource (.rsr)

Layers	**8-bit**	16-bit	32-bit
Bitmap	**Grayscale**	Duotone	**Indexed Color**
RGB	CMYK	Lab	Multichannel

The PICT resource is a PICT file that is contained in a Mac OS file's resource fork. This format is often used to create startup screens for software. While similar to a plain PICT file, you can avoid it if you are not doing software programming. You can edit a PICT resource file by importing it into Photoshop.

Pixar (.pxr)

Layers	**8-bit**	16-bit	32-bit
Bitmap	**Grayscale**	Duotone	Indexed Color
RGB	CMYK	Lab	Multichannel

The Pixar format is designed for high-end 3D applications (yes, Pixar makes movies and software). It supports RGB and grayscale images with a single alpha channel. If you create 3D animation, you may use this format for integration with third-party programs.

FORMATS THAT SUPPORT ALPHA CHANNELS

Do you need embedded transparency for use in multimedia, video, or animation programs? Then you might want to stick with file formats that support alpha channels. Be sure to check the manual of your software program to see which of the following formats are compatible:

- **Photoshop**
- **BMP**
- **ElectricImage**
- **Genuine Fractals**
- **JPEG 2000**
- **Large Document Format**
- **Photoshop PDF**
- **Photoshop 2.0**
- **Photoshop Raw**
- **PICT File**
- **PICT Resource**
- **Pixar**
- **SGI RGB**
- **Targa**
- **TIFF**

PNG (.png)

Layers	**8-bit**	16-bit	32-bit
Bitmap	**Grayscale**	Duotone	**Indexed Color**
RGB	CMYK	Lab	Multichannel

The file on the left is a PNG. Notice how the transparency is handled perfectly (even in the soft glowing areas). On the right is a GIF, which is an 8-bit image. Transparency is not handled as cleanly, and you will notice a white edge outside of the glow.

The Portable Network Graphics format provides lossless compression. It is increasingly common on the Internet, but not all browsers support it. The PNG format was created to be a patent-free alternative to GIF. Its major advantage is the PNG-24 file, which allows for 24-bit images (8 bits per channel) and embedded transparency. It is technically superior to GIF.

Portable Bit Map (.pbm)

Layers	**8-bit**	16-bit	**32-bit**
Bitmap	**Grayscale**	Duotone	Indexed Color
RGB	CMYK	Lab	Multichannel

This format is designed for lossless data transfer between many different applications. The Portable Bit Map (PBM) file format is also known as Portable Bitmap Library or Portable Binary Map. It supports monochrome bitmaps (1 bit per pixel). The Portable Bit Map format functions as the common language of a large family of bitmap conversion filters including Portable FloatMap (PFM), Portable Graymap (PGM), Portable Pixmap (PPM), and Portable Anymap (PNM). This format can be used to store floating-point images that can be used for 32-bits-per-channel HDR files.

QuickTime Movie (.mov)

Layers	**8-bit**	16-bit	32-bit
Bitmap	Grayscale	Duotone	Indexed Color
RGB	CMYK	Lab	Multichannel

The QuickTime Movie format is a cross-platform format developed by Apple. It is used for time-based media, such as video. As of Photoshop CS2, only ImageReady allows for the opening (and saving) of QuickTime movies.

Installing QuickTime is beneficial to Photoshop. By default it's on Macintosh systems, but it's a free download for Windows (www.quicktime.com). Having QuickTime installed unlocks more file formats.

Radiance (.hdr)

Layers	8-bit	16-bit	**32-bit**
Bitmap	Grayscale	Duotone	Indexed Color
RGB	CMYK	Lab	Multichannel

The Radiance format is another High Dynamic Range (HDR) image format. It allows for 32-bits-per-channel, which produces superior manipulation of exposure. This format was originally developed for the Radiance system. This is a high-end professional tool for visualizing lighting in virtual environments. The file format stores the quantity of light per pixel (not just the colors) to be displayed onscreen. Radiance (HDR) files are often used in 3D modeling.

Scitex CT (.sct)

Layers	**8-bit**	16-bit	32-bit
Bitmap	**Grayscale**	Duotone	Indexed Color
RGB	**CMYK**	Lab	Multichannel

The Scitex Continuous Tone format is used for high-end print work on Scitex computers. This format needs special scanners and rasterizing formats, and is designed for output of high-quality print such as magazines and art prints. CMYK images saved in Scitex CT format can have extremely large file sizes.

By using Scitex systems, a professional printer can produce images with very few moiré patterns. While Photoshop can create a Scitex CT file, you'll need specialized software to transfer it to a Scitex system.

SGI RGB (.sgi)—Optional Plug-in

Layers	**8-bit**	16-bit	32-bit
Bitmap	**Grayscale**	Duotone	**Indexed Color**
RGB	CMYK	Lab	Multichannel

The SGI RGB format is a somewhat uncommon file format that often appears in the computer graphics and simulation industry. The format was originally developed for use on SGI systems.

Softimage (.pic)—Optional Plug-in

Layers	**8-bit**	16-bit	32-bit
Bitmap	Grayscale	Duotone	Indexed Color
RGB	CMYK	Lab	Multichannel

Softimage creates professional 3D animation and modeling software. This optional plug-in allows for increased compatibility with Softimage's tools.

SWF (.swf)

Layers	**8-bit**	16-bit	32-bit
Bitmap	Grayscale	Duotone	Indexed Color
RGB	CMYK	Lab	Multichannel

The SWF format is a very popular Web format that is optimized for playing vector-based animations developed by Macromedia. SWF is pronounced "swiff" and the file extension was based on the original player Shockwave. Several programs can author SWF files, but the most popular is Macromedia Flash.

While optimized for vector playback, the format does support raster-based files. The SWF format is a streaming format. This means that the file plays as soon as enough of the file has downloaded. SWF files currently can only be written from ImageReady. Adobe recently purchased Macromedia, and users are hopeful for tighter Flash and SWF integration.

Targa (.tga)

Layers	**8-bit**	16-bit	32-bit
Bitmap	**Grayscale**	Duotone	**Indexed Color**
RGB	CMYK	Lab	Multichannel

The Targa format was originally designed for use on systems using the Truevision video board. The name is in fact an acronym meaning Truevision Advanced Raster Graphics Adapter. The Targa format predates Photoshop. It is a common format in the video industry (as it supports alpha channels), especially for PC users.

TIFF (.tif)

Layers	8-bit	16-bit	32-bit
Bitmap	Grayscale	Duotone	Indexed Color
RGB	CMYK	Lab	Multichannel

The Tagged-Image File Format is one of the most common and flexible formats available. It is widely used to exchange files between applications and computer platforms, and has a long legacy of compatibility. Older programs capped TIFF files at 2 GB, but starting with Photoshop CS, this barrier was changed to 4 GB. One benefit of TIFF is that it acts as a layered file within Photoshop, but is treated as a flattened file by other applications. Additionally, TIFF is the one of the few formats to work in a bit depth of 8, 16, or 32 bits per channel. High dynamic range images can be saved as 32-bits-per-channel TIFF files.

In the File Handling preferences you can modify how layered TIFFs are handled. While there, you can also turn on support for the Large Document Format.

Wavefront RLA (.rla)—Optional Plug-in

Layers	**8-bit**	16-bit	32-bit
Bitmap	Grayscale	Duotone	Indexed Color
RGB	CMYK	Lab	Multichannel

The Wavefront RLA format was designed to work with the Wavefront Data Visualizer. This is a scientific visualization package for volumetric data. While these systems are for high-end purposes, you may need to provide data to them.

Wireless Bitmap (.wbm)

Layers	8-bit	16-bit	32-bit
Bitmap	Grayscale	Duotone	Indexed Color
RGB	CMYK	Lab	Multichannel

This is the standard format for images on mobile devices such as cell phones. It is an optimized format, but only supports 1-bit color. This means that WBMP images contain only black and white pixels. The file format can only be accessed by choosing the Save For Web command.

Photoshop DCS 1.0 and 2.0 (.eps)

Layers	**8-bit**	16-bit	32-bit
Bitmap	**Grayscale**	**Duotone**	Indexed Color
RGB	**CMYK**	**Lab**	Multichannel

The Photoshop DCS format is an adoption of the Desktop Color Separations (DCS) format (a version of EPS developed by Quark—maker of page-layout software.) The original DCS format is referred to as DCS 1.0, but the more flexible format (referred to as DCS 2.0) allows for exporting images containing spot channels. The format is primarily intended for professional printing of CMYK images. To print DCS files, you must use a PostScript printer.

Adobe Digital Negative (.dng)

Layers	**8-bit**	**16-bit**	32-bit
Bitmap	Grayscale	Duotone	Indexed Color
RGB	CMYK	Lab	Multichannel

There are several competing raw file formats for digital cameras (most are proprietary to a particular manufacturer.) Adobe released the Adobe Digital Negative (DNG) file format to unify things. The concern is that proprietary formats will become obsolete more quickly due to company changes. The DNG format hopes to be the open standard model. The specs for this format are available to camera and software manufacturers, and Adobe has had relative success getting others to adopt it. For more information, visit www.adobe.com/dng.

The DNG format offers a unified solution for camera raw images. You can only save a DNG file from the Adobe Camera Raw dialog box.

Photoshop CS2 Import and Export File Formats

Adobe Photoshop offers great flexibility in reading and writing specialized file formats. These diverse formats are useful to specialized industries like printing, Web, and video production.

From Adobe Support Tech Doc #331305
www.adobe.com/support/techdocs/331305.html

Format (extension)	Mac OS Import	Mac OS Export	Windows Import	Windows Export
Adobe Illustrator (.ai)	X		X	
Adobe Illustrator Paths (.ai)		X		X
Alias PIX* (.pix)	X	X	X	X
Amiga IFF* (.iff, .tdi)	X	X	X	X
BMP (.bmp, .rle)	X	X	X	X
Camera Raw (.crw, .dcr, .mrw, .nef, .orf, .raf)	X		X	
Cineon (.cin, .spdx, .dpx, .fido)	X	X, +	X	X, +
CompuServe GIF (.gif)	X	X	X	X
Digital Negative (.dng)	X	X, #	X	X, #
ElectricImage* (.img, .ei, .eiz, .eizz)	X	X	X	X
EPS (.eps)	X	X	X	X
EPS with JPEG Preview (.eps)	X	X	X	
EPS with PICT Preview (.eps)	X	X	X	
EPS with TIFF Preview (.eps)	X	X	X	X
Filmstrip (.flm)	X	X	X	X
JPEG (.jpg, .jpeg, .jpe)	X	X	X	X
JPEG 2000* (.jpf, .jpx, .jp2, .j2c, .j2k, .jpc)	X	X	X	X
Kodak Photo CD (.pcd)	X		X	
Large Document Format (.psb)	X	X	X	X
MacPaint* (.mpt, .mac)	X		X	
OpenEXR (.exr)	X	X, §	X	X, §
PCX (.pcx)	X	X	X	X
PDF (.pdf, .pdp)	X	X	X	X

Format (extension)	Mac OS Import	Mac OS Export	Windows Import	Windows Export
Photoshop (.psd, .pdd)	X	X	X	X
Photoshop DCS 1.0 and 2.0 (.eps)	X	X	X	X
Photoshop Raw (.raw)	X	X	X	X
PICT (.pct, .pic)	X	X	X	X
PICT Resource (.rsr)	X	X		
Pixar (.pxr)	X	X	X	X
PixelPaint* (.px1)	X		X	
PNG (.png)	X	X	X	X
Portable Bitmap (.pbm, .pgm, .ppm, .pnm)	X	X	X	X
Radiance (.hdr, .rgbe, .xyze)	X	X, §	X	X, §
Scitex CT (.sct)	X	X	X	X
SGI RGB* (.sgi, .rgb, .rgba, .bw)	X	X	X	X
Softimage* (.pic)	X	X	X	X
Targa (.tga, .vda, .icb, .vst)	X	X	X	X
TIFF (.tif)	X	X	X	X
Wavefront RLA* (.rla)	X	X	X	X
Wireless Bitmap (.wbm,.wbmp	X	X, ¶	X	X, ¶
ZoomView (.mtx)		X		X

* Requires an optional plug-in from the installation disc.

+ 16-bit images only.

§ 32-bit images only.

¶ Using the Save For Web dialog box only.

\# Using the Camera Raw dialog box only.

Specialized Processes

Creating files for special uses often requires special processing. These techniques are fairly elaborate, so the short overviews here are meant for a clearer understanding of possibilities. The creation of specialized formats for the Internet, professional printing, or video requires a mastery of several interconnected skills. Let's take a quick look at converting to special purpose files.

Save For Web

VIDEO TRAINING
Save for Web

Preparing images for the Web is all about compromise. You must learn to balance appearance with file size. If a Web page takes too long to load, people will leave—which defeats the purpose of running the site. Fortunately, Photoshop provides a powerful command for compressing images and previewing the results: the Save For Web command.

Let's give the Save For Web command a try:

1. Open the file Board.tif from the Chapter 17 folder on the DVD-ROM.

2. Choose File > Save For Web.

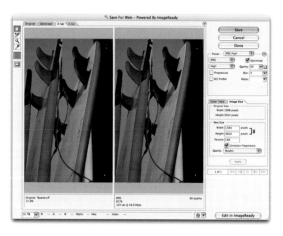

3. The Save For Web dialog box offers several important options for optimization and preview:

   • **Toolbox:** If you can't see the entire image, you can use the Zoom tool to make the image more visible. Additionally, you can use the Hand tool (or hold down the Spacebar) to drag and navigate around the image. Alternatively, you can click the Zoom Level menu in the lower-left corner and choose a magnification level.

- **Optimization tabs:** By clicking the four tabs at the top, you can choose to view the Original image, an Optimized view, 2-Up to view two versions of the image side by side, or 4-Up to view four versions of the image side by side. Being able to compare optimized images helps choose the right format and compression settings. In the case of this image, choose 2-Up.

- **Image Optimization Info:** The area below each image in the Save For Web dialog box gives you optimization information. You can see the current optimization applied, the projected file size, and the estimated download time based on a selected modem connection speed. Choose the JPEG High preset and you'll notice that the file has been reduced

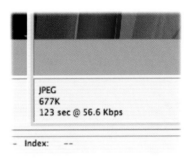

from 17.3M to 677K (a significant savings). However, the download time is 123 seconds on a 56K modem (you can right-click the time to choose another speed).

4. We need to further reduce the file size for Internet delivery. The first area to tackle is the actual image size in pixels. Click the Image Size tab and you'll see that the image is almost 2,000 pixels wide (which is much wider than a typical Web page). Type in a Height of 500 pixels, so the image can integrate easily into our Web page (even with a screen resolution of 800 x 600, a height of 500 would allow the image to display without scrolling up and down). Click Apply to resize the image.

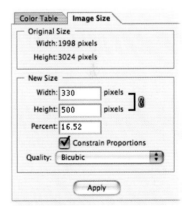

5. The file size has been significantly reduced, but it's hard to see the effects of the compression. Set the image magnification view to 100%.

6. Change the amount of Compression by either changing the preset (from High to Medium, for example) or adjusting the Quality slider. You will need to release the slider for the image to refresh. Try a setting of 45 to see the results, then experiment with other numbers. The image is now at just over 20K. This is more than a 99.9% reduction in file size and a fundamental change for Web delivery.

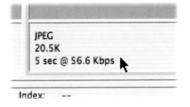

7. Towards the lower-right corner, you have the ability to choose to preview the image in a Web browser. If you don't see your browser of choice, just choose to Edit List.

8. Click Save to process the image and save a compressed Web-ready version. The original file will remain untouched, and its resolution and quality will be identical to its state when you launched the Save For Web command.

9. Experiment with other file formats such as GIF and PNG to see their benefits and limitations.

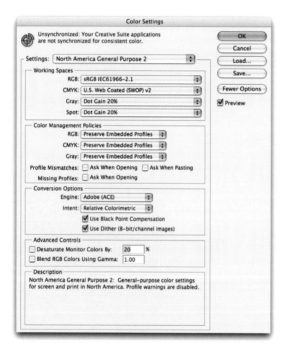

Convert to CMYK

While CMYK conversion is an everyday process for many users, several authors and trainers have developed some useful techniques. What I offer here is a proper workflow that will work for most users, on most images, in most environments. I encourage you to continue to explore prepress production through further reading. CMYK conversion can be a very tricky process, and it is essential that you have access to the color profile used by your output device. With all of these caveats said, let's take a look at the process:

1. Check your color management settings by choosing Edit > Color Settings or pressing Shift+Cmd+K (Shift+Ctrl+K). Choose North America General Purpose 2.

2. Open the file Bikers.tif from the Chapter 17 folder.

3. Choose View > Gamut Warning or press Shift+Cmd+Y (Shift+Ctrl+Y). Areas that are too bright or saturated for CMYK printing will be highlighted in gray. This is because the RGB space can represent a wider ranger of visible colors based on the additive method of color. CMYK printing instead uses the subtractive model, and it has a narrower range.

4. Select the Sponge tool (O) from the Toolbox. Adjust the brush to a large size with soft edges. Set the flow to a lower value such as 20% and the mode to Desaturate. This will gently soak up the color in the oversaturated areas.

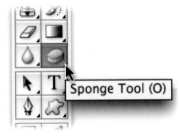

5. Carefully paint over the oversaturated areas with the Sponge tool. It may take multiple strokes, but you'll see the gamut warning go away. Repeat for other problem areas in the photo.

6. When all of the gamut warning has been removed, choose Image > Mode > CMYK. There should be no visible shifting in the colors.

7. Save the image in a print-ready format such as TIFF.

Add an Alpha Channel

We explored saving selections as channels much earlier in the book (Chapter 5, "Selection Tools and Techniques"). The alpha channel can be used to store transparency information, and it is particularly useful for video and multimedia users. If you are using Photoshop CS2, there are new actions for the video professional that I cowrote with Daniel Brown. These can speed up certain tasks for a video workflow. Two of these actions can create an alpha channel for multilayered graphics with transparency.

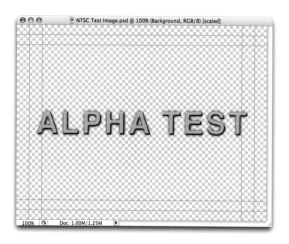

1. Open the file NTSC Test Image.psd from the Chapter 17 folder.

2. Make sure the Alpha Test layer is visible and others are turned off.

3. Call up the Actions palette and load the Video Actions by clicking the submenu. Choose the Video Actions set (you must have CS2 or later to access them).

4. Choose the Create Alpha Channels from Visible Layers action. You must see Photoshop's transparency grid for it to work.

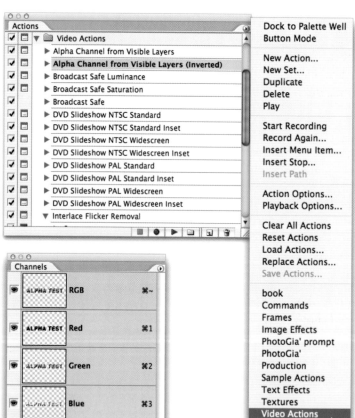

5. Click the Play Selection button to run the action. A dialog box comes up with instructions. Read it and click Continue.

6. A new alpha channel is added to the document. Save the file as a PICT, TIFF, or Targa file and choose to embed the transparency by including the alpha channel

There are many other issues related to creating graphics for use in video. I invite you to check out my reference site, www.PhotoshopForVideo. com. You'll find free training movies and links to my DVDs and other books for the video industry.

Include a Clipping Path

If you are preparing an image to import into a page layout program (such as Adobe InDesign or Quark Xpress), you may want to embed a clipping path. The clipping path embeds the transparency information into the file.

It's important to note that paths are vector-based; therefore, they have hard edges (and do not preserve softness or a feathered edge). Features like a drop shadow cannot be preserved when creating a clipping path (but can often be added in the page layout program). An alternative to clipping paths is to use an alpha channel (which can include a feathered edge).

Photoshop offers a few ways to create accurate clipping paths; we'll explore the easiest. Photoshop has a built-in wizard to help with the creation of clipping paths:

1. Open the file Ch17 Clipping Path.psd from the Chapter 17 folder.

   The Export Transparent Image Assistant only recognizes one layer, so it is a good idea to have a little human intervention.

2. Create a new, empty layer at the top of the layer stack.

3. Make sure only the needed layers are visible (in this case the type layer and the paw print).

4. Hold down the Option (Alt) key and choose Layer > Merge Visible. This will create a flattened copy on the recently created blank layer.

5. Choose Help > Export Transparent Image. A window opens displaying the interactive wizard.

6. You now must tell Photoshop how to determine transparency. The easiest method is to have the image on a transparent background, but you can also make a selection using any of your selection tools as well. The sample image is already on a transparent background.

7. The next window asks you to choose from Print or Online. For this purpose, choose Print.

8. Another window opens displaying advanced options. Choosing to embed Vector Data (if you have any) is usually all you need to select.

This path is functioning as a clipping path. When the path's name appears outlined, it is being used as a clipping path.

9. Name the file and set a destination. Photoshop automatically creates the path and saves the image in the right file format for PostScript printers (an EPS file). If you are using a non-PostScript printer, save the file as a TIFF.

Feel free to visit the Adobe Help Center (Help > Photoshop Help) for more information on clipping paths. You'll find advanced options on controlling the creation of work paths (which become clipping paths).

Building a Portfolio

18

If you want a job, you need a portfolio. Sure, a good-looking résumé with excellent credentials and references will seal the deal, but employers want proof. How do I know? Well, I've been on both sides of the table. I have interviewed for plenty of jobs over the years (some staff, others freelance). I've also been in charge of hiring for an agency and, now, for my own company.

No one is going to hire a creative professional solely on word of mouth or good grades in school (although both of those things help). If you are applying for a job in the creative industry, you're going to need a portfolio. This chapter looks at traditional printed as well as modern new media portfolios. It also discusses do's and don'ts when looking for that job.

JOEY NELSON/ISTOCKPHOTO

The Essential Portfolio

A good portfolio is a personal statement about a designer, photographer, or artist. As such, there is no one-size-fits-all approach that will work for each individual. The best advice is to look at samples of other people's portfolios. Many schools (especially art schools) will have student shows where graduating students show their work. Other colleges may have a job fair. If you are in school, start attending these events as soon as possible. For those who've already graduated, you can find a wealth of online portfolios on the Internet. The key step here is to start looking well before you need a portfolio so you can create one you like.

JOSUE CERVANTES/ISTOCKPHOTO

What Is a Portfolio?

A portfolio is a collection of your work samples that can be shown to prospective employers or clients. It should represent the diversity of talent and skills of the person behind it, but not try to show everything. Most folks need their portfolio in at least two mediums. For example, a photographer might have a traditional flat book with glossy prints, but may also want a Web site for an online presence and a DVD to leave copies of his work behind. Be sure to consider all of the scenarios in which you'll need to present your work to those who want to hire you.

What Goes into a Portfolio?

You want to show your versatility with your portfolio. Even if you only work on certain types of projects at your current job, be sure you have variety. For example, you might work for a manufacturing company, but don't only fill your portfolio with manufacturing-related work samples. Students in particular tend to put too much of their personal interests into a portfolio (most employers do not care about superheroes, street racing, or animé–sorry to disappoint).

THOMAS BROSTROM./ISTOCKPHOTO

What you want are several samples of work, ideally done for real-world clients. You may think it's impossible for a student to land "real" clients, but it is not. Oftentimes charities, religious groups, or local nonprofit organizations could use help with the design of their materials. You could offer to do the design work for free in exchange for 25 copies of the completed piece (always get extra) and a letter of recommendation for your portfolio. The other place to turn is internships (or even externships). Be willing to work for little (or no) money to get some real-world experience. This will significantly increase the perceived value of your portfolio.

What Stays Out of a Portfolio?

There is such a thing as too much. While you want variety, you don't want your portfolio to be thicker than the latest phone book. It is important to screen out the less-than-stellar examples from your portfolio. This can be accomplished through peer review or professional insight. Ask friends or colleagues to look at your work samples. Ask them to pick their favorites and least favorites. Repeat this with a few people, and the inferior samples will quickly be identified.

It's also a bad idea to fill a portfolio with spec projects. Unless you happen to work for a particular agency, no one wants to see your "spec" iPod ad. Fake projects scream a lack of experience. It is far better to have projects where you played a significant role in the execution (including concept, writing, photography, layout, etc.). Simply imitating others will not get you a job.

How Do I Present My Portfolio?

How you present your portfolio is mostly up to you, but certain job markets or industries may have traditions that you should respect. There are several ways to present a portfolio, including

- **Traditional flat book** with work samples mounted on pages.

- **Web site** with work samples and contact information. This method is ideal for designers who create in multiple mediums.

- **Coffee table books**, which can be created and printed from within Photoshop.

- **DVD portfolios**, which allow potential clients to explore the work on their own. Plus, work samples are only at screen resolution, which allays fears about leaving work samples behind.

- **Speaker presentations** using tools like PowerPoint or Keynote. A slide show is an excellent way to personally present your work.

- **E-book or electronic book**, which allows you to create a flat book and save it as a PDF, which is great for email delivery.

You may choose to create several of these portfolio types. We'll explore helpful Photoshop techniques for getting the job done.

How Often Should I Update My Portfolio?

Unfortunately, you're never done developing your portfolio. No job is 100% secure. You always need to be ready for that next interview. With that said, it's not a good idea to work on your portfolio at work. Be sure to update your portfolio a minimum of every 6 months. Certain mediums (like a slide show) are even easier to update and you should always be ready to show them.

Always save copies of your latest work and try to get printed or manufactured copies as well. Students should archive all of their work to disc, so they can update the best pieces and bring them together for the portfolio. Also, do not carry all of your work samples with you; rather, create a hard media archive, such as a binder of CDs or DVDs. Do not rely on a single hard drive, which can crash or get lost or stolen.

Professionals need to actively collect work samples as well. If you are working on a job, be sure to look at your employee handbook about work samples. Some jobs require you to get permission before keeping work samples. Additionally, be sure to credit the company that you did the work for when building a portfolio.

Creating a Portfolio

Photoshop is extremely useful when creating elements for or even producing entire portfolios. With its ability to open both raster and vector files, Photoshop can quickly process your images for print-, Web-, or video-based portfolios. You will likely need a few delivery methods for your portfolio, so keep reading to explore techniques and technologies that will help you show off your work.

Printed Portfolios

A printed portfolio is the most common form of portfolio for artists and photographers. Finding a physical portfolio to hold your work can be done using a simple Internet search. Be sure to balance size and cost. You want your portfolio to be portable but also show your work off at a reasonable size. Portfolios range in cost from $15–$500 plus; it just depends on the size, style, and craftsmanship.

Flat books

To fill a portfolio, you'll need good prints. The following options are useful for outputting your work:

- **Picture Package:** The Picture Package command (File > Automate > Picture Package) is extremely useful for fitting multiple items onto a single sheet. It includes presets for page sizes up to 11 × 17 inches, and you can create your own layouts. This will maximize your color prints by fitting the most images on a page and standardizing their size. For more information, revisit Chapter 15, "Actions and Automation."

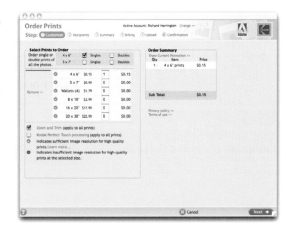

- **Print Online:** The Print Online command allows you to send your images to a digital "service bureau." Just choose File > Print Online and go through the guided steps to set up an account. Smaller images (4 × 6 inches) are very affordable, but larger images can get pricey. However, these are high-quality prints on photo paper.

- **In-Store Photo Prints:** Several stores, including drugstores like CVS and Walgreens and retail stores like Wal-Mart and Target, offer prints from digital files. Their pricing structure is very competitive, and many offer the ability to upload your files online, then have the prints sent to you or picked up in store. Be sure to crop your images to size, or use the Fit Image command (File > Automate > Fit Image) to match the size of your print.

Coffee table books

Using Adobe Bridge, which comes with Photoshop CS2, you can create your own coffee table books. The process is easy and fairly affordable.

1. Place 20 or more JPEGs into a single folder.

2. Launch Adobe Bridge from your computer or choose File > Browse from Adobe Photoshop.

3. In Bridge, navigate to the folder and select the images you want to use.

4. From Bridge, choose Tools > Photoshop Services > Order Photo Books.

5. Set up an online account (following the onscreen steps) or sign in if you have an existing account.

6. Click Next, the photos will upload to Adobe Photoshop services.

7. Once the images are uploaded, the onscreen instructions are easy to follow. Twenty-page books with 8.5 × 11 inch pages start at around $30.

Mac users have another alternative that doesn't involve uploading their images. You can create a photo book from within iPhoto. The prices are identical, but you have a few more options for layout and you can work offline. iPhoto also allows you to create much smaller books to leave behind with clients. One of the online options is to create soft-cover books (sized 2.6 × 3.5 inches). There's a minimum order of three, but they are priced below $5 a piece.

CREATE YOUR OWN POSTER

You can create an action to make your own poster from scratch. If you skipped Chapter 15, you'd better go back and read that first. This action is long, but worth making (if you are totally impatient, you'll find my copy in the Chapter 18 folder). Feel free to modify any of the colors or sizes.

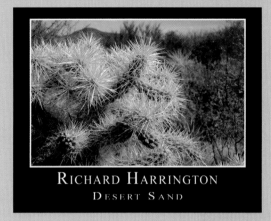

1. Activate the Actions palette.

2. Create a new set to hold your action or use an existing set.

3. Open a print resolution photo in the portrait aspect ratio.

4. Make a new action and name it Portfolio Poster - Portrait.

5. Choose File > Automate > Fit Image. Enter a width of 2100 pixels and a height of 2400 pixels. This will force the image to fit within a 7 × 8 inch area if printing at 300 ppi.

6. Choose Image > Image Size and uncheck the Resample Image box. Set the Resolution to 300 ppi.

7. Press Cmd+A (Ctrl+A) to select the image.

8. Choose Edit > Stroke and apply a 15 pixel stroke to the inside using white.

9. Double-click the Background layer and name it Photo.

10. Choose Image > Canvas Size. Click the Relative box and set the Width and Height to 15% with the anchor point center. Click OK to resize the Canvas.

11. Choose Image > Canvas Size. Click the Relative box and set just the Height to 20% with the anchor point to the Top. Click OK to resize the Canvas.

12. Make a new layer and call it Paper.

13. Press Cmd+A (Ctrl+A) to select all.

14. Choose Edit > Fill and fill with black.

15. Press Cmd+Shift+[(Ctrl+Shift+[) to send this layer to the bottom of the stack.

16. Press Cmd+R to call up your rulers. Right-click or Ctrl-click them and set them to measure in percentages.

17. Activate the Type tool and click the Center text button in the Options bar.

18. Position your cursor near the 50% point centered and below the photo.

19. Click and add your name and a title for the image. Modify the point size, leading, tracking, color, and style to taste.

20. Click the Commit button to apply the text.

21. Click Stop to stop recording. Test the action to make sure it works, and then save your set. You'll need to modify your label text for each image.

You can modify the pixel values for the Fit Image command if the picture has a landscape orientation. Just duplicate the action and double-click the Fit Image step. Type in a new width of 2700 pixels and a height of 2100.

PDF portfolios

By harnessing the power of the portable document format (PDF) you can quickly send your portfolio to potential clients. PDFs can be very efficient for email, and they also offer security options to prevent the extraction or printing of images. For more on PDF files, see Chapter 16, "Printing and PDF Essentials." Here are a few suggestions for creating PDF portfolios:

- **PDF Presentation:** You can choose File > Automate > PDF Presentation. This command allows you to place multiple images into a single PDF. It's a good idea to add captions to an image or create your own layout in Photoshop. You can easily create an 8 × 10 inch document and add images or text to the single page. Save each page, and then use the automation command to move them into one document.

Filename: Silhouette.tif \\ Copyright Notice: \\ Description: \\ Credit: \\ Color Profile: Untagged \\ Color Mode: RGB \\

- **Dr. Brown's Caption Maker:** Russell Brown from Adobe offers a very powerful script for adding captions to images. Dr. Brown's Caption Maker can add captions to your images as well as resize them to fit standard print and presentation sizes. You can download the script for free from www.RussellBrown.com.

Online Portfolios

Placing your portfolio online makes it readily available to potential clients or employers. The cost of hosting a Web page has decreased dramatically. Several reputable companies offer hosting plans for $99 a year (US) and will even register a custom domain name. While free email accounts are attractive, they don't send the right message to your audience. Students and professionals should both strongly consider getting their own Web site and email domain account.

Using Web Photo Galleries

Photoshop offers several useful Web Photo Galleries for showcasing your work. Some of the most effective ones include

- Dotted Border White on Black

- Flash Gallery 2

- Gray Thumbnails

- Horizontal Gray

- Table Minimal

- Vertical Slide Show 2

For the Flash savvy, you can even customize the Flash templates. Photoshop CS2 ships with two built-in templates, but a visit to Adobe's Web site will unlock more power:

- For the Mac: www.adobe.com/support/downloads/detail. jsp?ftpID=2960

- For Windows: www.adobe.com/support/downloads/detail. jsp?ftpID=2961 (for Windows)

(You can also find the Flash galleries download by visiting the generic downloads page, and then visit the Photoshop subpage).

From these Web sites you can download a third Flash template, as well as a sample file and the source FLA file. You can open the FLA file and edit it in Flash MX 2004 or later. These three templates are very different, and you can fully customize them. You'll find instructions on modifying and installing the galleries within the Read Me files in each folder.

Customizing Web Photo Galleries

If you are familiar with HTML (or at least an HTML editor like GoLive or Dreamweaver), you can easily tweak the built-in templates.

1. Navigate to your Photoshop application folder.

2. Inside, navigate the following path: Presets > Web Photo Gallery.

TIP

Impressing a Client

For event photographers, custom Web Photo Galleries are a great way to impress a client.

3. Duplicate the folder for a template that most closely matches your needs.

4. Rename the folder using a custom name.

5. Open the HTML files in a Web editor. *Do not* rename the pages. Modify the source code and embed new graphics as needed.

6. You can also modify the embedded graphics in the image folder. Place any new graphics in there as well.

7. Quit and relaunch Photoshop to load the template into your preset list. Try out the template to ensure that it works properly.

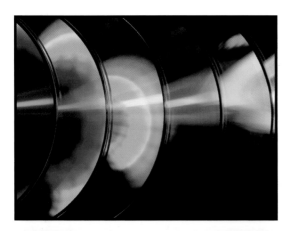

Electronic Portfolios

Electronic portfolios are very effective and affordable. They offer a great way to present your work to a live audience. You can also run them in kiosk mode in an entryway or at a portfolio show. Additionally, they are an easy way to leave a copy of your portfolio with a potential client or employer.

Sizing images for slides

The most common size for electronic portfolios is 1024 × 768 pixels. However, you don't have to design at this size. Some users prefer 800 × 600, whereas others may use high-definition size or widescreen sizes, depending on their monitor or laptop settings. What's important is to get your images sized properly for the screen. This will reduce the file size and load time for your presentation, as well as reduce the likelihood of crashes due to large files being loaded into RAM. Let's create an action and droplet to speed up this process:

1. Create a new set to hold your action or use an existing set.

2. Open a sample image.

3. Create a new action and name it Slide Sizer.

   We have to trick the action into recording a new Height and Width for Canvas Size. To do this, we will make the image just slightly bigger than we need for a 1024 × 768 pixel screen.

4. Choose File > Automate > Fit Image and set a Width of 1026 and a Height of 770 pixels (an extra two pixels in each direction). If you plan to use a different sized slide, use those numbers. Click OK.

5. Choose Image > Canvas Size. Make sure the Relative box is unchecked and set the value to pixels. Type in a size of 1024 × 768.

6. Set the Background Color to black (or another color of your choice).

7. Click OK. A warning will tell you the image is going to be clipped; click Proceed to continue.

8. Click Stop to stop recording the action.

9. You can now choose to batch process a folder of images or create a droplet for drag-and-drop ease. For more on batch processing and droplets, be sure to read Chapter 15.

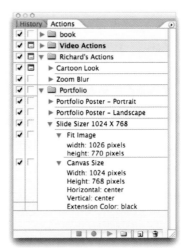

Using Apple Keynote

Apple makes an affordable presentation software package called Keynote. It is bundled as part of the iWork set. This package has several portfolio options designed specifically for designers. The Keynote templates also support High Definition video resolutions if you are using an HD monitor or laptop to

Keynote offers several themes that are well designed for photographers.

present. Keynote allows you to quickly import photos, and it offers advanced text animation and slide transitions.

Additionally, it can be used to output to several formats that your clients may want, such as PDF, SWF file, or even to DVD or a Web page. To find out more about Keynote, check out the iWork book published as part of the Apple Training Series.

Using Microsoft PowerPoint

Many users have access to the ubiquitous Microsoft Power-Point. This application is easy to use for creating basic slide shows. You can quickly import your sized images and create a slide show. PowerPoint files can also be saved as a QuickTime movie or a Web page. Additionally, you can download a free PowerPoint Viewer application that allows people to view (but not edit) your slide show. This can be useful to include on the CD or DVD in case you are presenting on a machine without PowerPoint or want to leave the electronic portfolio behind. Just visit www.Microsoft.com and type PowerPoint Viewer into the search field (the software is available free of charge for both PC and Macintosh computers).

ISTOCKPHOT

DVD Portfolios

DVD has been the most quickly adopted consumer technology of all time. You'll find a wealth of options available for playing back DVDs. The software and technology to create DVDs is both available and affordable for most users as well.

Sizing images for DVD

If you have Photoshop CS2, you already have the DVD Slideshow actions; these are part of the Video Actions set. They are designed to work with professional applications like Adobe Encore DVD or Apple DVD

Studio Pro. These programs recognize the specialized non-square pixels required for digital video usage.

If you are using a more consumer-oriented DVD tool (such as iDVD or Roxio Easy Media Creator) or do not have Photoshop CS2, record this action:

1. Create a new set to hold your action or use an existing set.

2. Open a sample image.

3. Create a new action and name it DVD Slideshow Prosumer.

   We have to trick the action into recording a new Height and Width for Canvas Size. To do this, we will make the image just slightly bigger than we need for a 722 × 536 pixel screen.

4. Choose File > Automate > Fit Image and set a Width of 722 and a Height of 536 pixels (an extra two pixels in each direction). Click OK.

5. Choose Image > Canvas Size. Make sure the Relative box is unchecked and set the value to pixels. Type in a size of 720 × 534.

6. Set the Background Color to black (or another color of your choice).

7. Click OK. A warning will tell you the image is going to be clipped; click Proceed to continue.

8. Click Stop to stop recording the action. If you have CS2, run the Interlace Flicker Removal action to approve the image's appearance on a TV screen.

9. You can now choose to batch process a folder of images or create a droplet for drag-and-drop ease. For more on batch processing and droplets, be sure to read Chapter 15.

Creating a DVD portfolio

Several options are available for creating a DVD portfolio. More professional options like DVD Studio Pro and Encore offer advanced features such as audio beds and transitions. These packages are becoming more common in college computer labs but are not standard on most computers.

However, affordable options like iDVD come bundled with Mac computers; for PC owners, Adobe Premiere Elements is a very user-friendly package for video editing and DVD authoring. Many disc-burning applications like Toast and Easy Media Creator offer limited DVD authoring as well, but these tools lack some of the more design-oriented features for menu customization that a creative portfolio needs.

At this point, creating a basic DVD has gotten so easy that many grade school children are able to complete the task. Be sure to explore your options and give it a try. DVD portfolios are a very affordable way to get your work out there for review.

Packaging the DVD

Creating a professional-looking DVD has gotten much easier. You can print directly on the face of certain brands of blank media (they are labeled as inkjet printable.) In fact, certain printer manufacturers, including Epson on a substantial number of printers, have a media tray for direct output. These printers start under $100 (US) and go up based on media size and budget. Be sure to also see some bonus tutorials on the book's DVD-ROM to get packaging ideas.

End of the Road

Have you reached the end of the road? Hardly. Photoshop contains a wealth of tools. What you have now gained is a firm foundation of knowledge. Many more techniques and specialized uses are worth exploring. And there is a wealth of Photoshop Web sites and books available to further your knowledge. A great place to start is with the National Association of Photoshop Professionals; be sure to check out its Web site at www.PhotoshopUser.com. Photoshop will be a core tool as you grow into other software applications. Continue to expand your Photoshop knowledge and the investment in time will pay back greatly.

Exercises

Exercise #1
Digital Painting

A popular technique is to turn a photo into a more painting-like image. There is no one-click answer, but a little experimentation can go a long way.

Exercise #2
Creating a Collage

Multiple images can be combined into a new composite image. This can be done for experimental or artistic purposes as well as to create an advertisement or cover image.

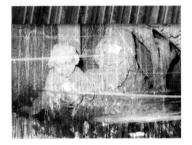

Exercise #3
Designing Speaker Support

Creating a custom background or series of backgrounds is important when designing a custom electronic portfolio. It also allows a designer to create a custom look for a client to use with Microsoft PowerPoint or Apple Keynote.

- Photoshop is an essential program
- Can be used to create content for use with other programs
- Use of Layers and Styles can enhance appearance
- Never have more than seven bullets per page

Exercise #4
Designing a Magazine Cover

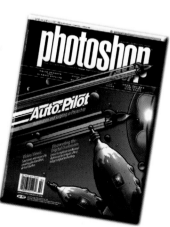

Designing a magazine cover is an excellent exercise to practice with type and layout. Precise positioning of elements as well as creative use of color and design are important to capture the audience's attention.

Exercise #5
Preparing Images for the Internet

Properly sizing and compressing images for the Internet is an essential skill. Finding the right balance of compression and image size is important to ensure that the end user can quickly download the images, yet still have them look good.

Exercise #6
Designing a CD/DVD Label

Whether you're creating a music CD for a band or a DVD label for a client, a professional-looking label is important. Use of text and effects are important to create a readable yet compelling design.

Exercise #7
Creating a DVD Menu

Designing a DVD menu is an important task. More and more projects are being distributed on DVD, and it is the most quickly adopted format in consumer technology history. There's a lot of ways a DVD menu can go (and it will depend on the DVD-authoring software used). But a lot of design work can happen in Photoshop, which allows design options to be fully explored.

Exercise #8
Artistic Reinterpretations of a Photo

Working with a single image and processing several ways is an excellent way to explore the power of filters. By creating unique looks through filter combinations, blending modes, and image adjustments, great design options can be created.

Exercise #9
CD/DVD Package

In this project, you'll create a label for a DVD or CD using an Amaray-style case. A template for printing is provided from a DVD replicator (each replication facility usually uses a custom template). The design will include text and photos, and a completed sample image is provided for reference.

Exercise #10
Preparing Images for CMYK Printing

Preparing images for CMYK printing requires special processing. Certain bright, saturated colors cannot be printed using the CMYK process. These out of gamut colors need to be reduced and brought into range.

Index